LIBERATION
THE UNOFFICIAL AND
UNAUTHORISED GUIDE TO
BLAKE'S 7

LIBERATION
THE UNOFFICIAL AND
UNAUTHORISED GUIDE TO
BLAKE'S 7

ALAN STEVENS
AND
FIONA MOORE

First published in the UK in 2003 by
Telos Publishing Ltd
5a Church Close, Shortlands, Bromley, Kent, BR2 0HP
www.telos.co.uk

This Edition 2014

Cover by Dariusz Jasiczak

ISBN: 978-1-84583-861-4

British Library Cataloguing in Publication Data.
A catalogue record for this book is available from the British
Library.

CONTENTS

ACKNOWLEDGEMENTS

We would like to acknowledge the help of, in no particular order, Jim Smith and Dianna Firmin (for reading and commenting on the text), Andy Hopkinson and Gary Holland (for providing us with invaluable archive material), Neil Faulkner, Betty Regan, Murray Smith, Jane Mather, Christine Lacey, Sarah Bellamy and Andrew Phillips (for insights into various episodes), Ann Bown and Maureen Marrs (for support and guidance), the people who made transcripts of the *Blake's 7* episodes available online (for obvious reasons), Ben Mann and Linda Tyrrell (our *Lexx* and *Farscape* experts respectively), Helen Parkinson and Ian Pritchard (fact-checking), Steven Allen, Sheelagh Wells, Joe Nazzaro, Alistair Lock, William Johnston, Chris Orton, Gary Russell, Andrew Pixley for reviewing the text, and for his work on Marvel Comics UK's *Blake's 7 Winter Special* and *Blake's 7 Summer Special* and Visual Imagination's *TV Zone*, Martin Dempsey, Steve Cambden, Patricia Merrick, Mark Oliver, Andy Lazell, Prof. Robert Moore, David Howe and Stephen James Walker, Derek Hambly, Paul Huzzey, Andy Holmes and Paul Taylor of Tenth Planet, Barking, and Ben Keywood and Andy Swinden from Galaxy 4 in Sheffield.

The people who, in one form or another, contributed interview material, anecdotes and reminiscences to this volume are (again in no particular order), Chris Boucher, David Maloney, Paul Darrow, Scott Fredericks, Pip and Jane Baker, David Bailie, Gareth Thomas, Steven Pacey, Jacqueline Pearce, Brian Croucher, Stephen Greif, Peter Tuddenham, Peter Miles, Jim Francis, Vere Lorrimer, Michael Keating, David Jackson, Jan Chappel, John Leeson, Harriet Philpin, Julian Glover, Isla Blair, Barry Summerford, Glynis Barber and Sally Knyvette.

The spellings of personal names, planets and so forth in this book have all been taken from episode credits and the original scripts for the series.

Some of the material which went into this book can be found at www.kaldorcity.com, in the Features section.

FOREWORD

The late Sydney Newman, legendary producer of *Armchair Theatre* and then Head of the BBC Television Drama Department, described the producer as a creative midwife. Looking back more than 25 years I clearly recall the birth pangs and the eventual delivery of *Blake's 7*.

It was my first outing as producer – a tenderfoot where managing budgets, hiring directors, designers and staff and dealing with publicity were concerned.

I had directed numerous episodes of serials and series as a freelance and was finishing a long stint on *Doctor Who*. The incumbent was Tom Baker and the titles included "Genesis of the Daleks" by Terry Nation, and "The Deadly Assassin" and "The Talons of Weng-Chiang" by the splendid Bob Holmes.

In fact, it was while I was on night location in Twickenham filming "Talons" that a message came for me from Ronnie Marsh, Head of Drama Series Department. Next day I met him with Terry Nation. Terry had a concept for *Blake's 7* and one script, "The Way Back". I thought it was pretty good and accepted the job of producer. It was intriguing, challenging and something that I felt that I ought to do.

And so the series was commissioned, with great faith in Terry to go away and write twelve consecutive scripts. Meanwhile, I began to recruit: directors – Michael E Briant, Pennant Roberts, Vere Lorrimer and Douglas Camfield – a script editor Chris Boucher, who was later to write so many excellent episodes; production unit manager Sheelagh Rees, set designer Roger Murray-Leach, composer Dudley Simpson, lighting Brian Clemett, Tony Millier and Clive Gifford (sound), A J Mitchell (electronic effects) and many others. Most were brought in from *Doctor Who*. Also, I began to cast the main characters. For a series, this was the responsibility of the producer. The directors cast individual actors in their own episodes.

I had exchanged the world of camera angles and rehearsing and directing actors for one of budgets and overall programme supervision. A good definition is: the director behind the camera and the producer behind the desk.

Before reading Alan Stevens and Fiona Moore's fascinating book, it may be useful to understand how popular drama programmes were made for thirty years between the 1950s and the 1980s. We worked a hybrid system – part film and part theatre – now outmoded except in the making of sitcom. This facilitated a fast production line.

Each fifty minute series episode would be rehearsed, camera rehearsed and videotaped on a consecutive ten day turn round but with only two days in a real studio. Other days were spent 'dry' rehearsing in a room with coloured floor tapes and bits of derelict furniture.

In the studio multi-camera recording – unlike the luxurious single camera shooting of today – would sometimes tape whole scenes non-stop. Little wonder that actors trained for the stage took to it so well. There were breaks between scenes but even these were frowned on in earlier days. Sydney Newman had at one time decreed that there should be only five recording breaks during the taping of a programme. Editing the heavy two inch video tape was difficult in those days and with only five joins to make, directors did not always attend the editing. They sent their production assistants instead. (*Blake's 7* always had a proper editing session and the directors were always there!)

Essentially, there was little latitude in the studio recording operation. Despite deadlines and enormous pressure to finish on time, producers and directors had to ensure that no part of the story would be missed. There were no later additions or pick-ups possible.

Of course, production teams coped well with all this and were trained to produce their programmes rapidly. There was a career line from assistant floor manager to production assistant and on to director and producer. They worked in small groups and there was plenty of work for them and for the budding writers.

The first series of *Blake's 7* was made on this turn round and without a dedicated studio for standing sets. The poor old *Liberator* interior had to be set and struck again and again. It began to look quite tired!

With so little time and money some of our creative designers had unachievable ideas and were naturally frustrated. Our shaky sets were spotted and later there was humour at the expense of the 'seven' body count for *Blake's 7*.

Yet Terry's scripts were sterling. The actors gave stalwart performances. Directors, designers and technicians worked hard and the appreciation and viewing figures went up. I am most grateful to them all.

Many teenagers watched on Monday evenings – an unusual placing for a space opera – and *Panorama*, which followed, inherited a large audience.

The making of later series was to become easier with more time and money available. Still, considering the tense effort to launch the first one I am delighted to see how much interest and enthusiasm is still shown for *Blake's 7*.

Alan and Fiona have unearthed a wealth of detail about the early development of the series and give us considerable information, with each season and episode broken down minutely. They have found interesting derivatives for characters, stories and plotlines and make a dense examination of relationships between the major characters. This is a shrewd, academic (and at times kindly) analysis. Occasionally they rightly have fun at the crudity of *Blake's 7* technology.

I am certainly in agreement with their praising of certain episodes 'where everything seems to come together'. Their concern at times about inconsistencies may have been partly my fault as I was constantly rearranging the broadcasting order of the stories. Also, I had a policy that if something did not work we should change it immediately. But many of the flaws they highlight result from intense pressure of production.

This book stirs memories of things that I had forgotten. I recommend it as a good read for enthusiasts.

David Maloney
July 2003

INTRODUCTION

Although *Blake's 7* is a series that many critics have derided over the years for its occasionally-poor special effects, sometimes-dubious costume design and overly middle-class casting, its legacy has nonetheless endured where other series with larger budgets have passed into obscurity. Because *Blake's 7*'s creators focused on powerful themes of human evil, rebellion, love and death, the series' message continues to be fresh long after its production has become dated.

THE BACKGROUND: THE MID-1970S

When discussing the contemporary influences of *Blake's 7*, most people refer to *Star Wars*, which was released in Britain eleven days before the first broadcast of *Blake's 7*. However, while it is true that *Star Wars* did have an influence on the programme, if only by making sci-fi a marketable commodity to television executives, and while it is true that there are some similarities between the premises of the two (roguish rebels versus fascist dictatorships in space), the links between them are very tenuous. The original *Star Wars* film is written in the vein of a *Flash Gordon* chapter-play, with clear-cut distinctions between good and evil, whereas in *Blake's 7* the dictatorship is constructed as a realistic, detailed society and the rebels are a very ambiguous lot indeed. In fact, rather than ask what the influences of *Star Wars* on *Blake's 7* were, it might be better to ask what *Blake's 7* had that *Star Wars* lacked.

Blake's 7 was created during a golden period in British television history. By the mid-1970s the medium had become established enough that it was no longer seen as a poor relation to radio or the theatre, as it had been in the 1950s (when much of the drama output had consisted literally of televised stage plays), but it was not yet so hidebound and formulaic that groundbreaking and innovative programmes were difficult to get commissioned, as would become the case in the 1980s. The great playwrights, producers and directors of the day were still interested in TV in and of itself as a medium (a viewpoint fostered in the previous decade by pioneering productions such as the ABC plays anthology *Armchair Theatre*), not just as a cheap substitute for film. Legendary stage and screen director Philip Saville (who had cut his television teeth on *Armchair Theatre*), in a 1976 interview about his *Play for Today* story *Gangsters* – later to be spun off into one of the most original serials ever produced on television – said: 'I see no reason why a new 'total theatre' should not come out of the TV studio.' Established writers, including Harold Pinter and Dennis Potter, also remained interested in the medium; Potter in particular felt that images drawn from pop culture were able to resonate more with viewers and have a greater emotional impact than high culture, and that television plays could thus produce a stronger effect in a wider audience than an opera or art film.

At the time, also, the BBC still had an ethos strongly influenced by original Director-General Lord Reith's doctrine that it should inform and educate as well as entertain. Consequently, BBC programmes, including those produced by the Drama Department, often focused on exploring serious issues and challenging perceptions: the plays of Dennis Potter (himself a fan of *Blake's 7*) explored issues of gender, sexuality and violence, while many series of the day employed the familiar conventions of the crime story or kitchen-sink drama to explore real issues of poverty, class differentiation, urban crime and immigration. Even an established show such as *Doctor Who* continued to push the envelope, by introducing gothic horror and adult themes to family programming.

At the time when *Blake's 7* was created, then, not only was sci-fi undergoing a revival, but many British writers and producers were actively exploring the possibilities for making popular TV programmes that pleased the crowds on one level while exploring serious themes on others.

GENESIS OF THE SERIES

The original concept for *Blake's 7* was devised by Terry Nation, one of the most influential television personalities of his generation. Previously best known for having created the Daleks (possibly the single greatest TV icon of the 1960s), Nation had written extensively for *Doctor Who, The Avengers, The Baron* and many other well-remembered series. Along with script editor Chris Boucher and producer David Maloney, he would take his concept and develop it into the series as it eventually appeared on screen.

One of the most misunderstood descriptions often applied to Terry Nation is the term 'hack writer.' A hack, simply put, is a writer who produces fiction with a view to making a living rather than art; unfortunately, in recent years, the term has also come to designate writers whose style is poor and whose stories are cynically-written. However, hack writing also makes for a good deal of discipline, an engaging prose style and an ability to present complex themes plainly and succinctly; Dickens, Hemingway and Heinlein were all hack writers. While Nation may not have been a Dickens or a Hemingway, it is no insult to call him a hack, and indeed, being able to work in this manner was one of his greatest strengths.

Nation, furthermore, was a politically astute hack. He was intrigued by the themes of fascism, collaboration, evil and the depths to which humans can sink in the name of greed and self-aggrandizement. He was also fascinated by George Orwell's *Nineteen Eighty-Four,* Anthony Burgess's *A Clockwork Orange* and Aldous Huxley's *Brave New World*, three novels whose themes of totalitarianism, resistance, class conflict and mind alteration would have a strong influence on *Blake's 7* as they did on his *Doctor Who* stories. In the early 1970s, Nation had developed a programme, *Survivors,* about an Earth where nine-tenths of the population have been wiped out by a plague, in which he had hoped to explore these themes in greater detail; however, producer Terence Dudley had increasingly steered the series in a different direction, aiming for more action-oriented scripts and fewer social dramas. This caused a bitter falling-out between Nation and Dudley, and the two were never reconciled. In 1975, with Dudley having effectively taken over *Survivors*, Nation pitched several ideas for new series to the BBC.

Most of his proposed scenarios were police dramas, but the one that attracted the attention of Ronnie Marsh, the Head of Drama Series Department (at the time, BBC Drama was split into three sections: Plays, Serials and Series) was a space opera with the provisional title *Blake's 7.*

It is clear that from the outset the series was intended to appeal to a wide variety of audiences. Marsh's notes for his meeting with Terry Nation of 9 September 1975, in which the series was initially pitched, refer to it as *'kidult sci-fi'*: *'A space western-adventure. A modern swashbuckler. <u>Blakes Seven</u>. Group of villains being escorted onto a rocket ship (transported) which goes astray & lands on an alien planet where inhabitants are planning to invade & destroy earth.'* Nation would later describe the initial concept of the series as *'The Dirty Dozen* in space.' Like *Doctor Who* at its best, it would thus have swashbuckling action and adventure to engage the interest of children and teenagers, but also deeper themes and grittier elements to attract a more adult audience – as is apparent from the comparison to *The Dirty Dozen,* a disturbing and brutal film still considered a classic today. The idea, furthermore, of a group of villains as the protagonists is more than a bit of a deviation from the norm of space opera. Although the alien-invasion storyline was soon (by 30 April 1976) abandoned in favour of the more familiar storyline of an ordinary man named Rog (later Roj) Blake discovering that he was once a rebel against the oppressive Federation, Nation was obviously hoping that *Blake's 7* would be what *Survivors* was not: a means of telling a deep, serious story with political overtones, through the familiar, enjoyable format of a space opera.

Nation would be assisted in this task by producer David Maloney, responsible for directing some of the best-remembered serials of *Doctor Who,* including Nation's own "Genesis of the Daleks"; Ronnie Marsh offered him the job because of his extensive experience with science fiction. Completing the main production team was Chris Boucher, who would remain as script editor for the entire run of *Blake's 7.* Originally, Maloney had approached Robert Holmes, with whom he had worked on *Doctor Who,* and who had a reputation for intelligent, sophisticated treatments of storylines, to be the script editor. Holmes had declined, but suggested his protégé Boucher instead; Boucher, under Holmes's influence, had written two acclaimed serials for *Doctor Who* (and would later write a third) and showed a good deal of depth and intelligence as a writer. Furthermore, Boucher's philosophy of scriptwriting is, in his words, to 'make the audience work,' preferring complex scripts in which the ideas are not all spelled out to the viewer, but can be discerned from careful observation of the characters and plot. Nation had, in the past, done his best work when coupled with a script editor who was able to enhance a tightly-plotted storyline with subtle, clever dialogue, and so Boucher was taken on. Like Maloney – and indeed like virtually all the writers and directors of the series – Boucher normally worked on a freelance basis, and this was his first full-time television post.

The result of the initial collaboration between Maloney, Boucher and Nation would be a series that was not only entertaining, clever and humorous, but also explored serious issues such as crime, punishment, legitimate government and feminism. It would, furthermore, contain continuing subtexts that carried some quite surprising messages about the characters and the society from which they originate.

SEASON A (1978)

SEASON A - CREDITS

Series Creator: Terry Nation
Script Editor: Chris Boucher
Producer: David Maloney
Title Music: Dudley Simpson

Cast:
Gareth Thomas – Roj Blake
Sally Knyvette – Jenna Stannis
Paul Darrow – Kerr Avon (A2 – A13)
Jan Chappell – Cally (A4 – A13)
Michael Keating – Vila Restal
David Jackson – Olag Gan (A2 – A13)
Peter Tuddenham (voice) – Zen (A3 – A13)
Stephen Greif – Travis (A6, A8, A9, A12, A13)
Jacqueline Pearce – Servalan (A6, A9, A12, A13)

Production Assistant:
Victor Mallett (A1, A5, A9, A12)
Pauline Smithson (A2, A4, A7, A11)
Christina McMillan (A3)
Geoffrey Manton (A6, A10, A13)
Tony Virgo (A8)
Jenny McArthur (A12) (uncredited)

Production Unit Manager:
Sheelagh Rees

Visual Effects Designer:

Ian Scoones
Mat Irvine (A4 (uncredited), A6 – A13)

Film Cameraman:
Ken Willcombe

Film Recordist:
Bill Meekums (A1, A2, A4)
John K Murphy (A3, A4)
Andrew Boulton (A5)
Graham Hare (A6, A8)
John Gatland (A7, A9 – A13)

Film Editor:
M A C Adams (A1, A2, A4 – A6, A10 – A13)
Martin Sharpe (A3, A7)
John S Smith (A8)
David Martin (A9)

Studio Lighting:
Brian Clemett

Studio Sound:
Clive Gifford (A1, A4, A6, A7, A10, A12)
Tony Millier (A2, A3, A4 (uncredited), A5, A8, A9, A11, A13)

Special Sound:
Richard Yeoman-Clark

Electronic Effects:
A J Mitchell (A3 – A13)

Series Videotape Editors:
Sam Upton
Malcolm Banthorpe

Costume Designer:
Barbara Lane (A1 – A9)
Rupert Jarvis (A8 (uncredited), A9 – A13)

Make Up Artist:
Eileen Mair (A1, A2, A5)
Marianne Ford (A1 – A4, A6 – A13)

Graphics Designer:
Bob Blagden
Ron Platford (A13)

Incidental Music:
Dudley Simpson (A1 – A7, A9 – A13)

Stunt Co-ordinator:
Frank Maher (A2, A4, A6, A8, A9, A11, A12)
Peter Brayham (A3, A10)
Stuart Fell (A9)

Designer:
Martin Collins (A1, A5, A7, A13)
Roger Murray Leach (A2, A4, A8, A11)
Robert Berk (A3, A4 (uncredited), A6, A12)
Chris Pemsel (A9)
Peter Brachacki (A10

SEASON A: INTRODUCTION

The series' first season was one of experiment and change, as the cast and production team developed the format, appearance and characterisation of the *Blake's 7* universe, and rose to the challenges of working around practical limitations.

The first obstacle faced by the production team was the fact that the series was put in as a replacement for the police drama *Softly Softly: Task Force*, and consequently inherited its relatively low budget. Ian Scoones, the visual effects designer, was more than a little indignant at the lack of money, especially as *Star Wars* was imminently due to be released in the UK. Maloney, Nation and Boucher therefore realised from the start that the series could not be the type of pure science fiction that relied on very extensive effects work – in which it would be unable to compete with the standard set by *Star Wars* – but must also incorporate elements of historical and crime drama, comedy, and contemporary thriller. 'That's what television drama is all about,' explains Boucher. 'If you haven't got the budget to afford George Lucas-style effects, you instead rely on interesting characters and interesting words.' In a similar vein, Maloney remembers that a copy of the draft script for each episode would always be sent to Richard Wilmot of the BBC's Design Department: 'Richard was the Estimator, and he would work out how many man-hours the building of the various sets would cost. I would always get hold of the draft script before it was handed over to him and if it read, "they enter a vast room", I would cross that out and write, "they enter a middle-sized room", and if it read, "they enter a middle-sized room", I would put a line through that and write, "they enter a small room", and I had to do that with every draft script so the whole thing would be affordable. The same counted for extras. If the script said, "fifty soldiers storm through the doorway", I'd cross that out and write "two!"'

This did not, however, prevent the occasional unfortunate decision to promote gimmicks over plot: the absurd-looking 'Federation Security Robot', seen in "Seek-Locate-Destroy" and "Project Avalon", was originally intended to be a regular feature, but it was unreliable and unconvincing. Even a publicity photo of the robot with Jan Chappell and Sally Knyvette did little to boost its profile, and it was ignominiously dropped. More successful, though no less troublesome, was the three-foot model of the *Liberator* spacecraft (referred to in early Nation scripts as *Liberator One*). Devised by set designer Roger Murray-Leach, its front-heavy construction made it very difficult to mount and fly.

A more prosaic hitch in the season's production came when Stephen Greif ruptured his Achilles tendon playing squash prior to the studio recording for "Orac" and had to be doubled by extra Barry Hayes in several shots.

The series was originally slated to run for 26 episodes, split into two blocks of 13. The cast were initially contracted with options on the BBC side, which meant that the BBC could let any cast member go at any point, but that they could not leave without the BBC's consent. A fixed fee was also included in the contract, to ensure that if one actor became particularly popular, they could not use this as a bargaining chip.

Terry Nation was assigned the task of scripting the first 13 episodes, not only because the series was his 'baby', but also to allow for it to be promoted on the basis of his strong public profile; it was also agreed that he would end the first season on a cliffhanger and resolve it in the initial episode of Season B, after which he would have the option of writing further stories. An examination of early drafts of the scripts indicates that Chris Boucher had a good deal of input from the start, particularly in terms of characterisation and dialogue enhancement; the scriptwriting procedure generally involved Nation writing the first draft, Boucher and Maloney making suggestions on it in the form of detailed notes, and then Nation writing the final version. Towards the end of the first season, as Nation began to find the tight writing schedule difficult, he would simply submit the drafts and Boucher would rewrite them – although Nation had the final say, and even on these later episodes the plot remained essentially unchanged from the first drafts, however skimpy, to the final version.

While the series' early episodes were in development, one Nation script, "The Invaders", was rejected; and, more prosaically, a few episode titles were also changed: "The Way Back" and "Cygnus Alpha" were originally to have been the titles of the third ["Cygnus Alpha"] and first ["The Way Back"] stories respectively, with "Prelude" also appearing on early versions of "The Way Back", and "Breakdown" was initially known as "Brain Storm".

Perhaps the most significant changes to be made in this developmental period, however, were in the area of characterization. Originally, 'Blake's 7' were indeed to have been Blake plus seven others; as well as Avon, Gan, Vila and Jenna, the regulars would have included Tone Selman, Brell Kline and Arco Trent. 'Terry was very keen on the number seven,' recalls Boucher. 'He believed it was lucky.' This large a cast, however, was soon to prove a problem in scripting terms: in particular, Kline gets virtually no lines in all of the draft scripts of the first three stories. Dev Tarrant was originally called Cral Travis, introduced in the first episode and then reintroduced (with an eyepatch and mechanical arm added) in an abandoned story called "Locate and Destroy" (which, despite its title's similarity to that of the televised episode "Seek-Locate-Destroy", actually resembled a cross between "Duel" and "Deliverance", with Travis attacking the *Liberator* and Jenna being kidnapped by primitives on a war-torn planet). Later, Travis would become a separate character, retaining the physical attributes that he was given in the abandoned script. Servalan was originally a minor (male) character, Shervalan, and Travis's crew went from being 'androids' to 'cyborgs' to 'mutoids'. Cally was a late addition to the team, intended to balance out the gender mix of the regulars; she was explicitly described as being like an Israeli terrorist girl in early drafts of "Time Squad" (and there appear to have been elements of Chris Boucher's *Doctor Who* creation Leela, a plainly-spoken primitive warrior woman who was herself named after a female Palestinian hijacker called Leila Khaled, and Kali, the Hindu goddess of death, in the mix as well).

The characterisation of some of those who would be retained as regulars also underwent changes. Vila was originally depicted as an urbane, wise-cracking criminal along the lines of *The Saint*; the original conception of Jenna appears to have been as something of a gangster's moll, being strongly tempted by Avon's offer of wealth in "Cygnus Alpha" and described as touching the money he holds out 'sensually'; and Cally, who was originally to have been able to read minds as well as send telepathically, was more explicitly alien, and came from the planet Saurian Major, where Blake first encounters her in "Time Squad", rather than Auron, as eventually established on screen. (An early proposal that Jan Chappell would sport red hair, scarlet makeup and red contact lenses, in keeping with director Pennant Roberts' idea of shooting Saurian Major through a red filter, was abandoned when the character's planet of origin was changed, as well as for reasons of practicality.) Avon as he appears in the series – a self-interested, ruthless, ambitious figure with a certain sort of leadership quality – is an amalgam of two antagonistic figures in the original draft scripts: Arco, who plots against Blake but develops a grudging respect for him after Blake saves his life, and Avon, a self-serving, treacherous coward who follows Arco.

It is worth noting that Boucher had a certain influence on the development of the characters, as many lines of dialogue establishing characterisation emerge from his rewrites. The original draft of "The Web", for instance, has Avon explaining to Gan how the *Liberator*'s regenerative technology works, but lacks the little jabs at Gan's intelligence throughout the sequence which appear in the final version. Boucher appears to have had a good deal of input into the characterisation of Avon in particular. (He is on record as saying: 'There was not a line of Avon's on which I did not have some form of influence'.) Vila also changes somewhat over the course of the series as transmitted: originally he seems to have been thought of as a slippery, devious character with a harder edge, as evidenced by his portrayal in "The Way Back" and "Breakdown". (Brian Croucher, who later was to be cast as Travis for the second season of *Blake's 7*, was originally considered for the part.) Later, prompted perhaps by Keating's style of performance, this ambiguous edge softens and Vila becomes more solidly a humorous figure.

One of the most striking things about the regulars from a twenty-first century perspective is the fact that they all have decidedly received pronunciation accents; even Gan and Vila, the 'working-class' characters, speak in measured, RADA tones. (The same holds true for most of the supporting cast, although here and there – Arco in "Cygnus Alpha", for instance – one does encounter a regional or working-class accent.) The most likely explanation for this is the domination of the space-opera market by American series like *Star Trek* and *Lost In Space*; although American regional accents are heard in all such series, the untrained UK ear has more difficulty in distinguishing between these than between more familiar accents, and consequently most of the characters sound, to a UK audience, the same. However, it may also be due in large part to the ethos of the BBC in the 1970s, where the use of the RP accent – or "BBC English" as it is sometimes termed – was still strongly favoured in all types of production.

The society from which the characters come is, significantly, not a post nuclear one. Although this idea was put forward in publicity material, it never formed part of the series itself. (Publicity writers frequently engaged in flights of fantasy that bore not the slightest resemblance to the intentions of the production team.) By the 1970s, enough was known about the effects of radiation to have allowed for the convincing depiction of a landscape ravaged by nuclear war, had that been the intention. However, the ground outside the dome in "The Way Back" is green and fertile; the water is good; and apparently-normal people (to say nothing of owls) live outside. The costumes of the Federation guards resemble chemical-warfare suits to a greater degree than they do radiation suits.

As with the characters, the political focus of the series also undergoes a gradual shift; originally, Blake's campaign is directed against the Terran Administration, the government of Earth; later, after he is exiled from Earth, the Terran Federation (which encompasses Earth, the other Federation-aligned planets and the military administration, Space Command) becomes his main target.

It is also worth taking a look at the technology of the *Blake's 7* universe. Much of it is plainly ludicrous in real scientific terms. (A good example is the automatic hull-sealing mechanism seen in "Space Fall"; if a flying object had really penetrated both the outer and inner hulls of a spaceship, the personnel would be dead before any sort of sealant foam could have blocked the gap). However, the technology is intended more for effect than for realism. The spaceships, for instance, act (like those in many other space operas) effectively like 18th-century sailing ships, facing off against each other on a two-dimensional rather than a three-dimensional plane, and continually tacking and drifting; planets seem to be effectively like islands in an ocean. The ubiquitous *Blake's 7* plot convenience of having the *Liberator* seemingly hanging over a planet undetected also makes sense only if one thinks in terms of ships dropping anchor in isolated coves (as witness the line in the second season episode "Shadow", in which it is explicitly stated that the *Liberator* takes a particular orbit to avoid detection). Other aspects of the series follow the 18th-century line; the sequence in "Seek-Locate-Destroy" in which Prell transmits a message by 'courier' to Travis echoes the sending of letters by messenger, and Nation's early descriptions of the *Liberator* guns have them as 'sword-like'. (Scoones' original design, resembling *Star Wars* lightsabres crossed with 18th-century rapiers, and his final design, a shorter but still long-barrelled weapon, kept to this theme.)

The computers are effectively a projection of the computer technology of the immediate pre-Microsoft era onto the future. Unlike contemporary computers, the ones we see here are all solid state; Avon has to physically alter them to reprogram them, rather than fiddle around with software, and Gan's limiter is a solid-state device. Descriptions of computers as being 'online' also refer to their being switched on rather than to their being connected into networks. As 1977 was the eve of the 'information revolution,' when cheap personal computers, programmed by writing pieces of software onto a standard hardware system, became widely available, this particular projection of computing technology onto the future is something of a historical curiosity. Conversely, Orac, a computer whose creator's personality seems to have become imprinted onto him, is both a foreshadowing of later software-based systems and of the novels of William Gibson and his contemporaries.

As envisioned by Nation, the title sequence would have involved a series of punch-cards bearing the portraits of the regulars coming out of a computer into a tray marked 'Enemies of the State,' plus a journey rushing through space (with portraits of the regulars overlaid) towards a planet, then the screen filling with fire and smoke. This imagery, something of a cross between *The Prisoner* and a 1930s sci-fi chapter-play opening sequence, effectively symbolises how the writing and production teams viewed the series at its outset. This was developed into the more traditional 'space' and 'oppression' themed sequence for transmission.

From its first broadcast, *Blake's 7* was popular with viewers. Although "The Way Back" garnered an audience of only 7.4 million, this relatively low figure can be attributed, at least partly, to the fact that it went out during the New Year's schedule and at 6:00 pm (one and a quarter hours earlier than all the other episodes bar "Orac", which went out at 7:05 pm). After a small drop for "Space Fall" (which scored only 7.3 million due to that night's episode of *Coronation Street* featuring the death of Ernie Bishop), by the third episode the figures had improved dramatically, climbing by 1.2 million and staying consistently above the 8.0 million mark for the rest of the season, peaking at 10.9 million on "Seek-Locate-Destroy" and hovering between 8.8 million and 10.6 million subsequently. This success can be attributed partly to tireless work by its scripting and production teams, and partly to the timeless themes and ideas that the stories explored.

A1: THE WAY BACK

UK TRANSMISSION: Monday 2 January 1978: 6.00pm – 6.50pm
DURATION: 47:06
VIEWING FIGURE: 7.4m
CHART POSITION: 72
WRITER: Terry Nation
DIRECTOR: Michael E Briant

CREDITED CAST: Robert Beatty (Bran Foster); Robert James (Glynd); Jeremy Wilkin (Tarrant); Michael Halsey (Varon); Pippa Steel (Maja); Gillian Bailey (Ravella); Alan Butler (Richie); Margaret John (Arbiter); Peter Williams (Dr Havant); Susan Field (Alta Morag); Rodney Figaro (Clerk of Court); Nigel Lambert (Computer Operator); Garry McDermott (Guard)

UNCREDITED CAST: Les Shannon, Derek Southern, John Henson, Sandy Sinclair, Barry Summerford, Mort Jackson, Tony Powell, Chris Holmes, Frank Arbisman (Guards); Beryl Nisbett (Screaming Woman Prisoner); Frank Arbisman, Reg Turner, Peter Roy, Derek Holt, Barry Hayes, Alan Crisp, Michael Mungarvan, Reg Thomason, Beryl Nisbett (Prisoners/City Dwellers)

SYNOPSIS: Roj Blake, an ordinary man living on Earth, is persuaded to come to a meeting outside the domed city in which he resides. Once there, he learns that he had been a rebel against the Administration, but was arrested and brainwashed into becoming a model citizen. Before he can learn more, the meeting is broken up by guards; the rebels are killed, but Blake is arrested. As his conditioning appears to be breaking down and Tarrant, the undercover security agent who betrayed the group, is afraid that Blake may expose him, Blake is put on trial for offences against children in order to destroy his credibility as a political activist. He is found guilty and sentenced to deportation to the planet Cygnus Alpha. Blake's lawyer, Varon, and his wife Maja investigate the situation and discover the truth, but are assassinated by government forces. Blake leaves Earth on a prison ship (with, among others, a smuggler pilot named Jenna and a thief named Vila), vowing to return.

ANALYSIS: "The Way Back" is *Blake's 7's* pilot episode, and the script is almost totally Terry Nation's work, with little input from Chris Boucher. Although it is peppered with familiar Nation ideas and plot devices, it contains a clever subtext, regarding oppression, social control and surveillance, which would be picked up on in subsequent episodes.

One of the great strengths of the story lies in its portrait of a totalitarian society; one of Nation's favourite themes. Although Nation frequently drew inspiration from Nazi Germany for the portrayal of such societies, here he is clearly drawing on Soviet Russia, via Orwell's *Nineteen Eighty-Four*. We see women in power and, although there are no Black or Asian actors (such casting being not yet *de rigeur* in British television), the Federation is clearly multiethnic: Foster is played by Canadian actor Robert Beatty (in a performance head and shoulders above those of the rest of the supporting cast), one guard affects an American accent; and one of the female rebels wears a headscarf. The low budget of the production actually adds to the effect; the impression we get is not of a self-aggrandizing Nazi-style dictatorship, but of a drab Socialist state full of cheap, shoddy goods. The society is clearly stratified, as can be seen in the differently coloured tabards (with rebels and criminals marked as outsiders by their flamboyant clothing), although it is not wholly clear whether this stratification is class – or function – based, or even, as Ven Glynd wears a darker shade of red than the two barristers, both.

This can also be seen in Blake's treatment by the regime. Doctor Havant's attempt to convince Blake that he has imagined the whole situation by saying that individuals create their own realities is a common device of totalitarian regimes, and recalls O'Brien's psychological-torture technique in *Nineteen Eighty-Four*; i.e. you are of course entitled to your own opinion, but mine is more valid than yours. The idea of discrediting a political activist dangerous to the regime by accusing him of committing a shameful crime is also in keeping with the activities of the Soviet Union and the Chinese Communist Party; in early drafts of the story, Blake was a schoolteacher, which would have made his purported 'crime' all the more horrific. (This idea was eventually dropped due to the prohibitive costs of hiring child actors.) There is, however, the ironic fact that in implicating Blake, the Administration has itself committed the very crime of which it would later accuse the rebel, highlighting the fact that all totalitarian regimes are inherently corrupt.

The central point of the story is that of Blake regaining his memory of having been arrested and brainwashed, and discovering that he has been set up by the government to live a lie. Ravella, the girl who reveals this to him, is dressed similarly to Blake and is very close in colouring to Gareth Thomas, making her a kind of ghost of Blake's earlier self, showing him the way back to the past. It is here, however, we reach the main apparent logical flaw of the story: how is it that, in four years, nobody has approached him? It cannot be that people are afraid to, as Blake would surely have noticed this. Likewise, it cannot be that they are universally doped into submission, despite the reference to mind-altering drugs. Glynd, Havant, Morag and many of the others are quite clearly capable of rational thought – even, in the case of Varon, of doubting the system – and Glynd mentions casually that many believe Blake's original trial to have been a set-up, suggesting that Varon is not unique. Furthermore, we later learn that Blake worked on the Aquitar project for the development of a teleport system, which would seem too complex for somebody to do in a mind-altered state. Similarly, there is no suggestion that he has moved from one city to another where nobody knows him; indeed, this would seem to be contradicted by the events of the script.

What is possible, however, is that Blake was downgraded. We learn later in the series that Blake is a member of the highest grade of the society, an 'Alpha'; however, it is left unclear whether or not he remained an Alpha after his confession. Societies with a politically-ignorant underclass kept in line by drugs or other attention-diverting devices form the premises of *Brave New World* and *Nineteen Eighty-Four*; the citizens about whose opinions Glynd is concerned would thus, as in *Nineteen Eighty-Four*, be those of the drug-free (and potentially revolutionary) middle – and upper-classes. Furthermore, in both novels, the social division between the underclass and the elite is so great as to be virtually unbreachable. The people we see walking in the area where Ravella meets Blake move slowly and appear dazed, which is not the case with Glynd and his colleagues; Blake himself never refers to having been approached by revolutionaries, or to having noticed that people treated him strangely. Furthermore, Ravella states that Blake's food and water have been laced with suppressant drugs. It seems therefore that Blake has been downgraded and kept, like his fellow labourers, in a drugged stupor, making it impossible for him to foment rebellion, difficult for higher-grade revolutionaries to find him, and very unlikely that he would notice it if they did.

A further suggestion within the subtext of the script is that Blake is a kind of walking loyalty trap. People who associate with him are automatically under suspicion (hence the deaths of his colleagues and siblings); it is possible that he continues to exist as a temptation to those hoping to foment rebellion. Anyone who approaches him would be arrested (even, perhaps, turned in by Blake, as he threatens to do to Ravella and Richie), and Blake himself could be easily reconditioned to forget such an incident. In "Voice from the Past", we will later learn that he is conditioned to respond to certain stimuli (in particular a high-pitched tone, like that played under Havant's words in the mind-conditioning scene in "The Way Back"); this time, however, the trauma has been great enough to break through his programming. Although Ravella is allowed to continue associating with him without being arrested, this would appear to be a means of getting her unwittingly to betray other rebels, and it is significant that she dies the night that Blake goes to the meeting.

Similarly, the Varon plot, which looks like a series of Nation clichés (everything tying up too neatly at the trial; Dev Tarrant appearing at the courtroom; the unerased attendance records; Glynd dropping the 'inadvertent' hint about the tunnels; the conversation between Glynd and Havant, in which Glynd tells

Havant to answer the phone only to him in such a way that Varon hears; and Varon somehow managing to fool Havant's secretary into sending him the records), could easily add up to a test; a loyal citizen, if faced with the attendance record discrepancies, would have ignored them or failed to act on them, as in *Nineteen Eighty-Four*, and the computer operator who reports the breach in security, after taking the bribe and showing Varon the prohibited files, must be an undercover agent, or else he would have been implicated in Varon's crime. Nation had constructed similarly convoluted subtexts before (in *Doctor Who*'s "The Daleks' Master Plan", for instance), and was well known for reusing ideas that he knew would work; the idea of mental manipulation and the prediction of human behaviour is, furthermore, one that will recur throughout the series.

Finally, the story sets up a sort of teasing sleight-of-hand with regular characters that will continue for several episodes. The title, *Blake's 7*, strongly suggests that he will have at least six supporters; throughout the story, candidates for this role (Ravella, Richie, Varon, Foster and Maja) are continually being introduced and then killed off. The genuine supporting characters, Jenna and Vila (with Michael Keating giving a remarkably sinister performance, which he would, sadly, never match again), are not introduced until more than halfway through the story and are relatively minor figures in it. Despite the episode's drawbacks, then, there are also hints to the viewer that everything may, in this series, not be exactly what it seems.

In summary, "The Way Back" is a series of standard Nation story elements worked together into a new scenario about entrapment in a totalitarian state. The series shows clear promise at this point as having an intelligence that belies its production values.

A2: SPACE FALL

UK TRANSMISSION: Monday 9 January 1978: 7.15pm – 8.10pm
DURATION: 52:00
VIEWING FIGURE: 7.3m
CHART POSITION: 73
WRITER: Terry Nation
DIRECTOR: Pennant Roberts

CREDITED CAST: Glyn Owen (Leylan); Leslie Schofield (Raiker); Norman Tipton (Artix); David Hayward (Teague); Brett Forrest (Krell); Tom Kelly (Nova); Michael McKenzie (Dainer); Bill Weston (Garton)

UNCREDITED CAST: Clinton Morris (Wallace); Roy Pearce, Mark Collins, Harry Fielder, Robert Watson (Guards); Stuart Myers, Terry Sartain (Crewmen); Reg Turner, Mike Mungarvan, Eric Kent, Barry Hayes, Michael Reynal, Reg Thomason, Kenny Whymark, Mark Holmes, Peter Roy, Alan Crisp, Derek Holt (Prisoners); Juliette James (Jenna's Mother); David Bache (Avon's Brother)

SYNOPSIS: On the prison ship *London*, Blake, who has incurred the enmity of sadistic first mate Raiker, plots rebellion with the aid of Jenna, Vila and fellow convicts Gan and Nova. They enlist the help of a computer expert, Avon, to put the ship's computers out of action; the revolt, however, is unsuccessful and the conspirators are forced to surrender when Raiker begins killing the other prisoners. Shortly thereafter, the *London* encounters an alien ship that has drifted away from a space battle; after three of his own crew have died or gone mad when attempting to board it, the ship's captain, Leylan, sends Blake, Avon and Jenna across. Avon and Jenna are caught by the ship's psychedelic defence mechanism; Blake, however, is able to resist and the three successfully get the ship away from the *London*, killing Raiker in the process.

ANALYSIS: "Space Fall" (which was recorded prior to "The Way Back", in order for the actors to become more familiar with their roles before performing what would be their on-screen debut) is, in essence, a retelling of "The Way Back" in microcosm. As a result of this retelling, however, we get a startlingly grim portrayal of political cynicism as well as some interesting hints about the backgrounds of the series' protagonists.

Like "The Way Back", "Space Fall" portrays a shoddy and shabby society presided over by a corrupt administration. The very name of the ship, *London*, points to its representing a whole city in miniature. Like Ven Glynd, the ship's captain Leylan is an apparently decent chap who in fact turns a blind eye to the torture, murder and sexual abuse practiced by Raiker; we have once again a savage, uncivilised periphery (Cygnus Alpha/outside) contrasted with an oppressive, surveillanced, civilised centre (*London*/the dome). We have the prisoners' food and water being heavily dosed with suppressants, and finally, at the end of the story, we have a honey-trap that, once again, is foiled.

At first glance, the relationship between Leylan and Raiker appears to be a case of an ineffective captain losing control of a psychopathic first mate. However, there is quite clearly more going on than this. The first indication is when Leylan says to Raiker 'We have a woman prisoner... be discreet'; the implication being that Leylan knows that Raiker will make an attempt to molest Jenna (as indeed he does), but that he is willing to turn a blind eye so long as there is no open trouble. The casual nature of this exchange also suggests that similar things have happened before. Later, when Leylan gives Raiker carte-blanche to quell the rebellion, he has no qualms about handing control over to Raiker, or about Raiker's tactic of killing prisoners to get Blake to surrender. (It is worth noting that, in "Cygnus Alpha", Leylan does not count prisoners in his list of casualties.) It is only once Raiker becomes indiscreet –

killing a prisoner after Blake has surrendered, or openly declaring his intentions for Jenna to Leylan before witnesses – that Leylan steps in.

This, ironically, explains the survival of Blake, Avon and Jenna under conditions when it would have been much easier to have them executed. If Leylan is to make good on his threat to file a report, he will need anti-Raiker witnesses, as otherwise he himself would also be strongly implicated. We have seen this behaviour with regard to new boy Artix: Leylan never says anything negative in Artix's presence, and part of his apparent outrage over the shooting of the prisoner may well be the fact that Artix is nearby; in Artix, Leylan has a ready-made witness for his own good behaviour. Raiker's suggestion that Leylan send the prisoners over to the ship thus takes on an additional implication as a form of burying the hatchet between Raiker and Leylan. Leylan's talk of a pardon is acknowledged both by himself and by Blake to be a lie; if nothing else, he hasn't the authority to grant one. Raiker is suggesting that the prisoners should be killed – either by the ship's defences or by him once they have secured the ship – quashing any bad blood between himself and Leylan, ensuring that Leylan drops his threat to file a report without loss of face, and providing both with the kudos for having captured the alien vessel. Although Leylan does file a report on the mutiny in the end, it is after Blake has escaped, and will return to attack the system that condemned him; Leylan's punishment for having allowed the revolt to take place (he makes no mention of how it was put down) would be far less than that for having failed to warn the authorities that Blake is now at large and armed.

A final parallel can be seen with regard to Dainer, the guard whom Vila distracts with magic tricks. When we first see him, he is quite amiable; as a guard, he cannot believe that Vila's actions are innocent (as illustrated by the fact that he will not accept a drink until Vila has tasted it first), but he's willing to let him get away with things, in exchange for the magic show. Once the mutiny starts, however, he abruptly becomes ruthless, gunning down unarmed men in cold blood. On the *London*, the prisoners are allowed a degree of tolerance provided they don't openly break the rules; once this has happened, however, all bets are off.

One of the new regulars, Gan, also has some interesting hints about his character. (Once again, Nation is coy as to who the regulars will be; there is nothing in the initial portrayal of Nova to suggest that he is to die an early death – indeed, the 'bright young lad' is as much a stock figure of such dramas as the 'roguish thief' – and there is no indication at the end of the story that Gan and Vila will re-encounter their former comrades.) Gan is a seemingly simple giant who, we later learn, is fitted with a 'limiter' to prevent him from carrying out particular sorts of behaviour. Apparently, however, this behaviour does not include harming other people; we see him threaten a guard (smiling as he does so), and disarm two others by applying painful pressure to their forearms. Indeed, there is evidence that he may even be able to kill; we see a group of prisoners, with Gan restraining a guard by the arm and the scruff of the neck, looking for the armoury, and, when we next see them, the guard is gone and they still apparently have not reached their destination; it is unlikely, given the situation, that the guard escaped, and Gan is the prisoner in the best position to have killed the guard. (Although the extra later reappears in the background, this does not necessarily mean the character survived, as the lack of budget at this stage means that extras were frequently re-used: in "The Way Back", the men wandering in the corridors of the dome are all later to be seen in prison cells and awaiting transportation, and then, a scene later, are back in the dome.) In "Cygnus Alpha", Leylan reports five crew deaths; the story accounts for only four, suggesting that one guard died in the mutiny. The possibility that Gan can, in fact, kill (and his motives for doing so) will be dealt with again in the series, with interesting consequences.

The story's climax, finally, involves Avon, Blake and Jenna being tested by the alien ship's defences. The clear implication is that the ship defends itself by showing an image of someone dear to the intruder, in such a way that they will run to them and be killed by the ship: Jenna sees her mother being attacked by Federation guards, and earlier, one of the *London* crew cries out '…what are they doing to you?' upon entering the flight deck. Blake, however, has been doing a lot of thinking about the nature of memory and truth of late – as we are aware – and so is not deceived by the illusion of his siblings, whom he knows to be dead.

The fact that Avon's brother is the one whom he sees suggests that Avon and his brother have – or have had – a strong relationship. Furthermore, the fact that, unlike Jenna and the guard, Avon does not see his brother in peril, but simply calling for him, suggests that Avon's brother is somehow inaccessible to him. Although Avon never mentions him again, or searches for him like he does for Anna Grant, it is unlikely that the brother is, to his certain knowledge, dead; the fact that Blake knows his siblings to be dead breaks the illusion for him, and it is unlikely that Jenna or the guard would be affected by the sight of a person they knew to be dead in peril. He may have disappeared in such a way that his death is fairly assured (as is common in totalitarian states), or to such a degree that Avon does not know where to start looking for him; we do not know. One way or another, we do know that Avon is strongly attached to the memory of a brother whom he cannot contact. This gives a strong clue to the nature of Avon's obsession with Blake; the love-hate nature of their relationship suggests that Blake may, for Avon, be a substitute for the vanished sibling, for whom he feels love but also, possibly, anger arising from his disappearance.

"Space Fall" is thus a fairly straightforward story of rebellion on a prison ship which, through its subtexts, both reinforces the messages of the first story and gives us insights into the minds of the characters who have been established as the series' central figures.

A3: CYGNUS ALPHA

UK TRANSMISSION: Monday 16 January 1978: 7.15pm – 8.10pm
DURATION: 52:00
VIEWING FIGURE: 8.5m
CHART POSITION: 54
WRITER: Terry Nation
DIRECTOR: Vere Lorrimer

CREDITED CAST: Brian Blessed (Vargas); Glyn Owen (Leylan); Norman Tipton (Artix); Pamela Salem (Kara); Robert Russell (Laran); Peter Childs (Arco); David Ryall (Selman)

UNCREDITED CAST: Clifford Diggins, Del Baker, Frank Henson, Nick Hobbs (Hooded Figures/Stuntmen); Clifford Diggins (Double for Blake); Cy Wallis, Reg Thomason, Richard Sheekey, Michael Reynal, Christopher Holmes, Alan Crisp, Monty Morris (Prisoners); Malcolm Taylor, Donald Stephenson, Brian Moorhead, Philip Webb, Clive Barrie, Andy Dempsey, Ray Sunby, Terry Sartain, (Hooded Figures); Harry Fielder (Security Guard); Leslie Schofield (Raiker – Flashback to "Space Fall")

SYNOPSIS: *London* lands the remaining prisoners on Cygnus Alpha, where they encounter Kara, a priestess of the religious group that rules the planet. Meanwhile, Blake, Avon and Jenna explore the alien ship, which acquires the name 'Liberator' after its enigmatic computer, Zen, communicates telepathically with Jenna. They discover a teleport system, and Blake goes down to Cygnus Alpha to offer the other prisoners the chance to come with them. When he finds them, he learns that everyone who lands on Cygnus Alpha develops a disease, 'The Curse of Cygnus,' necessitating regular doses of a drug, and thus that they cannot leave the planet. Blake is captured, taken to the high priest, Vargas, and, when he refuses to give Vargas the *Liberator*, is tortured and imprisoned. Most of the other prisoners are uninterested in escape, but Gan, Vila, Selman and Arco, together with Blake, plot to disrupt a human sacrifice by staging a battle, during which Selman and Arco are killed. Jenna teleports the survivors back up, accidentally bringing Vargas along; she teleports him into space, killing him, after he has revealed that the disease is not fatal and the drugs are placebos.

ANALYSIS: By this point in the season, the writing and production teams have achieved full rapport, producing a story that, although the script is marred by a flaw, has an excellent plot, good casting and lovely production values.

"Cygnus Alpha" gives us our third iteration of a totalitarian society (in this case, a theocratic one), demonstrating that, even on the outskirts of civilisation, oppression persists. We have surveillance, both human and divine; we have social control which is as much by the individual as by the state (the prisoners are not being held against their will and, when offered freedom by Blake, most choose to stay, simply because it seems the easier option); we have state-sanctioned torture and abuse (and, upon seeing Blake's condition after torture, Arco blames the victim, telling Blake that he should have stayed out of trouble); we have control using drugs (in the form of Vargas's Big Lie, that the drugs consumed in the religious ceremonies keep them alive); we have guards who attack Blake in a scene reminiscent of the flashbacks in "The Way Back". Sexual abuse is not mentioned, but we do have sex as an agent of social control: while Kara is visibly attracted to Gan, her kissing him seems to be as much a way of getting the most powerful man in the new group on her side as anything.

Here, however, we also see an interesting variety of ways in which belief factors into the system. Vargas is portrayed as a complex figure (although Blessed's performance does unfortunately degenerate, at the end, into dull top-volume ranting), aware of the lie upon which his religion is based, and wanting the *Liberator* for the power it will bring him personally, but at the same time firmly believing in his god, and wishing to increase the prestige of his faith. Kara also firmly believes, to the point where she will not intervene in the sacrifice of Gan. Laran, finally, is plainly interested in personal achievement only, despite his mimicry of Kara's religious speech.

The religion itself maintains, in form and symbolism, a close parallel with Christianity. Its symbols include the St Andrew's cross (not quite close enough to the Christian cross to incur the wrath of conservative viewers), and a stylised left hand, in a literally sinister inversion of the belief that Christ sits at the right hand of God. Kara also speaks of the 'rebirth' of the new converts (and the *London* crew, in an echo of this, put the prisoners in the 'berthing chamber'), Vargas's purple robes recall those of bishops, and the drug is distributed in a way reminiscent of communion, complete with plainsong chant. The fact that the drugs are visibly a familiar UK brand of extra-strong mints is something of a joke on the viewer, as their falsity is in this case not a production flaw, but a plot point.

The secondary plot, with the crew exploring the *Liberator*, is mainly a means of introducing the ship and its abilities. We learn that it is very fast, and can travel in 'negative hyperspace.' We also learn that it contains roomfuls of clothes and jewellery (the latter of which provides a serious temptation for Avon to abandon Blake); an armoury that prevents people from taking out more than one gun at a time (while seemingly doing nothing to prevent people from acquiring more than one once they have been removed from the armoury itself), and a teleport platform. (Curiously, at this stage the *Liberator* appears to have a *second* teleport platform, which is never seen again, suggesting either a last-minute design change or a slip of communication between director and scriptwriter.)

The computer, Zen, is, however, the most impressive part of the ship. It gets into Jenna's mind and learns, it seems, not only the humans' language but also their standard units of time and distance. It also chooses the name *Liberator* for the ship – and, by implication, chooses its own name, 'Zen' – from Jenna's thoughts. The name it chooses for itself is significant: Zen Buddhism is popularly known for the practice of telling of little parables (koans) that have many, complex meanings upon which the devotee is expected to meditate. Zen, similarly, does not give direct answers, but leaves the crew to figure out the meaning of its statements: as it says, 'Wisdom must be gathered. It cannot be given.' The name *Liberator*, however, also refers to Zen's actions as much as it does to the ship's role in 'liberating' the trio from Federation control; Zen allows the crew freedom of action, rather than guiding or directing their behaviour.

It is therefore unfortunate that the main flaw of the story lies in the *Liberator* sequence. We are told early on that the Earth-Cygnus Alpha trip lasts eight months, and later that Blake's revolt occurs about four months into the trip. The boarding of the *Liberator* appears to take place not long after the revolt. However, when we encounter the crew here, little time has passed since they have boarded the ship, and yet the *London* has already reached Cygnus Alpha. One possible explanation is that the *Liberator* travels through time during the 'negative hyperspace' jump; in that case, however, one might ask why Blake says, upon arriving at Cygnus Alpha, that they must 'get down there and rescue the others,' when he would not, at this point, have realised that he had travelled in time.

Finally, this story reveals more details about the central characters. As well as establishing the extent of Avon's greed, it also gives us a sequence in which Jenna flirts with Avon, and Avon reciprocates with a flirtatiously-phrased threat, foreshadowing later hints regarding his attitude to the opposite sex. We also experience Nation's sleight-of-hand with Blake's followers once again; Arco, who dies in this episode, was originally intended by Nation to be one of the Seven (the character was dropped for reasons of cost, and because writing for a large regular cast was proving problematic), and is as well-portrayed as Vila or Gan, with Peter Childs matching the performances of the best of the regular cast.

The most significant development is, however, accorded to Gan. At the outset of the Cygnus Alpha sequences, Gan becomes the unofficial leader of the prisoners; this is a primitive world, and so the strongest man, not necessarily the brightest or the most able, rules. In this story, it is quite plain that he is capable of killing; we see him in the fight sequence leaning on a spear to drive it into someone on the ground, and grinning as he does so (as he does earlier when he threatens to break Arco's limbs off). He also seems compelled to follow Kara – who later dies after warning him of an attack (her death appears to have been a fairly late addition to the script) – when she appears out of the mists. When we next see him, furthermore, he is kneeling in front of a crucified figure bearing the sign 'so perish unbelievers'; early versions of the script describe Gan as looking at this point 'like a man at worship.' A parallel will subsequently be set up between this crucified (therefore Christlike?) figure and Blake, who will be accused of being an 'unbeliever' and tortured in a room containing a cross. Later, when Blake gives his ultimatum to the other prisoners, the first one across the line is Gan, illustrating his faith in Blake. Gan is therefore a man with a belief in his leader and a flaw in his character.

"Cygnus Alpha" may contain a serious plotting error, but this is more than made up for by the characterisation, script and effects (including having the actors, in the location sequences, performing in front of a back-projection screen of the lunar surface and the landing bay). Almost all the major elements of the first series are now in place.

A4: TIME SQUAD

UK TRANSMISSION: Monday 23 January 1978: 7.15pm – 8.10pm
DURATION: 51:25
VIEWING FIGURE: 8.9m
CHART POSITION: 39
WRITER: Terry Nation
DIRECTOR: Pennant Roberts

CREDITED CAST: Tony Smart, Mark McBride, Frank Henson (Aliens)

UNCREDITED CAST: Roger Weighton, Nigel Sibley, Ian Lawrence, Geoff Cryer, Stephen Lyons, John Aston, Gus Roy*, Roy Pierce, George Fechter*, Paul Barry, Barney Lawrence, Mark Annandale (Guards)
*Not in finished episode

SYNOPSIS: *En route* for the Federation-controlled planet Saurian Major, the *Liberator* stops to answer a distress call, and picks up a small capsule containing three cryogenically-suspended aliens – guardians, it transpires, of a gene bank – one of whom has died in transit. While the survivors are revived, Blake, Vila and Avon teleport down to Saurian Major to meet the resistance forces there, only to discover that the resistance have all been killed bar one: Cally, a native of the planet Auron, capable of telepathic projection (although not, it seems, of reading minds). She joins forces with the others to attack the Federation's communications complex. Meanwhile, Jenna is attacked by the guardians; Gan goes to check on them, and Jenna later finds him injured and in pain from the action of the limiter implanted in his skull. The two fight off the guardians – including a previously unsuspected fourth – and bring the expedition party back to the ship; Cally agrees to join the crew.

ANALYSIS: "Time Squad" (originally scheduled as the sixth episode, then moved back to fourth to replace the aborted script "Locate and Destroy") is a fairly uneven story, involving as it does a plot thread with a subtext that outweighs the text to the point where the text actually makes little sense. Despite this, it has been one of the most influential stories on later television shows, in particular *Babylon-5* and *Buffy the Vampire Slayer*.

Another point against this story is that it is poorly directed. Much of the lighting is too harsh, and the low-budget feel, an asset in some episodes, here gives us television's least convincing nuclear explosion, and a pair of warriors wielding what look like salad forks. The acting, however, is very good, apart from that of a few overly melodramatic stuntmen. The script also builds up the regular characters nicely, leaving aside a regrettable (and rapidly-abandoned) attempt to recharacterise Jenna as a high-kicking warrior babe. Zen continues to speak in riddles, refusing to tell the humans straight-out what he knows about the capsule, but dropping broad hints that they shouldn't go over to it; by the time he speaks directly on the subject, the truth has already become obvious to them. Blake is clearly in control; he presents his plan to go down to Saurian Major as a *fait accompli*, which goes virtually unchallenged. (In an early draft of the script, he says that the ship is a democracy: they talk it over, argue about it, and then do it his way.) Avon is now established as an oppositional figure; he cooperates with the others, but regularly threatens to leave, and is quite aggressive towards Blake.

This episode also sees the introduction of a new regular character, Cally, and consequently the end of the teasing hints as to who the titular 'seven' will be. For a while, the possibility is left open that the frozen guardians will join the crew, and that Cally will get killed storming the reactor. Only at the conclusion is it made clear that Cally will be staying. Straight away a rivalry is set up between her and Jenna; Jenna, who has up until now been the only woman among the crew, makes a pointed remark at the end of the story about the dangers of letting aliens onto the ship. She might well have reason to do so; Blake and Jenna have up until now been rather affectionate, Jenna flirting with Blake in the cell and hugging him when he returns successfully from Cygnus Alpha, and Blake patting Jenna on the shoulder when he goes to the teleport in this episode. The relationship between Jenna and Avon, however, continues to be hostile, and Cally quite clearly looks up and down Avon's body suggestively when she first sees him. A sexual dynamic is thus now beginning to be felt on board the *Liberator*.

Cally is said to have come from the planet Auron to help the resistance on Saurian Major. As terrorists go, however, she is not very competent; she is fanatical and willing to die for her cause, but does not know enough to check for the presence of Avon and Vila when she encounters Blake, and Blake bests her easily in a fight. At the end, furthermore, when Blake suggests that she stay with the crew, Cally says that she cannot go back to her people because she 'has failed,' which seems a bit of an odd remark considering that she has in fact succeeded in her mission to blow up the reactor. There must, it appears, be another reason why she does not want to go back, which will be revealed in due course.

As in the previous episode, however, Gan's characterisation is particularly of note. Gan is not stupid; he is shown here to be a competent member of the ship-flying team. He is also the first crewmember to speak out in support of Blake. However, it is in this story that we find out that he has a limiter (which is symbolically echoed by Zen's apparent inhibitions, and Blake's significant remark that disabling the limiters on the reactor will allow it to blow sky-high). The concept is first flagged up when Gan suggests that Zen might have a limiter and Vila replies that Gan is scaring him, although what seems to scare Vila is not the idea of limiters, but of Zen being under control from an outside force. However, Zen clearly is not under outside control, as the technology of the capsule is patently too primitive to influence a computer of Zen's sophistication; also, Zen actively prevents the crew from bringing the capsule aboard, which would seem counterproductive, if that was indeed the intention of its makers. Zen's limitations are therefore internal to the computer itself. Although Zen is prevented, by its programming, from giving direct warnings, it seems that, when the crew are threatened, it will try to work around its limitations.

Gan's limiter is of a different order. This can be first seen in the sequence in which he and Jenna talk on the flight deck about whether or not to stay. Gan explains that he has to remain with Blake: 'I want to stay alive. And to do that I need people I can rely on. I can't be on my own.'. When Jenna asks what he means, he tells her, obliquely, that he killed a guard who killed his 'woman,' and complains of a headache; as Jenna leaves to check on the guardians, we see the top of his head with the implant in it. When Jenna returns, having fought with one of the guardians and locked the door on them, Gan makes explanations – which sound rather like excuses – for the guardian's behaviour, and says that he will go and investigate. When we next see him, he is inside the capsule where the cryogenic units are stored; he fails to answer Jenna's summons, but instead extends his left (again, sinister) hand; after Jenna has fought off the second guardian, he emerges, in visible pain, and collapses, but his only actual injury is from his fall. All this raises a number of questions: Gan is lying close to the gene banks that the guardians are programmed to protect, and yet they do not appear to have killed or even fought with him (as both he and they are uninjured). There is no rational reason for him to have climbed into the capsule; indeed, it would seem to have been putting himself at risk.

The explanation appears to come from his rambling statement to Jenna after he emerges from the capsule. He says: 'Couldn't stop them... implant. Limiter. Not possible for me to kill now.' Quite clearly he cannot mean killing in general, as we have seen him harm and even (by implication) kill people over the past few episodes; in this story, when Jenna hands him a gun, he takes it and grins, rather than handing it back with an explanation that he can't kill. However, if we assume that the limiter prevents him from killing under certain circumstances, it is very telling that it activates when he is alone on the flight deck with Jenna. Gan's speech continues: 'Never wanted to.' Again, this is untrue, as he would at least have wanted to kill the guard whom he says killed his 'woman.' However, if he means that he didn't want to kill the guardians, then he must have some other reason for being in the capsule. He says: 'They kill... anyone, everyone who isn't theirs'; the fact that the guardians have left him alive suggests that, on some level, he is identifying himself with them. He concludes by saying: 'The other one; I saw his face. Jenna... despises us.' However, the guardian is simply doing the job for which he has been programmed, and cannot despise anyone. If, however, he meant that *Jenna*, to his mind, despises both him and the guardians, then we have a different complexion on things.

The picture that emerges from the subtext is, therefore, that Gan's limiter has been implanted not to prevent him from killing in general, but to prevent him from killing for sexual pleasure. Gan's limiter causes him pain when he is alone with Jenna. Furthermore, his story about the guard killing his 'woman' is too close for coincidence to the events of Cygnus Alpha, in which a guard kills Kara and Gan is, shortly thereafter, seen driving a spear into a guard; this is the first hint of a pattern with regard to Gan's disorder. Under those circumstances, it seems likely that he went into the capsule as bait in a trap for Jenna; when she comes looking for him, the guardians will attack her, and he will get a vicarious thrill. However, this plan backfires (again suggesting that it is arousal that triggers the limiter, not a particular action on Gan's part). This also explains why he has been able to kill before, and why he says that he 'needs people' around him; previously, he has been killing for survival rather than for pleasure, and, in circumstances in which he is surrounded by people, he has no chance to be alone with a woman. Towards the end of the story, he is prevented by the pain from the limiter from shooting the guardian that is attacking Jenna; again, it seems, not because he cannot kill in general, but because he cannot kill in situations in which he is aroused. Later we will discover that a verbal command from a member of the group Gan identifies himself with can override the limiter, but here Jenna doesn't speak, and the guardians are all mute. As with Cally's lie, the subtext regarding Gan's limiter (an individual form of social control, as opposed to the collective ones we have seen up until now in the series), will become more significant in episodes to come.

This subtext was evidently a later addition. An early draft of "Time Squad", which does not feature Zen attempting to prevent the crew from bringing back the capsule, makes it quite explicit that Gan's limiter is in place to prevent him from killing; he says as much to Jenna, and then later is described as being seen emerging from the capsule 'heavily injured,' and begging Jenna to 'stop them' rather than engaging in confused, quasi-psychotic rants about limiters. The final version, however, shows Gan with no injuries other than those sustained from his fall out of the capsule, and leaves it ambiguous as to what the limiter is meant to limit – other than that, following on from earlier stories, it cannot be killing.

"Time Squad" is a confusing and difficult-to-follow story. When observed carefully, however, it reveals much about Gan, the nature of his crimes, and his reasons for following Blake, as well as about the sexual dynamics on board the ship.

A5: THE WEB

UK TRANSMISSION: Monday 30 January 1978: 7.15 – 8.10pm
DURATION: 49:39
VIEWING FIGURE: 9.6m
CHART POSITION: 41
WRITER: Terry Nation
DIRECTOR: Michael E Briant

CREDITED CAST: Richard Beale (Saymon); Ania Marson (Geela); Miles Fothergill (Novara); Deep Roy, Gilda Cohen, Ismet Hassam, Marcus Powell, Molly Tweedley, Willie Sheara (Decimas)

SYNOPSIS: The *Liberator* is drawn off course into a viscous, web like substance when Cally, possessed by an alien force, sabotages the ship. The force controlling Cally then briefly takes over Jenna and orders Blake to land the ship on a nearby planet; Cally suspects that the intruder is the Lost, a group of scientists exiled by the Auronar. Blake teleports down to the planet alone and encounters two beautiful humanoids, Geela and Novara, as well as a group of ugly dwarflike beings, the Decimas. These, it transpires, are all the genetically engineered creations of the Lost, who survive as a corporate mind in a single body, Saymon. The humanoids explain that their power cells are nearly depleted; if they have full power, they can beam a fungicide onto the web, and are willing to do this in exchange for Blake's help in replenishing their power supplies. Blake complies, but when he learns that they also intend to destroy the Decimas, he objects. By this point, however, Avon has teleported down with the cells, and they are forced to surrender them. The *Liberator* is freed, and the Decimas finally invade the compound, killing Geela, Novara and Saymon.

ANALYSIS: "The Web" is an excellent story that has the misfortune to be overshadowed by a rather lamentable special effect: the risible man-in-a-fishtank form of Saymon. If one ignores this, however, one finds a clever, deeply disturbing narrative.

This story sees the fourth and – for the time being – last iteration of the fascist society, indicating that even far outside the Federation, there is both oppression and the possibility of revolution. Significantly, this final version is the one in which the revolution actually succeeds; equally significantly, the next story sees a departure from allegorical representations and a return to the Federation itself, where we will encounter a man and a woman (foreshadowed in Geela and Novara) who will become the main antagonists of the series.

In the first draft of the script for the episode, the details of the society were somewhat different. As Cally – and therefore the Lost – was a later addition to the cast, the expedition was originally an Earth one; the laboratory was a converted spaceship bearing the designation 'Space Laboratory Project IX. 1998.' Even leaving aside the fact that it is generally prudent, in science fiction tales of the future, to avoid specific dates, the transmitted version is much more effective; by making the mission alien and removing the spaceship, the writers have given the society more of a timeless, placeless feel. The production and casting in this sequence reinforces this; Novara and Geela are genuinely creepy, with Ania Marson being simultaneously beautiful and coldly mechanical. The Decimas, described in the original script as looking rather synthetic, on screen have an organic, lichen like appearance in keeping with the idea of the Lost having a fungus-based technology. (Saymon, by contrast, is rather less effective in the final version than in the original, in which he was described as a normal man inside a coffin-like life-support system.) The forest setting, with its strands of web and inflated weather balloons, keeps the spider's web theme going throughout and reinforces the isolation and 'alienness' of the planet.

In this particular totalitarian society, the means of control is genetic. The Decimas have been genetically engineered as docile workers, and rebellious 'mutant' ones are killed; the Lost are prepared to wipe out the whole species in order to destroy the aggressive strain. Geela and Novara describe them in ways reminiscent of the attitudes of human ruling classes to their social inferiors, detaching themselves from the creatures and dehumanising them, even though we see one pleading for help and others crying over the death of a friend. Significantly, the people who appear to be the rulers are in fact part of the system; this has been hinted at in earlier iterations (e.g. with Ven Glynd in "The Way Back") but it is brought sharply to the fore in this case, in which Geela acts at one point as a literal mouthpiece for the society's true ruler (which itself is a corporate entity, not an individual). Blake, fittingly, is the author of the Decimas' deliverance; it is, if one thinks about it, ridiculous for the compound door to have been left open at this point, but it is appropriate in that it means that Blake is somehow responsible for the revolt.

In this story, for the first time, we see a successful rebellion. Which, we learn, is not a pleasant thing to witness. '*These* are what you wanted to protect?' says Avon to Blake, in a phrase that can be read as encompassing not only the Decimas, but the Federation people as well. While the viewer cannot help but sympathise with the Decimas, the sight of them trampling the bodies of Geela and Novara is a disturbing one. This ambiguity is also present in the sequence in which Blake looks out of the window at the rioting Decimas; it is difficult to tell whether the expression on the face of Gareth Thomas (whose performance in this story is of an even higher standard than usual) is sympathy, disgust, astonishment, or a mix of all three. Significantly, the Decimas go for the trappings of power first, rather than attacking the real oppressive force – Saymon – which they discover only after destroying everything else in the lab. Although they do, against all odds, succeed in their attempt to overthrow their masters, the ending of the story is ambiguous: will the Decimas succeed in setting up a new society, or will they be dead within the year? We are never allowed to find out.

The early scenes on board the *Liberator* afford a fair bit of character development. Gan is seen attacking a woman: he sneaks up behind Cally to disarm her, but only actually grabs her after Jenna has said: 'You're not Cally, are you?' Gan therefore commits his attack in a situation where, not only is he in a group, but has been told a split second earlier that the woman is not who or what she seems to be. Gan was also described in the original script (which, lacking the Cally plot, began with the crew attempting to determine why the ship was being drawn off course) as standing by Blake 'like a bodyguard.' We also revisit the Jenna-Cally antagonism briefly, when Jenna, seeing Cally holding Blake and Avon at gunpoint, says in an unsurprised tone, 'so it *was* you,' although she becomes a little more sympathetic after it becomes plain that Cally wasn't acting of her own accord. Zen, finally, is once again prepared to warn the crew about a danger – the bomb – and repair the damage after it's gone off, but not to disarm it for them, because, for him, 'preemptive interference in crew activity is forbidden'; as Blake notes: 'He'll clear up after us, but he won't stop us making a mess.'

Avon also benefits from further character development. Cally openly flirts with him over his computer equipment, saying coyly: 'I'm interested in your work'; he visibly gets the message, as he maintains eye contact for a full ten seconds afterwards. Once she has been disarmed a short time later, he grabs her by the throat – somewhat unnecessarily, as she is being restrained and is therefore helpless. Avon is thus violent to her for unstated reasons, which seem to have something to do with her flirting with him. More significantly, Avon's ambitions have now emerged fully; he is no longer talking about abandoning Blake and making off with the money, but he does say that Blake may not always be in charge, smiling broadly afterwards. At the end of the story, his remark about how balances of power change appears to refer less to the Decimas and more to himself and Blake. However, this ambition is tempered by Avon's association of Blake with his lost brother, of which Blake appears to be aware; when Avon saves his life by pulling him away from an explosion in Hold 3, Blake asks him, 'Why?', to which Avon responds, 'Automatic reaction, I'm as surprised as you are,' and Blake remarks, 'I'm not surprised.' Again, this ambition is a later addition to the story; the first draft had Avon talking about selling the *Liberator*'s technology and running away, but not about taking over the ship.

"The Web" consequently transcends its occasional technical limitations to produce a story that, like the situation of the Decimas themselves, is at once alien and familiar, touching and horrifying.

A6: SEEK-LOCATE-DESTROY

UK TRANSMISSION: Monday 6 February 1978: 7.15pm – 8.10pm
DURATION: 51:40
VIEWING FIGURE: 10.9m
CHART POSITION: 34
WRITER: Terry Nation
DIRECTOR: Vere Lorrimer

CREDITED CAST: Peter Craze (Prell); Peter Miles (Rontane); John Bryans (Bercol); Ian Cullen (Escon); Ian Oliver (Rai); Astley Jones (Eldon)

UNCREDITED CAST: Frank Maher (Stuntman/Guard); Astley Jones (Voice of Servalan's Secretary/Voice of Doctor); Kevin Sullivan (Robot Operator); Franklyn Arbisman, James Muir, Alan Forbes, Scott Thomas, Douglas Roe, Terence Ward, Lionel Sansby (Guards); James Muir (Medic); David Glen, William Wyatt, Jason Good, Michael Gordon-Browne (Laboratory Technicians); Jason Good, Michael Gordon-Browne (Interrogators); Straun Rodger (Unknown: not in finished episode)

> **SYNOPSIS:** The *Liberator* crew teleport down to the planet Centero and stage a raid on a Federation communications centre, with a view to stealing a message decoder. They cover their tracks by blowing the installation up. Cally, however, is overpowered by some of the base personnel she is holding hostage, loses her teleport bracelet, is knocked out in the explosion and left for dead by her comrades. Meanwhile, the

Supreme Commander of the Federation's armed forces, Servalan, has brought in an officer with the specific mission to eliminate Blake by any means necessary. This is Space Commander Travis, the man responsible for Blake's original capture (in events prior to "The Way Back"). Travis was disfigured by Blake and now has an eyepatch and a prosthetic hand, into which is built a gun. Travis goes to Centero and discovers that the message decoder is missing; he also finds Cally and has her interrogated. He sends via the decoder a message to the effect that Cally is alive and on Centero, to lure Blake back to the installation; Blake foils the plan by arriving before the trap can be set, overpowering Travis and rescuing Cally.

ANALYSIS: "Seek-Locate-Destroy" is one of the most crucial episodes of the first season, establishing not only the premise and formula of stories to come, but also introducing two powerful antagonists for the *Liberator* crew.

In some ways, Blake's raid on the installation is played out as a kind of roll call, establishing the character traits of the protagonists for the audience. Blake is the leader, coordinating it all and feeling guilty when things go wrong; Vila is a cheeky, witty and argumentative pick-lock (here, though, he is not that much of a coward; the scene where he engages two guards in conversation is pure *The Avengers*); Avon is a cold, sarcastic technical genius; Cally is a ruthless warrior babe with a tendency to speak in stilted terms (although her telepathy and alien origin are not mentioned); Gan is a strong giant with a personality disorder; and Jenna works the teleport (her piloting abilities made largely redundant by Zen, and by the fact that she has taught the others to fly the ship). Although "Seek-Locate-Destroy" has more the feel of a season-opener story, it is worth noting that this is the point at which the crew begin to act like freedom fighters and/or terrorists. It is here that the premise and pattern for the remainder of the series is established, hence the re-establishment of the characters.

Gan again gets more development. David Jackson's performance suggests sudden mood swings: he pushes the hostages into the storage area with unnecessary roughness, then mildly asks Cally: 'Can you handle it?' He then, abruptly, leaves Cally alone in a room with half a dozen strong men and goes to plant two mines in the corridor, where they will destroy the room when triggered; he doesn't go back to warn Cally of any developments, or provide her with backup. (Although he does help Avon remove the decoder, there are several points at which he could have checked on her, and doesn't.) Once they have returned to the ship without Cally, he does not remark on her absence, although he was the one who had the most to do with her on the ground, and when others do remark on it, he says little. In anyone else, this would be criminal negligence; considering his previous behaviour, however, what we have is Gan deliberately leaving a woman in an almost certainly fatal situation, at risk from both the explosives and the hostages.

This story also shows two particular aspects that distinguish *Blake's 7* from other series of the time. The first is that, unusually for a space-opera, we see evidence of the characters thinking, processing and living their lives between stories: Blake remarks of Cally that 'she was ashamed to go back to her own people because she had survived when the rest of the freedom fighters were massacred.' This suggests that Blake believes Cally to have been suffering from survivor's guilt following the massacre preceding "Time Squad" (and also that Blake himself may have similar feelings). The second is the portrayal of the Federation as people simply doing their jobs and getting caught in the crossfire: for the first time here, we see an ordinary man, Prell, who is taken hostage, fights back and helps the authorities. Although he may be on the opposite side from our heroes, we cannot help but sympathise, even admire him for his actions.

"Seek-Locate-Destroy" is also noteworthy in that it is an inversion of that standard television drama genre, the whodunit. Seen from the point of view of Travis and his supporters, this is a detective story with a lonely, alienated and intelligent protagonist, devoted to the system he comes from and with a vendetta against an old enemy, solving the central mystery. Here, however, we are expected to sympathise with the 'criminals,' and the 'detective' is the villain.

Travis is very much the focus of this story. He is the nemesis of Blake – in terms of Victor Hugo's *Les Miserables*, he is Javert to Blake's Valjean. He is also seriously unhinged. We learn that between receiving his injury at Blake's hands and the present, he has been responsible for a massacre on Auros, which included civilian deaths. Servalan has suspended the inquiry into his conduct and had him put to work hunting down Blake. Stephen Greif's performance adds much to the character; he strongly resembles Basil Rathbone, who is well-known not only for playing Sherlock Holmes, but also for appearing as Guy of Gisborne in the 1938 film *The Adventures of Robin Hood* (playing against Errol Flynn). This is echoed by a Robin Hood parallel running through this story: not only is Travis's plan vaguely reminiscent of the Sheriff of Nottingham's scheme to lure Robin into a trap using a bait he can't resist (an archery contest and the hand of Maid Marian), but the costumes of the expedition – in which we have two people dressed in green, one in scarlet, and a large man in brown – suggest Robin, the Merry Men, Will Scarlet and Friar Tuck. Darrow, significantly, was also cast as Avon on the strength of his performance as the Sheriff of Nottingham in the 1970s TV series *The Legend of Robin Hood*.

Travis is portrayed as something of a sadist. This is suggested by the tight-fitting leather costume, which implies a twisted sexuality as well as a man who feels the need to be in control. He smiles to see Cally in the life-support unit facing interrogation, referring to her as 'the property' of the Federation, and telling her that 'there may be a little pain, a little discomfort.' Significantly, however, he does not administer this pain himself; he is a sadist only by proxy. There is also a homoerotic aspect to the character; shortly before the scene with Cally, we see him looking at photographs of Blake, who is in obvious distress. Greif plays the character in a very macho way, but with a slight camp edge: leaving aside the homoeroticism implicit in any character devoted to the military life, it must be remembered that in the 1970s, homosexuality had been decriminalised in the UK for only a few years, and the tradition – dating from Shakespearian times – of using effeminacy as a symbol of villainy was still very commonly adhered to.

Another aspect of Travis's character is seen when he remarks that Blake's fatal flaw is loyalty. This would seem an odd observation, coming from a man who values loyalty to the Federation; however, what Travis means is loyalty to an individual. He remarks: 'He wouldn't abandon the girl, not Blake.' Travis, by contrast, orders his soldiers to ignore the potential risk to his own safety when attacking Blake. He identifies himself here with mutoids, individuals modified into cyborg soldiers at the beck and call of the Federation. It might also be suggested that his obsession with his injury – which also seems odd, as soldiers expect injury as a matter of course – might stem from the fact that it put his career at risk, and threatened his retirement on medical grounds; in disfiguring him, Blake has made Travis realise that he is in fact nothing *but* his career, and that outside of a military setting he is nothing.

This story also introduces us to a second antagonistic figure, Servalan. Dressed throughout in white – in what seems to be a conscious echo of Carrie Fisher's costume in *Star Wars* – and with a name recalling the Scarlet Pimpernel's nemesis Chauvelin, the character was originally written as a man. The change in gender clearly demonstrates the impact that a performance can have on a character: any one of Servalan's scenes could have been played by a male actor, but it would have been very different. As it is, Jacqueline Pearce's performance is nothing short of spectacular: cool and businesslike with Rontane and Bercol, she then imbues the brief scene with Rai with sexuality, before switching it off abruptly when Rai and Servalan have their disagreement, and is again businesslike with Travis. One might note how she looks slightly flustered when she learns that Travis has refused to wait, but by the time he has arrived in her office she is looking calm and relaxed, as if she were anticipating his every move.

The sequence with Rai is interesting, in that it seems to echo the theme of placing the group above the individual: it could, at this point, be read as a politician refusing to give up doing what she thinks is best for the Federation, even at the cost of personal relationships. Equally, however, it could be seen as placing the individual above the group; Servalan refusing to allow her personal agenda to be challenged by anyone, however close to her. In light of what happens later, the second interpretation seems closer to the truth.

Finally, the brief scene with two minor characters, Bercol and Rontane (wonderfully insinuating performances from John Bryans and Peter Miles), is, despite its brevity, crucial to the ongoing narrative. We learn that although there are stories circulating about Blake, the Federation is not officially acknowledging that he exists. We also hear about, but never see, the President; even now that

Blake is attracting attention at the highest levels, the politicians we meet are clearly part of the system rather than in total control of it.

At the end of the story, Blake, refusing to kill Travis, states that, if he does so, the Federation will just send someone else. This line reinforces the theme of individual versus group – it is the system that Blake is fighting, not particular members of it – but also sets up the Blake-Travis dynamic which will drive many of the subsequent episodes.

A7: MISSION TO DESTINY

UK TRANSMISSION: Monday 13 February 1978: 7.15pm – 8.10pm
DURATION: 51:12
VIEWING FIGURE: 9.6m
CHART POSITION: 46
WRITER: Terry Nation
DIRECTOR: Pennant Roberts

CREDITED CAST: Barry Jackson (Kendall); Beth Morris (Sara); Stephen Tate (Mandrian); Nigel Humphreys (Sonheim); Kate Coleridge (Levett); Carl Forgione (Grovane); John Leeson (Pasco); Brian Capron (Rafford); Stuart Fell (Dortmunn)

SYNOPSIS: The *Liberator* encounters a spaceship, the *Ortega*, drifting in a circular orbit. Blake, Avon and Cally teleport over and discover a dead pilot and unconscious crew. Once revived, the latter are revealed to be from the planet Destiny, which is afflicted with a fungal plague; the ship bears the cure, an expensive device called a 'neutrotope.' The crew are baffled as, although one of their number is missing and a life-rocket launched, the neutrotope is still present. The ship is now incapable of flying faster than light, so Blake offers to take the device back to Destiny while Avon and Cally remain to effect repairs and solve the mystery. The corpse of the missing crewman comes to light and a third crewman, Mandrian, is killed in such a way as to implicate his aggressive colleague Sonheim. Meanwhile, Blake discovers that he has been given an empty box, and hastens back to the *Ortega*. Avon, taking as his final clue a seemingly meaningless message scrawled by the dying pilot, identifies the murderer: Sara, Mandrian's lover, who locks herself into the flight deck to await rendezvous with a mystery ship homing in on a device on board the *Ortega*. Avon stages a subterfuge to draw Sara out, and Blake returns to teleport everyone over to the *Liberator*. Sara remains behind and is killed, along with the pirate occupants of the mystery ship, by a bomb planted by Blake.

ANALYSIS: "Mission to Destiny" is a very traditional mystery story, and as such unusual for *Blake's 7*. It is likely that Nation, who expected to be writing a police series rather than a space opera, decided to recycle one of his earlier ideas. Despite its unusual nature, however, it is a very watchable story, and the mystery well-designed.

There are other signs of Nation's recycling within the programme. Destiny's plight has been lifted wholesale from an abandoned *Blake's 7* episode, "Locate and Destroy", in which the Federation were behind the plague; hostile fungi have been seen before in *Blake's 7*, in "The Web". The crew's names also betray their likely sources: 'Dortmunn' (a name Nation had used previously, with slightly different spelling, in *Doctor Who*'s "The Dalek Invasion of Earth") and 'Kendall' suggest that Nation was looking through an atlas for names; Mandrian and Sonheim (another name Nation had used, with slightly different spelling, in his draft scripts for "The Dalek Invasion of Earth", although in that instance the character was renamed Campbell in the transmitted version) appear to have been called after a painter (Piet Mondrian) and a songwriter (Stephen Sondheim) respectively. Sara's surname was given in the script as 'Ovidial,' suggesting that Nation was either thinking of Ovid or Gore Vidal, or both. (Sara was another name that Nation had previously used for a prominent character in one of his *Doctor Who* stories: "The Daleks' Master Plan".) The name of the ship is, however, more significant: Jose Ortega y Gasset was a Spanish philosopher of the 20th century who opposed the Primo de Riviera dictatorship, supported the Republicans (although he later became disillusioned with politics) and also wrote a book, *The Revolt of the Masses*, in which he argued that ordinary people are incapable of self-governance. This story might seem to support Ortega's hypothesis, in that the ship's crew appear incapable of governing themselves. However, in this case an undemocratic element has been introduced into the mix, subverting the democratic process; this element is an insider who has made a deal with an outside force, not unlike the Communists in the Weimar Republic doing a deal with Stalin. There is also a parallel between the crew and the Seven themselves: there are two women, an aggressive and intelligent man, a small and humorous man, a leader figure and a secret murderer. As with the Robin Hood parallel in "Seek-Locate-Destroy", the analogy is partial only, but nonetheless present.

The mystery itself is carefully thought through. Sara has only one canister of sona vapour tranquillising gas, and no precise time of rendezvous – or way of communicating – with the pirates who wish to steal the neutrotope (they keep tabs on her via a homing beacon). Therefore her original plan must have been to knock out the crew with the gas, smash the controls to immobilise the ship, then kill Dortmunn, put his corpse in the life-rocket and launch it, thereby setting up a riddle to misdirect the crew. Rafford's death was not planned; he was killed only because the air vents on the flight deck had been closed, allowing him to escape the effects of the gas. Avon later suggests that Dortmunn may have been a red herring put in place to cover Rafford's death after the *Liberator* crew had teleported aboard, which would mean that Sara's original intention had been to keep the *Ortega* crew tranquillised until the pirates docked; however, as stated above, Sara did not know the time of the pirates' arrival and was limited to only one cylinder of gas. Also, it seems unlikely that she could have devised and acted on this plan in the short time available once Blake, Avon and Cally were aboard and searching. It is, however, reasonable to assume that she was surprised in the act of carrying out her plan, and this forced her to hide Dortmunn's body and launch an empty life-rocket instead before returning to her cabin to be found by Blake.

The astute viewer will, however, notice hints as to the murderer's identity in the story. In the first place, Rafford reacts to the unknown killer somewhat flirtatiously, suggesting a woman. In the second, Avon's remark to the effect that 'someone other than the killer already knows,' implies that it would have to have been one of the four people sharing rooms: Sara, Mandrian, Sonheim or Pasco. Later, after Mandrian is killed, it is clearly not Sonheim who did it (even leaving aside the cliché that in a mystery story, the man holding a weapon over the corpse is never the killer), as whoever killed Mandrian was the same one who sabotaged the cable, and the insulated saw used to cut it is not present: Sonheim has only a knife. Mandrian's death of course contains an additional poignant element, as he clearly knew that Sara was up to something by this point; although he cared enough for her not to voice his suspicions to Kendall, she was quite prepared to kill him in pursuit of gain. The crew, however, would prefer to believe that the killer is a stowaway rather than one of their own, and ignore the fact that it would have been very difficult for someone to have hidden for that length of time without being noticed; like many people, they avoid an unpalatable truth by concocting more palatable, albeit improbable, explanations.

The mystery story does contain one slight fudge. Kendall, we learn, is the only one with the molecular key and combination to the wall safe in which the neutrotope is kept, and yet, after explaining to Blake what it is, he apparently does not lock it back up (although he visibly has time to do so between that scene and the next), as he later asks Sara to fetch it for him. It would seem unsafe to leave the neutrotope unguarded under the circumstances, and also rather fortuitous for Sara that it is she he asks to bring it. It is unlikely that Kendall was in on the plan, as he would have been able to give her the code and to cover up for her. Although the fact that the *Ortega* crew trust Blake might also seem far-fetched, it is not completely implausible; if the *Liberator* crew were pirates, they would simply have stolen the neutrotope rather than engage in complex subterfuges. Also, not all of them do trust Blake, as can be observed in the scene in which Sonheim follows Cally; it is patently not because he wishes to apologise, as he sounds unconvincing when he makes this excuse, and she doesn't believe him either. It is, in fact, because he doesn't trust her and wants to see what she is up to.

The production quality on this episode is variable. The ship is a bog-standard science-fiction set, heavy on the corridors. The performances range from very good (Barry Jackson) to abysmal (with the usually-competent John Leeson and Carl Forgione seemingly not even trying). However, the presence of two games – one a chess game, the other a game played on multiple levels, like the mystery itself – is a nice touch, in that they highlight the complex, multilayered nature both of the story and of the series itself.

The strongest of the regular characters in this story is Avon. Gan, after having been built up considerably in earlier episodes, is virtually absent here, reduced to standing on the *Liberator* flight deck and feeding the others straight lines. Had he been featured more prominently, the Gan subtext might easily have clashed with the nature of the mystery story, which also involves a surface narrative with another, genuine, plot underlying it. With Avon taking centre stage for the first time, Paul Darrow shows himself to be very good in a leading role. Avon's character is developed throughout the story; he agrees to stay on the *Ortega*, it seems, because of intellectual caprice; he is a clever man intrigued by a puzzle. The fact that he stays also suggests that he is willing to trust Blake with the neutrotope and therefore, implicitly, with his life. His violent streak towards women comes out strongly in the scene in which he fights with Sara: he puts his hand on her breast at one point; their faces come quite close together, and the struggle develops a growing sexual undercurrent, ending when he punches her in the face. As she falls into the arms of Pasco and Grovane, he says: 'You'd better get her out of here... I really rather enjoyed that.'

Although Blake is not strongly featured in this story, we also see a new side to his character as well. He wishes to help the *Ortega* crew for humanitarian reasons, but shows a genuinely ruthless streak in deliberately planting a bomb on the ship to kill the pirates; he does not seem to feel at all troubled by this. Although Blake is a liberal, he can use violence quite matter-of-factly when he deems it necessary.

While it may be something of a departure from the series format, then, "Mission to Destiny" does not particularly suffer by its anomalous nature, and indeed, benefits from it in many ways.

A8: DUEL

UK TRANSMISSION: Monday 20 February 1978: 7.15pm – 8.10pm
DURATION: 51:13
VIEWING FIGURE: 10.0m
CHART POSITION: 45
WRITER: Terry Nation
DIRECTOR: Douglas Camfield

CREDITED CAST: Isla Blair (Sinofar); Patsy Smart (Giroc); Carol Royle (Mutoid)

UNCREDITED CAST: Christopher Holmes (Mutoid); Cliff Diggins (Double for Blake); Frank Maher (Double for Travis)

SYNOPSIS: The *Liberator* comes into the orbit of a seemingly deserted planet to recharge its depleted energy banks. While there, it is ambushed by Travis with three pursuit ships. At the climax of the battle, Blake and Travis are mysteriously transported down to the planet, where they encounter two female beings, the youthful Sinofar the Guardian and the elderly Giroc the Keeper. The two force Travis and Blake to fight a duel, without any weapons more sophisticated than machetes, and with a companion each – Jenna and one of Travis's mutoids respectively – to 'demonstrate the death of a friend.' Travis and the mutoid kidnap Jenna and lure Blake into a trap, which Blake foils; the two men fight, but when Blake has Travis at his mercy, he refuses to kill him. He is transported back to Sinofar and Giroc, who return him to the

Liberator and replenish its energy supplies. Travis is also allowed to depart unharmed, but with his mission unfulfilled.

ANALYSIS: "Duel" is one of those stories where everything seems to come together. The production, the performances, and the script are all fantastic, and unflawed by the kind of little hitches and plot conveniences that have plagued earlier episodes.

The production deserves special praise. The exterior sequences are all very good, as are the models – including the 'vampire bat' creature that bites Blake. Doubtless due to Camfield's influence, the studio lighting is also much better than that seen in a number of previous episodes. There are some outstanding directorial touches, including a cut from the apprehensive-looking Jenna to the wizened face of Giroc, which suggests the withering of beauty and is echoed later in a similar contrast between the old woman and the eternally beautiful but vampiric mutoid. The ten-minute-long space combat sequence is gripping, edge-of-the-seat stuff.

Sinofar and Giroc are, of course, pivotal to the story. The antiwar message derived from the aborted script "Locate and Destroy", which involved a planet being devastated by a Federation weapon and Blake deliberately stating that he will stop the cycle of aggression by not killing Travis when he has the chance. Sinofar and Giroc, however, make this into a more subtle, allegorical tale, almost mystical; together, they represent two-thirds of the Celtic maiden-mother-crone triad, but with the mother – significantly, given that the planet is now barren, the fertile third – missing, and with the thirds representing youth and death remaining. They also represent a people, highlighted in the small human figures carved on Giroc's staff. One might further note that they materialise only when people are about to kill (lending a sinister symbolism to their appearance before Gan, a known killer). The 'lesson' that they teach has to do with the choice not to fight; at the outset, Sinofar explains that if Blake and Travis choose not to engage each other in combat, they will not be in need of the lesson.

There is, however, more to it than this; at least part of the exercise is to recognise and acknowledge that killing is a pleasure, and yet to abstain from it. One might note that when they are first asked to state their grievances, Blake and Travis omit the personal aspects of their quarrel; at the end, however, Blake confesses that one reason why he did not kill Travis is that he would have enjoyed it. Sinofar then acknowledges that perhaps there is nothing more for Blake to learn. The story is thus more complex than a simple antiwar message, in that it acknowledges that violence can be a seductive thing.

Another part of the lesson is to demonstrate 'the death of a friend.' The choice of Jenna for Blake is interesting because, although Jenna clearly fancies Blake (as seen once again in her slightly dry '...yes,' when Blake says that Sinofar was very pretty), Blake hasn't shown much interest in her. It is not entirely ruled out – note that Travis, without knowing who Blake's companion is, automatically assumes it to be female – but although Blake seems to get on better with her than with the rest of the crew, he does not give open signs of wanting to develop a closer relationship. However, Sinofar and Giroc evidently feel that her death would be more of a blow to Blake than that of Vila, Cally, Gan or Avon, which suggests that there is a stronger feeling on Blake's part than he is willing to admit, or perhaps than he is conscious of himself.

The choice of Travis's female mutoid, the woman formerly known as Keera, is equally significant. Blake remarks dryly that it would be hard to find someone who could demonstrate the 'death of a friend' to Travis; however, it is very appropriate that it is a mutoid fulfilling this function. The identification between Travis and mutoids is flagged up in this script: we learn that mutoids exist to serve, and if one is dismissed from service, it ceases to exist. Travis also would cease to exist without a military purpose; he would be nothing. In this case, however, it is more than simply an identification that draws Travis to Keera; this is also a mutoid whose past he has taken the trouble to research.

This fact brings out a new dynamic in Travis's relationship with mutoids. Travis attempts to build a rapport with Keera, by telling her about her former life; but this attempt at reaching out rapidly turns to revulsion when he realises she isn't interested, and he acts with hostility towards her afterwards. Interestingly, also, her remark about how erasing the memory of a mutoid also erases its identity recalls what happened to Blake. It is unclear whether or not Keera's memory really is erased, as she pronounces her name differently to Travis, which could either be a conscious act of remembering, a memory being awakened, or simply her playing with the sound; one way or another, however, she is not interested in finding out more. Keera is a disturbing creature on many levels; the parallel is drawn between her and vampires, not simply by virtue of the needle in her arm, which allows her to drink blood when she doesn't have serum available, but also by virtue of the fact that she is dressed in black with a pale face and black-lined eyes. Travis may identify with mutoids, but he is also, on some level, repulsed by what they are. He is still, after all, human.

Greif's performance in this story is particularly worthy of note. Unlike in his earlier episode, he is not in the slightest bit camp here; the scene where he ambushes his opponent, puts the knife against his throat and says, 'Goodbye, Blake,' is particularly chilling. Despite this, the sadistic obsession with restraint is still there, as part of Travis's plan involves tying up Jenna. Elsewhere in the story, however, there are strong parallels set up between Blake's and Travis's actions, as each tries to outthink the other, both in the space-combat sequence and on the ground. Travis uses the same strategy as in his first story, luring Blake into a trap using one of his friends, and Blake again foils it through anticipating this.

The development of Gan also continues in this episode. He goes down to the planet with Blake and Jenna; in narrative terms, this scene would function well with only two people, and the obvious thing is to send down Blake and Jenna, who will later become the focus of the story, however, Nation has chosen to include Gan in order to highlight an aspect of his character. Once on the surface, Gan emerges into a clearing with a cruciform figure in it (as in "Cygnus Alpha"); he calls to Blake, then later in the scene he turns around and sees two women, one young and pretty, one old and looking at him admiringly (as she will look at Travis later). When the women seemingly vanish, he expresses concern that his limiter is malfunctioning, which both draws attention to it and reinforces suggestions in earlier episodes of a connection between the limiter and Gan's reaction to women. At the end of the story, Gan asks what Sinofar was like. 'Of course, you never saw her,' replies Blake. 'No,' lies Gan with a smile. We also see, however, Gan's faith in Blake; when Vila suggests the possibility of him and Jenna not returning, Gan refuses to discuss it.

Finally, this story reveals some striking aspects of Avon's character. Paul Darrow gives a very commanding performance;

having been established as a dominant figure in the previous episode, Avon is not about to give up power. We also see, as in his encounter with Jenna in "Cygnus Alpha", Avon's tactic of disconcerting people through invading their personal space, refusing to step aside for Vila, and leaning in aggressively towards Blake. Avon has some of the best lines in the episode, such as when he is dryly doubting that Travis's scaffolding is a 'recreational aid,' or summarising the situation by remarking: 'Blake is sitting up in a tree, Travis is sitting up in another tree. Unless they're planning to throw nuts at one another, I don't see much of a fight developing before it gets light.' The most significant statement, however, is when Avon says: 'I have never understood why it should be necessary to become irrational in order to prove that you care, or, indeed, why it should be necessary to prove it at all.' The first phrase is easily understood – it isn't going to do Blake any good if Avon stays up all night watching him – but the meaning of the second is more difficult to discern. It seems to run as follows: if you care, and the other person knows that you care, you shouldn't need to have to keep proving it. Here, Avon is saying that he *does* care what happens; who, precisely, he cares about in this case is, however, not directly stated. At the end of the story, when all the others – Vila, Gan and Cally – are urging Blake to kill Travis, Avon smiles slightly and shakes his head. He knows that Blake won't do it, and that it is the wrong way to solve the problem. Although Vila calls Avon a 'machine,' Avon not only cares, but seems to understand Blake's mindset better than Vila does.

Despite the fact that the basic idea behind "Duel" has been a science fiction staple for many years, it is easily one of the best episodes presented to this point. It features consistently good production, scripting and acting, combined with a tight story and strong character development.

A9: PROJECT AVALON

UK TRANSMISSION: Monday 27 February 1978: 7.15pm – 8.10pm
DURATION: 52:30
VIEWING FIGURE: 9.7m
CHART POSITION: 36
WRITER: Terry Nation
DIRECTOR: Michael E Briant

CREDITED CAST: Julia Vidler (Avalon); David Bailie (Chevner); Glynis Barber (Mutoid); John Baker (Scientist); John Rolfe (Terloc); David Sterne, Mark Holmes (Guards)

UNCREDITED CAST: Stuart Fell, Cyd Child (Stunt Artistes / Subterrons); Stuart Fell (Double for Mutoids); Frank Maher (Stuntman / Guards); Roy Pearce, George House, Peter Whitaker, Eddie Le Roy, Leslie Weekes (Scientists); Chris Holmes, Michael de Wilde, Christina Halstead, Roberta Kingsley, Monique Briant (Mutoids); Kavid Ianson, Kelly Varney, Bruce Guest (Prisoners); John Cannon, John Jenson, Doug Roe, Peter Dukes (Guards); Bunty Garland (Double for Avalon); Gaye Hopkin, David Charles, Jay Dyer (Subterrons / Mutoid)

SYNOPSIS: On a frozen planet, Travis stages a raid on a resistance meeting, kidnapping a rebel leader named Avalon and leaving her supporters for dead. Elsewhere, the *Liberator* crew are preparing to rendezvous with Avalon; Blake and Jenna teleport down to the planet and meet the massacre's sole survivor, Chevner. Aided by Vila, they proceed to the command centre where Avalon is being held and rescue her, despite fierce resistance from the guards. Back on board *Liberator,* Blake's examination of a captured rifle, which has been doctored to deliver non-fatal charges, leads him to suspect that they may have been set up. Initially, Chevner is suspected, but they then discover that the woman they have brought on board is in fact an android double of Avalon, programmed to crush a small capsule that will release a short-lived but fatal virus into the *Liberator's* atmosphere. Avon reprograms the android and Blake teleports with it back to the surface; he forces Travis to surrender the real Avalon by threatening to have the android crush the capsule. As a result of the project's failure, Travis is suspended from duty by Servalan, pending a full enquiry.

ANALYSIS: "Project Avalon" is another Travis-versus-Blake story, in which the two characters twist and turn to anticipate each other's moves. While perhaps not as allegorical as "Duel", it does show strong character and narrative development throughout.

It is worth noting at the outset that some time has passed between "Duel" and "Project Avalon". Travis is here pursuing a strategy very different from that which he outlined at the end of "Duel", and he refers to having made two attempts to kill Blake which were thwarted by his superiors' insistence that the *Liberator* be taken intact (and which therefore cannot be the two encounters we have seen before). There is also mention of assassination attempts on Servalan, which have taken place off-screen; and, on the *Liberator*, the suspicion between Jenna and Cally appears to have cooled. Again, in this episode, it is strongly highlighted that the characters have lives outside of what we see on-screen.

In contrast with those of the previous story, the production and performances in "Project Avalon" are of a variable standard. The casting of David Bailie as Chevner is inspired; although the role is not a large one, Bailie makes it into more than it is through improvisation – for instance, grinning at Vila's jokes and starting forward slightly when Travis calls Avalon's name (as if to claim that he is she, or to physically shield her from Travis) – and by doing his own stunts. By contrast, the choice of Julia Vidler to play Avalon leaves a lot to be desired; she appears to be aged about 18-25, and doesn't seem much like a leader of rebels. In production terms, the stock footage sequence that opens the story works well, but the effects scene showing the inside of the Avalon robot's head is appallingly bad.

There are some continuity problems in the scripting, too. Curiously, Jenna and Cally have 'swapped roles', with Cally learning how to pilot the ship and Jenna suddenly developing a past encounter with a resistance leader. The fact that the android can teleport up to and down from the *Liberator* with impunity also seems rather odd, as otherwise the teleport system appears, from what we see in the first three seasons, to transport only living matter and things directly adhering to it; it is possible, however, that the android contains *Terminator*-style organic components.

On a more positive note, Travis is again strongly portrayed. The scene in which he asks for a prisoner on which to test the virus is wonderfully evocative of the low value placed on human life in fascist states; when the mutoid asks what she should do if there is no suitable prisoner in the detention area, he snaps: 'Then detain one!' Likewise, Travis is willing to deliberately allow his own fellow soldiers to be killed simply to make Blake's escape suitably convincing. At the end, Travis is even willing to kill himself, and conceivably everyone else in the room, in order to end Blake's life. Travis's death-wish, previously implicit in his remarks to the effect that Blake should kill him when he has him at his mercy, is here made explicit. Significantly, Servalan makes him lower his gun-hand, suggesting both that she is aware of his death-wish, and that he will obey her as his superior officer, even if it means losing his chance of killing Blake.

Travis's sadism-by-proxy is also present. He likes seeing Avalon strapped down, although he does nothing to her himself. When the (male) prisoner is killed in the virus-testing experiment, we get two close-ups on Travis's face: in the first, he is tense, staring and breathing hard; in the second, his eyes are wide and, as he approaches the window of the room, he is seen to be smiling. When Servalan says, 'Satisfied?' he says, 'Completely!' This double-entendre highlights the fact that the satisfaction Travis obtains from the sight may have to do with more than just the successful completion of the experiment.

Servalan, by contrast, is not only cold and detached throughout, but there is a conscious mirroring of her with the mutoid; the way the shots have been set up, the mutoid is continually behind her, imitating her movements, and creating a parallel between two emotionless women. It is also worth noting that Servalan has the only male mutoids in the story; all of Travis's mutoids are female (and, we learn, can stand quite low temperatures). Again, we see her ability to seemingly switch her sex drive on and off at will: she is businesslike with Travis, until the point at which she tells him that his superiors are not pleased with his actions but that she will support him unofficially, when she starts smiling flirtatiously and running her finger along the trimmings of his uniform. Then, the moment that she speaks the word 'officially,' her manner is again businesslike. Whether this performance is an attempt to impress Travis, lure him to her side, harass him, or something else, is unclear at this point.

The character of Avon continues to develop. He takes control of the ship, giving the orders and arguing down Cally and Gan. He is as much a leader as Blake, and his decisions are as sound as Blake's, albeit more aggressively put. (Blake, incidentally, is here seen breaking a man's neck, in another of his periodic displays of ruthlessness.) We also, however, see a different side of Avon in the scene in which he finds Cally unconscious; he touches the blood on her face and rubs it between his fingers, and then caresses her cheek and neck. When we next see her, she has been placed in a chair and Avon has left the room. Although Avon has previously given evidence of a cruel streak with women, it seems to be brought on by being attacked, used or obstructed, rather than a broader-based disorder like Gan's, so there is no suggestion that the sight of her induced him to emotional distress. Most likely, he leaves her alone because he is reluctant to admit to feeling affection.

For Gan, however, this story contains some crucial sequences. When the expedition party returns to the *Liberator*, Gan is detailed to take Avalon to her quarters. At some point between then and when we see her next, her clothes have been changed and her tunic, containing the capsule with the virus, has gone missing. Gan is the only person with the opportunity to have obtained it at this point, and there is no reason for Jenna to have taken it into the teleport bay (as Gan suggests). It thus appears that Gan is trophy-hunting. Furthermore, when Avalon comes onto the flight deck, Gan is seen swallowing a pill with water; he is having headaches again, which are visually connected in this scene with Avalon's presence. Gan is very – even, one might say, overly – solicitous to her, putting his arm around her shoulders and repeatedly asking if she is all right. He stammers a lot, and keeps looking at her, seemingly disconcerted by her presence. In the teleport bay, however, when Jenna says, 'Gan, that's not Avalon,' he lunges for her throat; as with Cally in "The Web", he can be violent with her because she is neither who nor what she seems to be. The fight sequence that follows is excellent, avoiding the fake appearance of the combat scenes in "Time Squad" by using close-up shots and a hand-held camera to give the action an urgent quality. However, Gan is an enthusiastic participant, seemingly damaging the robot's servomotors (which make labouring noises for the rest of the story) with the sheer force of his attack, rather than holding back or asking for explanations.

"Project Avalon" therefore not only develops the Blake-Travis and Travis-Servalan axes of the ongoing narrative, but also builds on the Gan storyline in a way that will be picked up on in the next episode.

A10: BREAKDOWN

UK TRANSMISSION: Monday 6 March 1978: 7.15pm – 8.10pm
DURATION: 51:22
VIEWING FIGURE: 8.8m
CHART POSITION: 41
WRITER: Terry Nation
DIRECTOR: Vere Lorrimer

CREDITED CAST: Julian Glover (Kayn); Ian Thompson (Farren); Christian Roberts (Renor)

UNCREDITED CAST: Sue Crosland (Double for Jenna); Michael Gaunt (Voices)

SYNOPSIS: While piloting the *Liberator*, Gan suddenly becomes violent, attacking first Jenna and then Blake. When he is tranquillised and restrained, the crew learn that part of his limiter has burnt out, and that he needs immediate neurosurgical attention. After the crew reject all of Zen's suggested locations for this treatment as impractical, Avon suggests XK-72, a neutral space station that he has been investigating as a potential bolthole should he no longer wish to stay on the *Liberator*. Getting there, however, necessitates traversing a dangerous area of space without computer aid, as Zen refuses to function in this region. At XK-72, the crew enlist the help of Kayn, a neurosurgeon, who rapidly works out their identities and alerts the nearest Federation base, buying time for its pursuit ships to get there by refusing to work on Gan. Avon has meanwhile decided to leave the *Liberator* for XK-72, but while there, he learns of Kayn's deceit and returns to warn the others. Blake forces Kayn to repair Gan's limiter, then teleports the neurosurgeon back to XK-72 and prepares to evade the pursuit ships; the station, however, is hit by a plasma bolt meant for the *Liberator* and destroyed.

ANALYSIS: "Breakdown" (originally to have been entitled "Brain Storm") is where many of the hints and suggestions regarding Gan and his condition come sharply into focus. (Terry Nation's story "The Invaders" would have given Gan a very major role, involving him fighting a murderous alien duplicate of himself, but had been abandoned prior to production.)

The Gan we see in this story is not, as Blake suggests, simply reacting against stress (since Gan still tries to kill when he appears to be perfectly calm) or, as Avon guesses, at the mercy of scrambled signals (as Avon says, it's not his field; he could be misinterpreting the limiter's faulty attempts to hold Gan back). After the limiter has cut out completely, in the scenes in the infirmary, we see a trace of Gan's true personality. Far from a mindless killer or, despite Avon's cheap shot in "The Web", slow and stupid, he is cunning and ruthless; he feigns unconsciousness, manipulates Cally into removing his restraints and grabs her, smiling cruelly as he strangles her. Later, with Avon, he deliberately attacks the computers – although this action will reduce the crew's chances of survival – because he knows that this will upset Avon more than simply attacking him.

Despite his intelligence, however, he is at the mercy of his behaviour patterns. The initial scene in which he attacks Jenna and, when Blake warns him to stop, turns on Blake, echoes his description of killing a guard who killed his 'woman.' Later, when he is prevented from attacking Cally by a limiter surge – not by a man – he deliberately goes in search of a man, Avon. A pattern has been set up to which he keeps, even if the circumstances are different. The fist that we see him clenching initially is once again the left; his attempt to break Blake's neck mirrors Blake's attack on the guard one episode earlier. It is telling that Kayn assumes Gan to be a psychopath without knowing anything about him bar that he has a limiter, suggesting that the limiter is used only for the most dangerous cases. At the end, when Gan asks if they could have removed the limiter and Blake says that it was not possible, it is significant that at no point prior to this have Blake and the others even discussed this possibility; they may not know the reason why Gan has the limiter, but they aren't about to risk having it removed.

Blake's leadership qualities come across strongly in "Breakdown". On the face of it, his style might seem rather manipulative: we see another display of ruthlessness, when he threatens dispassionately to destroy Kayn's hands. He also seems to use aspects of his crew's personality to keep them from leaving: Avon's feelings about his brother, Cally's idealism, Jenna's interest in him and Vila's lack of anyplace else to go. However, he states that he will not force anyone to stay and, as we have seen in "Duel", the fact that he uses Jenna's feelings for him doesn't mean that he does not reciprocate. Something about Gan, furthermore, means that Blake will take great risks to save him; it seems that Gan's faith in Blake blinds him partially to the fact that Gan is a murderer. Blake appears to think that, if Gan has faith in him, and Gan seems to be a simple soul, then Blake truly is a man of the people. As Vila notes, Blake, for all his seeming ruthlessness, has a conscience.

Avon, by contrast, is making good on his threat to leave the crew. We again see negative sides to his character; he grabs Jenna such that Blake has to shout at him to make him let go; he is willing to sell the teleport (although not to the Federation or anyone who will share it with them); and he advocates turning back rather than going through the vortex, even though this will mean Gan's death. However, when he learns what Kayn has done, he changes his mind and returns to warn the crew. The most obvious motivation for this appears to be a desire to protect someone on the ship, although whether it is the whole crew or simply Blake is still unknown. Another factor, however, seems to be the ambitions of Farren, the station administrator; Farren wants Avon on XK-72 for the things that he can bring them, to the point where he, the rule-bound bureaucrat, is willing to bend the rules. Avon, though, cannot be unaware that such a person is likely to use him, and to maintain a hold over him, and he, being an independent, selfish sort, would not tolerate such a situation.

Cally, in this story, appears to have undergone a shift in role, playing nurse to Gan and whinging about inhumane treatment.

This is not, however, incompatible with her terrorist activities (and her namesake Kali is the goddess of birth as well as of death); the acts of sabotage by environmentalist and animal-rights groups demonstrate that a liberal ideology need not mean a total abstention from violent means. Vila, for his part, has an unusually ruthless and clever scene in which he takes a gun, concealing his actions from the rest of the crew, and threatens Kayn without their knowledge; although Keating plays this jokily, it seems to be a holdover from an earlier, more devious Vila.

Farren's charge Kayn, however, is not so much ambitious as he is selfish. When we first see Kayn (an assured performance by Julian Glover), he is very anti-authoritarian, shouting down Farren and seemingly interested in Blake's plight: sentiments with which the audience can sympathise. However, as Blake notes, simply because someone is neutral, that does not make them well-disposed towards rebels: although Kayn is anti-authoritarian, it is only as it applies to his immediate personal circumstances, and he views the Federation as a force for stability. The situation of XK-72 *vis-à-vis* the Federation appears to be one in which there is outward independence, but actually a certain amount of reliance on the Federation to keep order, much like the position of many countries *vis-à-vis* the USA today. (Note that Farren, in his fight with Kayn at the end, is more concerned about maintaining the appearance of neutrality than genuinely worried about the *Liberator*.)

Kayn also is willing to use the ambitions of his assistant Renor to get his own way. Renor is somewhat selfish – he is interested not in the crew's politics, but in meeting celebrities, and, like Artix in "Space Fall" and Laran in "Cygnus Alpha", is a favourite Chris Boucher character, the ambitious young man. Although he might seem more sympathetic than Kayn, his desire for advancement means that he will not disobey or report Kayn, whatever moral objections he may have to Kayn's behaviour. He flirts with Jenna – she looks him up and down suggestively when he comes on board, and he reciprocates. The subsequent exchange between them works on three levels: Jenna has been told by Blake to get close to Renor – which she clearly interprets as meaning sexually, saying that she may not be his type – but there is no suggestion that she particularly fancies him. The words she speaks are therefore probably indicative of her true feelings for him; however, she says them in such a way as to suggest that she is flirting, but playing hard-to-get. The three layers of meaning are: the uninterested words, the interested tone and, under it all, the real lack of interest in Renor.

The exchanges between Kayn and Renor show Kayn at his worst. He is willing to use Gan's deteriorating condition to buy the pursuit ships more time ('What sort of a doctor are you?' asks Renor); we also see him gaining enjoyment from playing with the lives of the crew, saying, 'I haven't decided yet,' when Renor asks whether or not he plans to report them to the Federation, although he has clearly made up his mind already. Finally, at the end of the story, Kayn goes completely over the edge, beating Farren to death with a blunt instrument. Although he calls Gan a psychopath, it seems that in this case, it takes one to know one.

This episode not only showcases Gan's true nature, and that of his condition, but we also see development on the part of both Blake and Avon, and reinforcement of the idea that there are degrees of neutrality, and that there is no guarantee of who will support and who will reject Blake and his cause.

A11: BOUNTY

UK TRANSMISSION: Monday 13 March 1978: 7.15pm – 8.10pm
DURATION: 51:57
VIEWING FIGURE: 9.6m
CHART POSITION: 40
WRITER: Terry Nation
DIRECTOR: Pennant Roberts

CREDITED CAST: T P McKenna (Sarkoff); Carinthia West (Tyce); Marc Zuber (Tarvin); Mark York (Cheney); Derrick Branche (Amagon Guard)

UNCREDITED CAST: Stanley Hollingsworth (Stunt Driver); Derek San-Sellus, Neville Rofaila, Geronimo Sehmi (Amagon Guards); Doug Charlton, Rex Browne, Bob Sutherland, Ronald Nunnery, John Aston, Paul Berry, Barnie Lawrence, Keith Norrish, Andy Dempsey (Federation Guards); Roberta Gibbs (Double for Cally)

SYNOPSIS: Blake and Cally teleport down to an unnamed planet in order to find Sarkoff, the former President of the planet Lindor, who resigned his post and went into voluntary exile after having been defeated in an election. Sarkoff, however, does not want to return with them; even when they explain that the election was rigged by the Federation, who plan to incite Lindor into civil war, take over and restore Sarkoff as a puppet ruler. Blake ultimately convinces Sarkoff to return by threatening to destroy his prized collection of twentieth-century artefacts. Once more on board the *Liberator*, Blake and Cally find that it has been taken over by a group of Amagon bounty hunters, the leader of whom, Tarvin, has a previous acquaintance with Jenna; Jenna has seemingly turned traitor on the crew. However, this proves to be a ruse and the crew, together with Sarkoff and his daughter Tyce, overpower the Amagons and set course for Lindor.

ANALYSIS: "Bounty" is the first genuinely bad script presented by *Blake's 7*. The sheer effort of writing thirteen stories one after the other was clearly taking its toll on Nation; and Boucher, who, along with Pennant Roberts, did much rewriting on this episode, also appears to have been feeling the strain.

Although the script does have a number of clever lines (for instance, Avon's remark regarding the seemingly crippled spaceship that: 'The test is not whether you are suspicious, but whether you are caught'), it was found in production to be under running, necessitating some obvious padding: Sarkoff spends seventy seconds listening to a recording of singer Kathleen Ferrier, and Blake takes a full forty-five seconds to admire Sarkoff's home décor. Furthermore, there is some dire dialogue – notably, Cheney's somewhat suspect cry of: 'You two, round the rear!' – to say nothing of the guards' colour codes, which include Red Standby Alert (apparently meaning stand around and do nothing); Red Mobilisation (wander around outside the house) and Blue Mobilisation (allow the President and his daughter to escape accompanied by two terrorists in an old car). The exchange between Jenna and Tarvin about their night alone in the mountains unfortunately can be read as suggesting that Jenna saved Tarvin's life by distracting 300 customs guards. How she did this is left to the imagination.

The direction of the story is less than inspired, with the fight sequences being a particular casualty. In addition, the director has chosen to cast only Asian men as the Amagons and put them in headscarves. This, coupled with Tarvin's lines about wealth being the only thing that matters and selling his grandmother, lends the production a racist undertone even by 1970s standards. As Nation reportedly intended the story to be a comment on late-1970s peacekeeping activities in the Middle East, the Amagons' portrayal is rather ironic.

The character of Sarkoff (to say nothing of his more-than-slightly-camp headgear) is inconsistent with his stated profession. He acts more like a king than a career politician: having made it to President, he should be shrewd enough to know when he is being used. Although there are cases of politicians being forced out of office, they generally try to get back into power afterwards; Churchill, whose painting hangs in Sarkoff's residence, is a case in point. (The painting, incidentally, appears to be the scorched remains of the Sutherland portrait of Churchill, presented to him by both Houses of Parliament on 29 October 1954, which he famously loathed; on 11 January 1978, just over a month prior to the commencement of studio recording on "Bounty", the fact came to light that Churchill's wife Clementine had destroyed this painting after her husband's death). The Federation's strategy more directly recalls the Nazis' plans for the Duke of Windsor (the former King Edward VIII), notably their intention to bring him in as the puppet ruler of Britain. However, it wouldn't do for Blake to be seen to be supporting a monarchy, hence Sarkoff has to become, somewhat uncomfortably, the leader of a democracy. The sequence in which he, seemingly deserted by his last supporter, listens to a record of 'Blow the Wind Southerly' (the lyrics of which express the fear that a loved one might never return from a journey) is really rather poignant, making Blake's ruthless smashing of the disk doubly effective; however, Sarkoff's portrayal as pompous, self-indulgent and – since he, an allegedly anti-Federation politician, is happy to accept Federation hospitality – hypocritical rather subverts this intention. The fact that we do not find out that Tyce (who was a late addition to the script by Boucher) is his daughter until the end could lend a nice ambiguity to her role, as it is unclear whether she is truly loyal to him or simply a gold-digging little tart who wants to be First Lady of Lindor, but the actress is not quite able to pull it off.

Finally, the plot in general has a number of poorly-thought-through aspects. The scene in which Cally jumps off a wall and knocks out a guard (apparently another late addition) makes no sense in script terms and, furthermore, makes a mockery out of lines like Cally's 'Something has alerted the guards,' which would fit if the sole evidence of the rebels' presence was the tripped alarm, but not when she has just brutally clubbed one of them unconscious. There is no explanation for why Blake and Cally are carrying around what appears to be a bright red picnic hamper, or for why Tarvin doesn't check Tyce for concealed weapons. The guards are unbelievably thick – standing in the smoke for what appears to be quite some time before realising that they've been tricked – and are rather impolite to Sarkoff, considering that they are supposed to be masquerading as an honour guard. Tyce suggests as a hiding place for Blake and Cally a set of mine workings 20 miles away, which seems a little excessive. Gan's going over to the Amagon ship makes sense in plot terms: Vila is too cowardly to go over, Avon too suspicious, and for Jenna to go over would reflect poorly on everyone else's masculinity, so it must be Gan. However, Gan has no motivation for undertaking a potential suicide mission (and in this case, it can't be his murderous impulses: he has no idea what is on the ship, and the fact that the Amagons fake his voice later on suggests that he was not deceiving the crew willingly). The only possible explanation is that this is some sort of atonement for the events of "Breakdown", but offering to get oneself killed seems to be a poor way to apologise for beating the hell out of one's crewmates. Jenna's traitor act is the least convincing in the series: had it been Avon who seemed to betray the crew, it would have made sense, but Jenna has shown too much affection for Blake for her betrayal to have any ring of truth.

Despite all the problems, this story isn't entirely bad. The idea of Sarkoff collecting 20th-century artefacts and getting their use slightly wrong (cutlery as décor, for instance) is a rather nice dig at present-day romanticism about the past, and the idea of 'natural history' coming to mean history in the sense of the study of past things that no longer exist is also clever. We get more backstory on the Auronar: according to Sarkoff, they do not originate from Earth, and the Auron ambassador to Lindor, Leeharn, has apparently exiled himself. (Note that Cally does not respond to Blake's inference that it was due to his having failed, or to Sarkoff's that it was due to Sarkoff having failed him.) We also get a clever series of shots when Avon and Jenna go to teleport Gan back to the *Liberator*: Zen warns Vila that the voice isn't Gan's, Vila calls the others on the intercom – and then time is rolled back briefly, so that we see Avon and Jenna in the teleport bay just before Vila calls them.

Although "Bounty" does have one or two enjoyable aspects, on the whole, it is easily the poorest story of the season, and it's probably best that it was positioned between two stronger examples.

A12: DELIVERANCE

UK TRANSMISSION: Monday 20 March 1978: 7.15pm – 8.10pm
DURATION: 49:11
VIEWING FIGURE: 9.0m
CHART POSITION: 36
WRITER: Terry Nation
DIRECTOR: Michael E Briant and David Maloney (uncredited)

CREDITED CAST: Tony Caunter (Ensor); Suzan Farmer (Meegat); James Lister (Maryatt)

UNCREDITED CAST: Terry Plummer, Terry Richards, Billy Horrigan, Chris Webb (Stunt Scavengers); Pat Garman, Harry Fielder, Steve Kelly, Ron Tarr, Bill Hemmings, Joe Santo, Steve Ismay, James Linton, Derek Suthern, John Hogan, Reg Woods, Ian Munro, William Perrie (Scavengers)

SYNOPSIS: The *Liberator* crew, having witnessed the explosion of a small spacecraft, go down to the radiation-ravaged planet Cephlon to search for survivors. They find one, who is badly wounded, and teleport him to the ship, but Jenna is attacked by primitives and loses her teleport bracelet. Gan, Avon and Vila go down again to search for her. The survivor of the crash, Ensor, is the son of a brilliant scientist (also named Ensor). The elder Ensor will die if he does not get microcells to power his artificial heart and access to a surgeon; they have done a deal to sell a device called Orac to the Federation in exchange for both, plus a hundred million credits. Young Ensor takes Cally hostage, and insists that Blake fly the *Liberator* to the planet Aristo. We also learn that the ship's explosion was deliberately engineered by Servalan, so that both Ensors would die, allowing her to go to their base and steal Orac. Meanwhile, the expedition team are rescued from the primitives by a woman named Meegat, who hails Avon as a divine figure; a long time ago, it was foretold that a man would come and launch a rocket containing genetic material from her people, so that their race might continue on another planet. Avon complies with her request in exchange for help rescuing Jenna and, their bargain concluded, the crew leave; Blake and Cally, meanwhile, have overpowered Ensor, who dies from his wounds.

ANALYSIS: "Deliverance" is a somewhat unusual story for the first season. In production terms, the difference lies mainly in the fact that the location work is directed not by the story's principal director, Michael E Briant, but by producer David Maloney. As Maloney recalls: 'Michael said that he couldn't do it for some reason. I didn't go too deeply into that because I was quite looking forward to flexing my own directorial muscles again, so I went ahead and did it myself.' In scripting terms, the exceptional aspect of the story is that it has three plots running concurrently throughout: the Travis-Servalan plot, the drama on board *Liberator*, and that on the planet Cephlon.

The initial scene with Travis and Servalan clearly demonstrates how much their relationship has changed since "Seek-Locate-Destroy". In contrast to the earlier story, Servalan keeps Travis waiting for some time after he enters her office, while she completes some minor calculations; as she herself notes, he would not have taken such a deliberate insult, even from a superior officer, before being stripped of his duties. She uses her sexuality as a weapon against him, keeping things strictly businesslike until she tells Travis that the surgeon she has sent with Ensor is Maryatt, at which point she becomes briefly flirtatious; later, when she tells Travis her full plan, she gives him her glass and lounges on the sofa with her skirt falling away to show the full length of her legs.

Servalan's choice of Maryatt is also a deliberate attack on Travis. She specifically chose the surgeon who fixed Travis's injuries – and thus saved his life – for a mission in which the surgeon will be killed, then framed as a deserter, meaning that his wife and children will be sent into slavery. For most people in the military, the service is a family, and one that looks after its own; this would particularly be the case for Travis, who has no known family or other relationships outside of those connected with his career. This incident thus effectively involves one part of the family deliberately killing a family member; Servalan also clearly knows that this particular surgeon is one with whom Travis has a personal connection. By forcing him to comply with this scheme, Servalan has made a direct attack on Travis's world and, by association, on his ego.

In this sequence, also, we get an account of the Ensors' plan, albeit with some details missing. It seems that they have approached Servalan and offered to give her the location of their base in exchange for Maryatt, the microcells and a hundred million credits. It is unexplained how they intend to stop her from taking the money back again once she has Orac, and unclear why they would give up so valuable an asset in the first place. Such details will be revealed in the next episode, "Orac", but at this point it is enough to note that young Ensor takes Maryatt (who, it is stated, is to act as hostage) to the base by a roundabout route, although we know that Servalan has been told its location by the Ensors, as they have threatened to destroy Orac if she tries to take it by force. The main flaw in their plan is that they do not realise that Servalan is ruthless enough to kill one of her own, and that she wants Orac for herself, rather than on behalf of the Federation. Thus, instead of paying the money (which would alert the Federation to the purchase), she arranges a double-cross. Young Ensor and Maryatt will be killed; Ensor's father, without the microcells, will die; and she can then collect Orac at her leisure. Secrecy is of the essence; she files no flight plan and involves Travis specifically because she has a hold over him; he wants his command back and she, the Supreme Commander, is the one who can give it to him.

Young Ensor, however, has not been killed, and winds up on the *Liberator*. The most notable thing about the *Liberator* sequences is the fact that the roles originally written for Avon and Blake were swapped around by Boucher (ostensibly for logistical reasons) in the final version of the script: Blake would have gone down to the planet, and Avon remained on board, had Nation's original intention been followed. This has the effect of bringing the two characters closer together in personality terms, and blurring the boundaries between them. Furthermore, the role-swap is, rather cleverly, turned into a plot point; the fact that Avon takes the leader role changes the situation from a routine expedition into one in which Avon is attempting to prove himself as someone who could take over for Blake (and, again, raises the question whether he returns for Jenna out of a sense of duty, or of affection, or simply because he wants to prove his leadership abilities).

The storyline on Cephlon is the most interesting of the three. Once again, we see some rather dodgy behaviour from Gan: when he senses danger, he leaves Jenna alone and walks up and over the crest of a hill. When he teleports up, although he was the last to see her, he doesn't ask where she is, and when Blake asks him, he lies, saying that she was right behind him (when she was plainly some way away, and, since he'd asked her to stop there, he would know this). The door to Meegat's domain may open for Avon, but it does not open for Gan, placing him implicitly in the same category as the primitives. He later says: 'When it comes to killing, remember my limiter,' a phrase which, although it implies to the audience that he cannot kill because of the limiter, in fact does not actually *state* anything of the kind. He then remarks on having enjoyed beating up the attacking primitives to Vila (who responds: 'You're as mad as Meegat'). Jenna's kidnapping, incidentally, is another plot point salvaged from the unused "Locate and Destroy"; what the primitives intend to do with her is unclear, although one might speculate, from the shot of the – apparently entirely male – tribe around a large fire in front of the tents, that they intend to spit-roast her.

The relationship between Avon and Meegat is also telling. Meegat (whose name is an anagram of 'gamete,' a sexual reproductive cell) is a woman, dressed in a rather flimsy vestal-virgin outfit, who is waiting for a man to come along and fire off a rocket full of genetic matter. Avon is initially wary of her, suspecting that he is being lured into a trap (which of course he is, albeit, as it transpires, one of mutual benefit). Typically, he uses her throughout; he refuses to help her until he gets Jenna back, and at several points is clearly playing along with her (evidently failing to find her obsequious act impressive) in order to get what he wants. Avon does show sexual interest in her (she, for her part, cannot take her eyes off him); he holds her hand and, when he leaves to rescue Jenna, touches her face as he did with Cally in "Project Avalon". But they only ever seem to have sex on a symbolic level – if nothing else, they never seem to have the time.

The act of firing the rocket marks the end of their relationship. Although Avon seems rather to enjoy being identified as a god, his last onscreen words to Meegat are to the effect that his appearance seems 'a poor reward' for her long wait. Avon does not offer to take her along on the *Liberator,* nor does he stay with her; he simply leaves her on the radiation-soaked planet with the rest of her people. When asked, 'Did she really think you were a god?' Avon replies, 'For a while,' suggesting that she became disillusioned with him. Although this disillusionment is in some ways necessary – as it allows both Meegat and her people to move on after their mission of guarding the hatch and awaiting their saviour has come to an end, perhaps even to find new purpose – on a personal level, it is an act with an edge of cruelty. At the end, Blake remarks on Avon's abdication of his divinity, 'I don't like the responsibility either,' a phrase that compares and contrasts his situation with Avon's. Blake is responsible for his crew, and, had Avon stayed with Meegat or brought her along, he would have been responsible for her; the difference between the two is thus that Blake stays with his crew, whereas Avon will abandon responsibility if it is more convenient for him.

"Deliverance" is a strikingly allegorical piece that highlights the similarities and differences between Blake and Avon, and flags up changes in the Travis-Servalan relationship. Furthermore, it ends with a few unresolved points, and leads into the last story of the season.

A13: ORAC

UK TRANSMISSION: Monday 27 March 1978: 7.05pm – 8.00pm
DURATION: 51:47
VIEWING FIGURE: 10.6m
CHART POSITION: 27
WRITER: Terry Nation
DIRECTOR: Vere Lorrimer

CREDITED CAST: Derek Farr (Ensor); James Muir, Paul Kidd (Phibians)

UNCREDITED CAST: Derek Farr (Orac/Satellite); Barry Hayes (Double for Travis); Tony Caunter ([Young] Ensor – flashback to "Deliverance"); James Lister (Maryatt – flashback to "Deliverance")

SYNOPSIS: Following on from the events of "Deliverance", the *Liberator* is *en route* to Aristo with the microcells for the older Ensor's artificial heart, when the crew discover that those who teleported down to Cephlon have contracted radiation sickness, and there are no decontaminant drugs in the surgical unit. Meanwhile, Travis and Servalan arrive at Aristo before the *Liberator*, and approach Ensor's base through a system of underground tunnels in a ruined and partially flooded city. Once the *Liberator* reaches Aristo, Zen is briefly taken over by Orac, which sets teleport co-ordinates for Blake and Cally; after landing, they are guided through a system of defences (including a force barrier impenetrable to the teleport) to Ensor's laboratory. Ensor supplies them with drugs, and agrees to teleport up to the

Liberator, with Orac, to have the microcells fitted; before they can do so, however, they are attacked by Travis and Servalan and forced to navigate the system of tunnels to the surface. Ensor dies during the journey. Upon reaching the surface, Blake and Cally discover Travis and Servalan there before them; however, Avon and Vila teleport down and rescue their crewmates. On board the ship, Orac is revealed to be a super computing device that can link to any computer containing Tarial cells, and thus its knowledge is virtually limitless; it can even make predictions, which it demonstrates by prophesying the destruction of a ship that appears to be the *Liberator*.

ANALYSIS: "Orac", as the final story of the season, not only ties up some of the plot threads from the previous episode, but also leaves us with an unresolved mystery in the form of a cliffhanger that will lead into the first episode of Season B.

In this story, we learn that the Ensors are much less naïve than Servalan's account of their proposal in "Deliverance" made them seem. Here, it is made plain that they do not intend to sell Orac: when Blake reveals that the Federation will pay a hundred million for it, Ensor laughs and says: 'He's worth ten times that much.' Furthermore, one might well ask what he and his son would do with the money, as they show no signs of wanting to return to civilization. We also see that Orac is quite capable of taking over even as sophisticated a ship as the *Liberator*; it would be no problem for him to, say, take over the weapons systems of Federation pursuit ships and cause them to attack each other. Between Orac, his defences and the Phibian creatures haunting the tunnels, Ensor is quite unperturbed at the prospect of attempted invasion. The plan would seem, therefore, to be to let Maryatt go once Ensor Senior has had his surgery (presumably taking him outside of the system first); then, when Servalan comes for Orac, to use Orac and/or the defences to kill her and any escort.

Ensor Senior is also, it transpires, something of a shrewd customer when it comes to the natural dangers of the planet. The map he gives to Servalan leads her straight into the midst of the Phibians; it is also all but stated that he is responsible for the deaths of the members of the expedition that never returned, as we see their skeletons in the tunnels, killed, presumably, by Phibians.

Later, when Cally asks if the Phibians are dangerous he says, 'No, I don't think they'll harm us,' a statement that makes little sense, as earlier in the episode he expects the Phibians to kill Travis and Servalan. (A scene cut from the final version shows a Phibian mourning over the body of its fellow, killed by Travis.) It is, however, explicable if we assume that he is covering up for the murder of the expedition force, as it implies that he does not know that they were killed by the Phibians; here, however, it gets Cally into a dangerous situation.

Servalan's plan, described in the previous episode, comes to fruition here. She intends to kill Maryatt and young Ensor, wait for the old man to die, then collect Orac; she clearly does not realise Orac's full capabilities. She states that she is collecting Orac for the Federation, but this is plainly not the case: in the previous episode, she was concealing her actions from the Federation, and here she says to Travis that when they give Orac to the Federation, they will be very grateful; the implication of both these incidents, taken together, is that she intends to keep Orac and its abilities to herself until an opportune moment. (Travis, of course, has no real ambitions in this regard, being here only on Servalan's orders.)

At the end of the story, Blake remarks that telling the Federation that Travis and Servalan let him take Orac is a more fitting fate for them than death. It is possible that he simply assumes that the Federation will be less than pleased to discover that the Supreme Commander failed on a mission for them; however, it is also possible that Blake has guessed that Servalan has not informed her superiors of the scheme, given that she is on Aristo virtually unaccompanied. Travis smiles at the end of the story; he knows that, one way or the other, he will get the blame, and this appeals to his self-destructive nature.

There are a few elements in this story that show evidence of end-of-season exhaustion on the part of the scriptwriting and production teams. The opening recap on the *Liberator* is absolutely cringeworthy, taking place as it does in an alcove with a patio table and chairs that has never appeared before nor will do again; Avon, on two occasions, noisily scrapes his chair across the floor. We see Blake playing back some kind of *Star Trek*-style captain's log (also something he never does before or after), which makes no sense for a terrorist, as, if it fell into enemy hands, they would have hard evidence of Blake's movements. The events of the previous episode could easily have been conveyed through dialogue, and the most likely explanation for this sequence is that the episode was under-running, and/or that there was little time to write complicated lines. The episode also features a whacking great plot convenience, in that the *Liberator*'s well-stocked medical unit does not contain common anti-radiation drugs, and a moment of inadvertent humour when Cally appears to grope Jenna in the corridor.

Blake does not show conspicuous intelligence on this occasion. He sends Cally on ahead with Ensor while he pulls the roof down, ostensibly to stop anyone from following them. However, he had no knowledge that anyone was actually following them in the first place, and his actions waste time and allow Travis and Servalan to reach the surface before them, via another route. In addition, with Blake staying behind to sabotage the roof, Ensor is forced to carry Orac with Cally, which weakens the old man further and hastens his demise. As it turns out, they are only a few feet from the surface anyway, and if they had simply pressed on ahead, they would have got Ensor safely back onto the ship.

Gan, once again, is seen entering a room on the ship alone, rubbing his forehead and taking a tablet. Although he does later turn out to have radiation sickness, we do not know if this is the cause of his discomfort. Later, still on his own in the room, Gan has the communicator tuned to listen to the conversation on the flight deck, perhaps as a way of making him feel less alone. Finally, we see him hiding behind the teleport-bracelet rack, because, once again, he doesn't like being alone.

The most significant aspect of this story is the introduction of Orac, voiced for this episode only by Derek Farr. Although the eponymous device may appear, as Terry Nation's script describes it, 'not at all impressive; indeed, looking slightly botched together,' it is a sophisticated computer – 'a brain!' exclaims Ensor – that takes on aspects of his creator's personality. Significantly, Orac does not actually do this until after Ensor dies; it is as if, at his death, Ensor's personality, his soul even, is symbolically transferred into the machine. Orac also, living up to his name, is an oracle; he will prophesy, but his predictions are ambiguously worded. He does not say that the ship in the prediction is the *Liberator* – he simply says 'space vehicle will be destroyed' – and does not say when it will be destroyed, or where. The *Liberator* crew quite clearly have no idea what they have acquired; even the information that he has limitless knowledge, and therefore limitless power, does not cover all the possibilities. Ensor, from whom Orac has obtained his personality, keeps pets, which, perhaps, suggests something interesting about Orac's relationship with the *Liberator* crew.

Finally, the key to Orac's power lies in the fact that he can read any computer with a Tarial cell; these cells were developed by Ensor before he left the Federation, and not only do all Federation computers contain them, but Zen also appears to have them, or some kind of analogue. The significance of this will, however, not become apparent until the first episode of the next season. The last few minutes of the story make for a fantastic cliffhanger; the fact that the final shot depicts a ship very similar to the *Liberator* actually being blown up in space, without the frame of the viewscreen, leaves it ambiguous as to whether or not the *Liberator* itself has actually been destroyed, a fact that caused much speculation among contemporary viewers.

"Orac" is an intriguing conclusion to a season that transcends its limitations to produce a clever, intelligent and entertaining television series, with ongoing plots, complex characterisation and a political astuteness belying its pulp origins.

SEASON B (1979)

SEASON B - CREDITS

Series Creator: Terry Nation
Script Editor: Chris Boucher
Producer: David Maloney
Title Music: Dudley Simpson

Cast:
Gareth Thomas – Roj Blake
Sally Knyvette – Jenna Stannis
Paul Darrow – Kerr Avon
Jan Chappell – Cally
Michael Keating – Vila Restal
David Jackson – Olag Gan (B1 – B5)
Peter Tuddenham (voice) – Zen/Orac (B1 – B8, B10 – B13)
Jacqueline Pearce – Servalan (B3, B5, B6, B8, B10 – B13)
Brian Croucher – Travis (B3, B5, B6, B8, B10 – B13)

Stunt Co-ordinator:
Frank Maher (B1, B2)
Peter Brayham (B8, B9)
Leslie Crawford (B9)
Stuart Fell (B12)

Production Assistant:
Geoffrey Manton (B1, B7, B8, B9, B13)
Ralph Wilton (B2, B4)
Michael Brayshaw (B3, B5, B10, B11)
Jackie Willows (B6, B12)
Pauline Smithson (B6, B12)

Production Unit Manager:
Sheelagh Rees

Visual Effects Designers:
Mat Irvine
Peter Pegrum
Andrew Lazell (B2, B4, B6, B8 – B13)

Film Cameraman:
Peter Chapman (B1 – B5, B7)
Max Samett (B6, B8 – B13)
Paul Godfrey (B12)

Model Sequences:
Paul V Wheeler (B13)

Film Recordist:
Ian Sansam (B1 – B5, B7)
John Gatland (B6, B8 – B13)

Film Editor:
Sheila S Tomlinson

Studio Lighting:
Brian Clemett

Studio Sound:
Clive Gifford (B1 – B5, B7)
Malcolm Johnson (B6, B8 – B13)

Special Sound:
Richard Yeoman-Clark (B1 – B7)
Elizabeth Parker (B8 – B13)

Electronic Effects:
A J Mitchell

Senior Cameraman:
Dave White (B13)

Reg Poulter (B3, B6 (both uncredited))

Series Videotape Editors:
Sam Upton
Malcolm Banthorpe

Costume Designer:
June Hudson (B1 – B5, B7)
Barbara Kidd (B6, B8, B9 – B13)

Make Up Artist:
Marianne Ford (B1 – B5, B7)
Ann Ailes (B6, B8 – B13)

Graphic Designer:
Bob Blagden

Incidental Music:
Dudley Simpson (B1 – B10, B12, B13)

Designer:
Sally Hulke (B1, B7)
Paul Allen (B2, B4)
Mike Porter (B3, B5)
Gerry Scott (B6, B8, B9)
Steve Brownsey (B8, B9)
Ken Ledsham (B10, B11, B13)
Eric Walmsley (B12)
Ray London (B13)

INTRODUCTION: SEASON B

The second season of *Blake's 7*, unlike its predecessor, was fraught with problems from an early stage, with the result that – despite having benefited from a budget increase – it is arguably the season that shows the most variation in quality. Due to time pressure, behind-the-scenes arguments between writers, directors and actors and changes in the production team's relationships with each other, the second season comes across as confused and frequently inconsistent.

Work began on the season quite a long time in advance of the start of its production, with a complete draft of the original story order being developed by January/February 1978. The biggest change from the previous season was that the scripts were to be provided by a number of different writers, with Nation originally down to do five stories, including a two-part story for the end of the season. Boucher composed a document called 'General Notes and Baffle Gab Glossary' to explain to the new writers what the technical terms were, and invited them to view episodes of the first season. It was also decided that the overall plot of the season would involve a quest for Federation Central Control, which would finally be discovered in Nation closing two-parter, after a mid-season climax where Blake and his crew believe that they have found it, only to be confronted by an empty room.

At the same time as working on the series, Nation was trying to launch a TV movie called *Bedouin* and also planning to move to America. He was thus growing increasingly detached from his creation, and eventually contributed only three scripts to the season. He was also working less closely with Boucher, who was now editing the work of several different writers as well as writing three (later four) scripts himself. The Nation-Boucher writing partnership, which had resulted in the first season being fairly seamless, was therefore lost.

Another factor that affected the season was that a number of regular cast members decided to move on to other projects. Stephen Greif had been offered a part in a film, production of which would coincide with the recording of the season; he was also unhappy with what he saw as a lack of development in his role. By this point, however, at least one script featuring Travis had already been written and more were planned, so, with Chris Boucher halfway through writing "Trial", the decision was taken to recast the character. Brian Croucher, an actor known for his roles as villains and 'heavies,' took over the part. Sally Knyvette also expressed her intention of leaving and, even more problematically, Gareth Thomas informed the production team that he would not be renewing his contract at the end of the season. Plans were floated for introducing a 'substitute Blake' character at some point, possibly around the tenth episode. This idea was eventually dropped in favour of having Avon take over the central role.

To add to the complications, Nation decided early on that he wanted to kill off one of the regulars, in order to add an element of unpredictability to the show. Boucher recalls: 'It was Terry's instinct that you had to convince the audience that everyone really was under threat, and so the only way to do that was to kill someone.' According to Boucher, Nation met both him and David Maloney in the BBC bar and informed them of his decision, proposing Vila as the subject as he was not keen on Michael Keating's performance. Boucher and Maloney were vehemently against this, as Vila was popular with viewers. They subsequently went through the rest of the characters and eventually settled on Gan as the best candidate, as an internal BBC Audience Research Report had singled him out as the least popular. Later, with Sally Knyvette continuing to express her intention to leave the series, Nation was said to have been writing the deaths of Jenna and Vila into his end-of-season two-parter, but this idea was apparently never discussed with Boucher or Maloney, and did not get very far into development. All these developments, as well as the decision (which appears to have been made fairly late in the day) to retain Orac as a regular, meant a good deal of chopping and changing for the crew, with very little certainty as to who was leaving when, or even at all.

There is also a rumour that Nation had initially planned to write the Daleks into the two-parter; while Maloney has no recollection of this, Boucher remembers the plan being tentatively suggested by Nation, and being turned down 'politely but firmly' by the production team.

Politics in the outside world were also beginning to have an effect on *Blake's 7*. 1977 and 1978 saw a shift in climate with regard to acceptable levels of sex and violence on television. *Doctor Who* famously came under attack from Mary Whitehouse and the National Viewers and Listeners Association (the stories under criticism including three directed by David Maloney, with one, "The Deadly Assassin", being edited on its repeat to remove a sequence perceived as overly violent), and its new producer, Graham Williams, was given orders to lighten the tone of the series. Philip Martin's *Gangsters*, another series influential on *Blake's 7*, also came under scrutiny, with a debate being televised on BBC2 on 10 February 1978 over whether or not it was 'sending the wrong message.'

The *Blake's 7* production team had always exercised a degree of caution over the inclusion of explicit content; for instance, whereas the original script for "The Way Back" openly stated that Blake's alleged offences against children were sexual, this was merely implied in the televised version. In the second season, however, this toning-down becomes more obvious, with neither the nature of Blake's crimes nor the presence of Gan's limiter being mentioned again. The production also takes on a less 'gritty' and realistic quality; for instance, the crew's outfits in the first half of the season are elaborate, unreal, space-operatic confections. (Costume designer June Hudson says that Maloney instructed her to take this approach, but Maloney maintains that what he told her to do and how she interpreted it were two different things.)

The Gan subtext, also, had been dropped by sometime around the writing of "Redemption", even though "Pressure Point" could have been written so as to bring this subtext out. Boucher and Maloney, although they do not dispute that the Gan subtext is present in the first season, maintain that it was never actively articulated to them as such. (Boucher has remarked that, although sex killers are not his personal forte, Nation had featured them before in his writing.) The decision to move away from it must therefore have been Nation's, perhaps prompted by advice from BBC Head of Series Ronnie Marsh (who was a close friend of his) or by personal recognition that in the current climate it might be too controversial to reveal (as had been done some years earlier in *Survivors*) that one of the regulars was a sex killer. Gan is therefore killed off, but not in the way that might have been expected on the basis of the development of the character in the first season.

There were also problems with regard to Pip and Jane Baker's violent script "Death Squad", which was cancelled at a very late stage. This was ostensibly for cost reasons, although it is also true to say that Maloney did not like it: 'I thought it was better suited to *Space: 1999*, which Pip and Jane had then recently worked on.' Boucher agrees: 'It was okay, but on reflection perhaps not of the series.'

Vere Lorrimer was the only director who returned for the second season (the series being required under BBC rules to have at least one director on contract to the BBC as opposed to freelance). One of the new directors, George Spenton-Foster, proved controversial with the cast, as he was known to take likes and dislikes to particular actors, and had difficulties with Brian Croucher – an actor who likes to be aware of a character's background and motivations, and who will ask the director about these if they are not apparent from the script. Spenton-Foster, according to his colleagues, preferred actors simply to do what they were told (although he was known to be more lenient with performers whom he liked, such as Jacqueline Pearce, Paul Darrow and Scott Fredericks).

Jan Chappell and Sally Knyvette, meanwhile, regularly complained that they were not having enough to do. (Lorrimer frequently got confused over the fact that Jan played Cally and Sally played Jenna, calling them 'Jam and Jelly'.) It is fair to say that many of the new writers appear to have focused more on the male characters in their initial scripts.

The allocation of the second season to a Tuesday evening transmission slot, opposite *Charlie's Angels* on the ITV network, resulted in a noticeable drop in ratings (although they still remained impressive). Audience figures hovered around the 7.0 million mark, with the lowest-rated programme, "Horizon", gaining 6.3 million and the highest, "Star One", 8.2 million viewers.

The changes in regular cast, writing and production – no doubt coupled with other factors now unknown due to fading memories and the passage of time – meant that the series saw a lot of chopping and changing, with stories moving rapidly around the transmission order. There were also substantial changes in the relationships between team members, and some debate, both official and unofficial, as to how much sex and/or violence was appropriate in the stories. The result is that the second season contains some of the best regarded episodes in the series' history (e.g. "Trial", "Killer", and "Gambit") and also some of the most heavily criticised (e.g. "Pressure Point", "Hostage" and "Voice from the Past").

B1: REDEMPTION

UK TRANSMISSION: Tuesday 9 January 1979: 7.20pm – 8.10pm
DURATION: 49:40
VIEWING FIGURE: 7.9m
CHART POSITION: 50
WRITER: Terry Nation
DIRECTOR: Vere Lorrimer

CREDITED CAST: Sheila Ruskin (Alta One); Harriet Philpin (Alta Two); Roy Evans (Slave)

UNCREDITED CAST: Fred Haggerty, Les White, Terry York (Stuntmen/Alta Guards); David Charles, Gordon Somers, Paul Menzies, David Ponting, Peter Clare, John Curry (Alta Guards and Slaves); Peter Roy, Mike Mungarvan, Ray Faulkner (Alta Guards)

SYNOPSIS: Following Orac's prophecy (in the previous episode) of a *Liberator*-like spaceship being destroyed, Avon proposes that the best way to stop the prediction from coming true is to pinpoint the area of space where the incident occurs and then avoid it. Shortly thereafter, the *Liberator* comes under attack from two non-Federation spacecraft. This disables the control systems but does not destroy the ship. Zen appears to come under external control, and the crew are prevented from repairing the damage by the *Liberator* itself. The ship is boarded by an expedition force and taken to a massive space station called Spaceworld, located in the area where Orac predicted the explosion would take place. It transpires that here, there were once three planets in a perpetual state of warfare; one of them developed a supercomputer called the System, which now controls all three worlds as well as Spaceworld. The crew effect an escape, with the help of a slave-worker, while Orac interferes with the System; as they escape, the *Liberator* is pursued by a sister ship, which explodes – fulfilling the prophecy – when Orac takes control of its weapons systems.

ANALYSIS: "Redemption", as the first story of the new season, re-establishes the series' themes and protagonists. It also, however, establishes new characters and situations and, in one respect, rewrites the series' mythos.

Appropriately enough, "Redemption" references the early stories of the first season. We have, once again, a fascist society in which people are controlled by a combination of force, technology and (as the slave whom they encounter remarks on the fact that 'these young guards' don't know about the old lifts, implying a degree of free will on their part) an element of individual compliance as well. The apparent leaders, the Altas, are also a part of the system, and are reminiscent of Geela and Novara in "The Web"; there is also a parallel between the slave-workers and the Decimas, although here, it is the slave-workers who dehumanise the Altas. The guards' uniforms recall those of Federation troopers (in addition to which, the location used in this story had previously appeared as a Federation communications complex in "Time Squad"), and the presence of Blake and his crew again triggers a revolt as well as (on Orac's part) an attack on the System. The sequence where Alta One questions Blake is also a recap of earlier events, hence Blake's statement that his main point of reference for where they first encountered the *Liberator* is Cygnus Alpha (which serves to remind the viewer of the fact that Blake was bound for the prison colony at the time he took over the ship). Similarly, the gratuitous statement at the end of the story that the *Liberator* is now bound for Earth Sector not only references Blake's vow in "The Way Back", but also emphasises that their main fight is with the Federation. Finally, we have the crew breaking free of the System, highlighting the way in which the *Liberator* (whose creators have simply named it 'Deep Space Vehicle 2') allowed them to reject the (small-s) system of the Federation.

This episode is very reminiscent of Nation's *Doctor Who* story "Death to the Daleks", which also featured a living city, guarded by mechanical serpents, which rejected its inhabitants (as in the events on the *Liberator* in this episode); the slave is reminiscent of the "Death to the Daleks" character Bellal, who, similarly, hides in places that his oppressors do not know about. Both stories also have a heavy Freudian element, in this case involving a scenario of dominant women ruling an army of symbolically castrated men, who wield long, phallic, purple-lit weapons.

This episode, like "Seek-Locate-Destroy" in the previous season, acts to re-establish the main characters for the audience. Elements of the *Liberator* set are slightly redesigned – a reflection of the improved budget – and all the regulars are given new outfits, although some are less appropriate choices than others. (Vila's lemon-yellow trousers are particularly dire.) Blake is re-established as the leader; Avon is clever, ruthless and angling for Blake's job (although he seems to have a degree of feeling for his leader, putting his arm over Blake as if to protect him when they are knocked to the floor as the ship comes under attack). The scene in which Avon remarks of Blake, 'You looked as though you were planning something you didn't want the rest of us to know about,' is a character-establishing one, as is the sequence in which Blake asks Avon, 'Do you think you could forget your superiority complex for a moment and get on with it?' and Avon responds, smiling slightly, with 'All right,' suggesting either that he is agreeing with Blake's assessment of his own character, or acknowledging that he is getting at Blake, or possibly both. Vila is established as a coward who is good with locks, and Jenna as a pilot. Cally, for her part, gets very little to do, not even having a gratuitous mental-telepathy sequence.

Gan, however, has a re-establishment that is slightly different from those of the others. He is defined, in this episode, as a large man who beats up the System's guards on behalf of the group; there is no mention of his limiter, not even a side remark along the lines of that in "Deliverance": 'When it comes to killing, remember my limiter.' In fact, the limiter is never mentioned again; it is as if this aspect of Gan's character and passed has ceased to be. He never even so much as has a headache from now on. The scene in which the slave kills Alta Two, shocking her along the neck with one of the guards' weapons, with Blake then doing the same to a guard, would have worked better had Gan been the one attacking the Alta (with a command from one of his fellow-crewmembers); an opportunity that would doubtless have been taken in the previous season is avoided here.

This story also contains a significant subtext regarding Orac (voiced from this episode onwards by Peter Tuddenham). Orac, rather than the System, would seem to be the one behind the crew's predicament. If the two smaller spacecraft were capable of taking over Zen themselves, they would not have needed to attack and disable the *Liberator*. One might observe that the Altas do not establish control over Zen using the command code until they are physically inside the ship. (The guards have to use the consoles initially, implying that Zen is still, at this point, outside the System.) Furthermore, the snakelike cable that menaces Blake and Avon does not kill either of them, despite having ample opportunity; whoever is controlling the ship does not want to seriously harm the crew. Also, it is worth noting that the System has not come looking for the *Liberator* before, despite having had an entire season in which to do so.

Orac, however, is more than capable of taking over Zen, and of having alerted the System to the ship's whereabouts. Orac himself, furthermore, appears to be the one who destroys Spaceworld, as the grenades hurled in the closing stages of the story do not appear to do much damage, and the Alta's cries of 'Destruct!, Destruct!' suggest the triggering of a self-destruct mechanism more than anything else. (It is implied throughout that the System either has actual Tarial cells – pirated or otherwise obtained from the Federation – or a close analogue as part of its makeup.) Significantly, when Blake asks Orac to clear Zen from external controls, Orac responds that his systems are engaged with other tasks; most likely, these involve controlling Zen himself. When the crew return to the *Liberator* on Spaceworld, Zen obeys their commands; he has not been wiped or reprogrammed by the System. It is also probably not insignificant that when Avon tells Blake how to foil the prophecy, he does so in earshot of Orac (whose abilities all the crew appear to underestimate, even at the end of the story), and that the events involving the System seem to follow on from this incident. Blake uses the word 'redemption' to refer to the

System seemingly taking back its own ship; there is also, however, another meaning to the word, that of to liberate from captivity or free from distressing circumstances. Avon's remark regarding the prediction, 'That's because you're looking for the wrong things... it's a common enough failing,' might well have been written about the story itself.

Why, however, would Orac act in this fashion? The answer lies in the central premise of the story. This appears to be a reworking of a familiar theme in European mythology (from Achilles through to Macbeth), of a hero whose doom is foretold if particular conditions are met and, although s/he attempts to avoid these conditions, sooner or later the prophecy comes true. Prediction, as Avon remarks, is not immutable, but is the most likely outcome based on the known facts; Orac therefore, as he admits after blowing up the *Liberator*'s sister ship, has been setting up the facts in order to fulfil his own prophecy; effectively making the System work for him. Where Zen is something of a parental or professorial figure, watching over the crew but allowing them to make mistakes as long as these are not fatal ones, Orac is Ensor writ large: a brilliant but crotchety and selfish old man who keeps pets.

"Redemption" is a story that effectively restates the series' themes and objectives. However, the differences between this and the first-season stories suggest that some of these themes and objectives have changed.

B2: SHADOW

UK TRANSMISSION: Tuesday, 16 January 1979: 7.20pm – 10pm
DURATION: 50:32
VIEWING FIGURE: 7.6m
CHART POSITION: 87
WRITER: Chris Boucher
DIRECTOR: Jonathan Wright Miller

CREDITED CAST: Derek Smith (Largo); Karl Howman (Bek); Adrienne Burgess (Hanna); Vernon Dobtcheff (Chairman); Archie Tew (Enforcer)

UNCREDITED CAST: Les White, Fred Haggerty (Stuntmen/ Guards); Archie Tew (Voice of Duty Officer); Graham Kennedy Smith (Peety)

SYNOPSIS: The *Liberator* goes to Space City, a neutral satellite run by a criminal organisation called the Terra Nostra; Blake hopes to enlist their help in his fight against the Federation. They are, however, taken prisoner by their contact, Largo, and have to be rescued. In the meantime, Orac (who is acting strangely) has teleported Vila down to Space City, in exchange for which Vila has hidden him. (Vila later returns after a session of apparent debauchery.) Blake goes back for two of their fellow-prisoners, one an addict of a drug called Shadow, which is the source of much of the Terra Nostra's power. An analysis of a sample of Shadow reveals that it is derived from a partially telepathic plant called a Moon Disc. Blake directs the *Liberator* to go to the planet Zondar, from which Moon Discs originate. Cally searches for Orac and is seemingly rendered catatonic by him. On Zondar, Blake, Jenna and Avon discover that the Moon Disc growing operation is guarded by members of the President's personal security force, and thus that there is a high-level connection between the Federation and the Terra Nostra. The Moon Discs assist Cally in fighting off an entity that has possessed Orac, and the Moon Disc garden is destroyed by the *Liberator*'s neutron blasters.

ANALYSIS: Chris Boucher's first story to be transmitted suggests a slightly different take on the series' themes and characters from that established in the first season. The developments here go on to form the core of the second season.

The episode underwent one or two significant changes from its initial outline. This had Cally being forced to take the Shadow drug; however, as she is an alien, she did not become addicted, but instead began to develop new powers, including precognition and telekinesis, which manifested themselves erratically. The plot with the entity taking over the ship was more vaguely defined, and did not specifically involve Cally. The drug's effects were also fully described, as follows: 'It stimulates the brain so that the latent desires of the subject are isolated, amplified and fed back as vivid sensory dreams. Shadow guarantees pleasure, however the subject subconsciously defines it.'

Leaving aside improvements in production values – with "Shadow" featuring sets with ceilings and splendid model shots, including a lovely dissolve from a model of the exterior of Space City, to its interior and then to the interior set – the most notable development in these opening episodes of the second season is with regard to Blake. The titular character has undergone a slow personality shift, which seems to originate in "Deliverance", in which he effectively took on Avon's role. Although he seems largely unchanged in "Orac", here and in "Redemption" we see a much harder, more self-interested Blake than before. He states that he has no concern with other worlds, just Earth (an assertion supported by the fact that in "Redemption", he was not interested in freeing the slaves on Spaceworld). This contrasts with his outlook in the previous season, when he took an interest in what happened to the Decimas and the population of Lindor. He is willing to do deals with known criminals to achieve his ends – excusing his behaviour by saying, 'That will make us winners.... That's the only excuse for fighting' – and uses Bek and Hanna quite openly, coming back for them not through sympathy, but because Hanna has a supply of Shadow. After working with the Terra Nostra is ruled out, Blake's next plan is to coerce the organisation into working with him by threatening its ability to distribute Shadow – again, he is willing to allow them to continue their criminal activities so long as they support him – and he abandons this idea only when the connection between the Terra Nostra and the Federation becomes apparent. In destroying the garden on Zondar, Blake causes the deaths of lots of innocent creatures – intelligent, helpful and telepathic – simply because a drug can be made from them, which seems like burning down fields of poppies merely because one can obtain opium from the seed pods. Although he says that he is sending the Federation and the Terra Nostra a message, the means are rather cruel. Jenna also gets in a dig at Blake, saying that she doesn't think he cares if Cally comes out of her coma or not.

Blake is not, however, without conscience. Avon (who, we have seen, appears to understand Blake better than any of the others do) suggests that his anger towards the crew has more to do with his worries about Cally. Blake also urges Bek to take up the fight against the Terra Nostra, saying that he will return in three years and see how he is getting on, and allows him to press the button that fires the neutron blasters. It is worth noting that Avon, who gets most of the best lines in this story, still follows Blake.

Gan's character continues to change. As interpreted by Boucher, he doesn't mention the limiter (which the writer considered a plot constraint); he also seems to have become the ship's 'conscience', objecting to deals with the Terra Nostra and empathising with Cally. However, there has not been a radical break with the Gan of the previous season; he is also interested in the fact that telepathy means the Auronar never have to be alone. The most obvious rationalisation is that Gan is changing for the better; the limiter is actually doing its work and steering him away from murderous acts. Earlier, we saw a Gan who kills men and attacks women; eventually, though, the headaches that he was getting as a result of the latter activity must have caused him to stop trying to find ways around the limiter.

Orac, finally, has discovered that there are reasons for tolerating the *Liberator* crew other than simple amusement. In this story, Orac has encountered something more powerful than himself, and capable of taking him over. He has also discovered, over the course of his possession experience, that he needs help from others; as well as Vila being required to hide him, it is Cally who saves him in the end. On Aristo, he had control of a small flying device, and probably other external units as well; here he has nothing of that kind. It is for this reason that Orac, with his almost limitless power, permits Avon to place within him an explosive charge that will destroy him if there is any attempt to tamper with his communication channels; he has recognised that he needs limits, and people to watch out for him. The crew are thus not so much pets to him now as they are a necessity.

Other characters also develop, but not as radically. Avon kills someone on-screen for the first time, but otherwise seems very much unchanged; we may note that, although it is Bek who taunts him in the cell, he directs his intimidation tactics towards Bek's sister, Hanna, instead, in another display of aggression towards women. Zen intervenes directly in crew affairs, but only because there is a threat to the safety of the ship from the possessed Orac, which is beyond their abilities to cope with. Finally, although this is very much a Cally-focused episode (the actress having complained about her lack of representation in other stories), there is little development for her; although her telepathy gets a thorough airing, it is still left unclear whether she is an alien or not. (Although Vila describes her as an alien, Avon says that she is more human than he is, and Orac refers to her as a 'human'.) The only new revelation is that she is capable of telekinesis when she has help, an idea that will later reappear in "Sarcophagus".

This episode also pits Blake against the Terra Nostra. This name has multilayered connotations; most obviously it references the Cosa Nostra, or the Mafia, but it also means 'Our Earth' in Italian. This flags up the fact that in this case, the ruling powers control both legal and illegal aspects of society; the Terra Nostra is simply the flip side – the shadow, as it were – of the Federation, and is supported, albeit clandestinely, at the very highest levels of society. Boucher has said of this story: 'It seems to me that major crime syndicates like the Mafia have to be part of the establishment, because it isn't possible to run an organization like the Mafia without being very, very close, and indeed part of, the power structure.' Once Largo – who appeared to have been set up as the story's main villain – dies midway through the episode (and not through the intervention of any of the regulars), the Terra Nostra fade into the background. This conveys a sense that there are other stories out there than that which directly concerns the viewer, and that the Terra Nostra is much bigger than Blake and his crew. Finally, Blake's attempt to approach the Terra Nostra for help demonstrates powerfully how, if one involves oneself with criminal elements, one winds up behaving exactly like they do: as Gan notes, either you become a pusher in helping them supply the drug, or you renege on your deal, in which case you become a cheat. Much as Bek states that he would like to see the Terra Nostra grovel – just as Largo caused him to do, making him in some ways no better than Largo – we see here how the system contaminates even those of firm moral convictions.

We also learn more about crime and punishment in the Federation. We discover in this story that Jenna was on the *London* not because of the nature of her crimes, but because she had refused to transport drugs for the Terra Nostra, and it is implied that Largo set her up for a hard fall. Elsewhere, Vila refers to juvenile detention wards; there are thus other forms of punishment on Earth than transportation. It seems that, unlike the 18th-century deportation of criminals to Australia on which the idea is based, you have to be a genuinely hard case to get sent to Cygnus Alpha: as well as a woman who was set up by the underworld to receive a particularly severe sentence, the transportees that we encounter here include a convicted child molester, a serial killer, and a kleptomaniac who has had his head adjusted by the best in the business only to learn that it won't stay adjusted (and who has apparently been in and out of other sorts of penal institutions from an early age). What this suggests about Avon is rather disturbing; either his was a particularly high-profile case (and thus, like Jenna, he was being made an example of), or there is an element of Avon's character that has not yet come fully into focus.

"Shadow" gives us more details about the Federation and the way in which it operates than we have previously had, and also about the effect that their lifestyle is having upon the series' protagonists.

B3: WEAPON

UK TRANSMISSION: Tuesday 23 January 1979: 7.20pm – 8.10pm
DURATION: 51:41
VIEWING FIGURE: 6.4m
CHART POSITION: 108
WRITER: Chris Boucher
DIRECTOR: George Spenton-Foster

CREDITED CAST: Kathleen Byron (Fen); John Bennett (Coser); Scott Fredericks (Carnell); Candace Glendenning (Rashel); Graham Simpson (Officer)

UNCREDITED CAST: Harry Fielder, Reg Turner, Bob Smythe (Guards)

SYNOPSIS: The *Liberator* is *en route* to the Federation Weapons Development Base when the crew learn that the installation is on maximum alert. This is due to the theft of a device called IMIPAK by a Beta-grade weapons technician, Coser, who has fled to a deserted planet with a bond-slave named Rashel. Meanwhile, Servalan has had two clones made of Blake by a non-Federation group called the Clonemasters; the first is killed by Travis, the second she takes with her to the planet where Coser is hiding, following the instructions of Carnell, a psychostrategist (a profession whose members specialise in predicting human behaviour). As Carnell foresaw, Coser hands the weapon over to the clone Blake, believing him to be the original. IMIPAK's action is twofold; its victims are 'marked' for death by a projector, but do not die until the second half of the weapon, the key, is activated. Blake, Avon and Gan teleport down to the planet, and are marked by Travis with the projector; when they find Servalan, she reveals this and seemingly allows them to leave (so that the Federation will believe that they, not Servalan, have IMIPAK), intending to use the key on them shortly thereafter. However, Rashel (whose presence was unknown to Carnell) and the clone Blake get IMIPAK back from Servalan and Travis, mark them with it, and then order them to leave the planet, which they are now free to explore on their own.

ANALYSIS: "Weapon" (originally entitled "The Armourer"), the first script Boucher wrote for the series, is an exploration of the nature of freedom, control and the relative power of society versus individuals. These themes, however, are expressed not so much through the actions of the main characters, as through those of the villains and guest cast.

The story, which is hampered by a slightly hasty production (Spenton-Foster having made the unusual decision, when faced with industrial action at the BBC, to rush the production rather than ask for a deadline extension), is also the episode in which Brian Croucher makes his debut as Travis. As well as the change of actor, Travis appears to have undergone a change of personality. It is very easy to attribute this character shift to Croucher's different take on Travis, and indeed some of it does come from the difference in acting styles between the two performers. However, much of the unaccustomed violence, insolence and near-lunacy of this new Travis was actually scripted. Indeed, the story was written before Greif took his decision to leave the series. The script refers to Travis having visited a 'retraining therapist,' a euphemism suggesting a forced mental reprogrammming to re-mould Travis's personality into a form better suited to his superiors' needs. This retraining process – an echo of the social conditioning used to mould the young Travis into a Federation soldier – appears to have failed; he has gone from a disciplined, if somewhat obsessive, officer, to someone who cannot stop himself from killing the duplicate Blake, even though he knows it to be a clone. Had Greif been still in the role (or had Croucher been established in the role from the outset), it would have been even more apparent to the audience that there had been a sea-change from a disciplined officer to an insolent psychopath as a result of the retraining.

The IMIPAK storyline also echoes these themes of power, control and hierarchy. The designer of IMIPAK (which stands for Induced Molecular Instability Projector and Key) is a man with a grudge against the hierarchical nature of the Federation; as a Beta-grade technician, Coser is assumed not to be intelligent enough to create a weapon of IMIPAK's quality. Anticipating that he will have the credit for his achievement stolen, he takes the weapon, kills everyone else at his workplace, and escapes in the company of a member of the lowest grade of all. Although we never get a complete picture of how the 'grading' system works, the implication is that it is an examination-based meritocracy. Such a process has been known to fail individuals, even groups; although Coser may know that he is smarter than his grade classification suggests, nobody will believe him, as it begs the question why, if he was so bright, he didn't do better on his exams. Even Coser does not entirely believe it himself; his choice of companion is so far down the social hierarchy that there is no possibility of her outranking him, and his last desperate statement to Servalan as she prepares to kill him – 'I didn't mean it' – suggests that, although Coser resents the power structure of the Federation, he is unable to prevent himself from thinking in the same terms. Elsewhere, he reveals that he does not like Rashel calling him 'sir', partly because he himself had to show similar deference to others. At the same time, however, Coser also resents it when Rashel shows any sign of independence, at one point threatening to kill her if she disobeys him again. In the same scene, when she mentions that a disobedient bond-slave could be 'modified,' he does not even acknowledge that she has rights over her own body. This also highlights Coser's hypocrisy: for all he goes on about the injustices he has faced, her plight is far worse than his.

Rashel, for her part, gives us virtually the sole glimmering of hope that there is a way out of this system. Initially, she goes with Coser, not out of love nor out of a sense of rebelliousness, but apparently simply because he, a higher grade, has ordered her to do so. Later, she suggests that the original inhabitants of the installation deserted it 'because they were free.' At this point she has a partial understanding of the nature of freedom; she sees it here as the ability to do what one wants, without fear of reprisal. At the story's climax, she commits the ultimate act of disobedience in 'marking' Servalan and Travis and thus enslaving her masters. The end of the story sees her with a more mature concept of freedom; she is confined to the planet and agrees to share it with the clone Blake, but she is free to do as she likes with it, and their relationship is one of mutual respect, even of love, rather than of power and reprisal.

Carnell also reflects the themes of power and hierarchy, but in a different way. In "Weapon", Carnell appears to take on an almost authorial role; he is the instigator of Blake's, Travis's and Servalan's actions. By suggesting to Servalan a scenario in which Travis would unwittingly kill himself along with Blake, Avon and Gan, Carnell has solved her predicament of being politically incapable of dismissing Travis and yet finding him too dangerous to use. Carnell is visibly willing to employ every psychological weapon at his disposal to achieve his ends; when Servalan flirts with him in the same way that she did with Travis earlier in the episode, Carnell, unlike Travis, flirts back. Later, he also briefly gives a suggestive look (an action that Scott Fredericks deliberately placed in the scene) to an officer who delivers a report, implying that for him, flirtation and sex are ways of getting what he wants from people. We also learn that a psychostrategist takes every human and environmental factor involved in a particular case into consideration, and that Carnell was supplied with data, biographical and otherwise, on everyone and everything involved. Carnell is able to predict with reasonable certainty the time at which Coser will leave the weapons installation, the fact that he will fake his own death in doing so, and the point at which he will have descended sufficiently into madness for the arrival of the clone Blake to seem unremarkable to him. (Note that, once again, it seems that the Federation's middle grades are the social segment most affected by Blake's activities.) In fact, Carnell's strategy is foiled only by virtue of the fact that Rashel's presence has not been reported to him, therefore introducing a random element; not only does she take charge at the end, but, as she is the only factor unaccounted for in the scenario, she seems to have been the cause of Coser's acting earlier than predicted. However, while it is understandable that the Federation officials should overlook her presence – given that they would neither consider her worth gathering data on nor think that Coser, a Beta-grade, would have anything to do with her – one can only puzzle over why, if Carnell is so omniscient, he not only neglects to take her presence into account, but also fails to realise that his informants would not consider her important.

For all his abilities and apparent superiority, it seems, Carnell is as much a product of the system as any of the other Federation (and ex-Federation) characters. Unlike the Clonemasters (whose actions are instrumental in the foiling of Carnell's plan), Carnell comes to Servalan's office, not vice-versa; he speaks of the value (or lack of value) of careers, money and respect; he plays chess. Carnell, for all his sense of superiority, can no more totally divorce himself from the ingrained attitudes of the Federation than Coser can. This also explains the other problematic aspect of "Weapon" – the fact that Carnell is willing to let someone as dangerous as Servalan have possession of something as powerful as IMIPAK. One would think that he would at least recognise the potential risk to himself, if not to others. If he had intended Servalan's actions to fail – specifically, if he had deliberately overlooked Rashel's presence – that would be one thing, but the fact that he speaks the line 'and my second mistake was not asking for my fee in advance' after the officer with the report has left the room suggests that the fact of her presence genuinely did not occur to him. Carnell may be able to manipulate the actions of others, but he fails to acknowledge the potential consequences of his own actions.

By concentrating on characters other than the regulars, then, "Weapon" not only broadens our understanding of the society in which they live, but develops insights into what it is to be part of, or to reject, the system.

B4: HORIZON

UK TRANSMISSION: Tuesday 30 January 1979: 7.20pm – 8.10pm
DURATION: 50:28
VIEWING FIGURE: 6.3m
CHART POSITION: 93
WRITER: Allan Prior
DIRECTOR: Jonathan Wright Miller

CREDITED CAST: William Squire (Kommissar); Darien Angadi (Ro); Souad Faress (Selma); Brian Miller (Assistant Kommissar); Paul Haley (Chief Guard)

UNCREDITED CAST: Kelly Varney, Martin Clarke, Jennifer Ellen, Valerie Hastings (Slaves); Al Wade, David Charles, Paul Bassett, Ceri Morgan, Adrian Varcoe, Paul Strike, Jay Eden Winn, Samura Khan, Mike Kenwright, Paul Menzies, David Pople, Brian Chaplin, Les Hill, John Curry (Slaves/Guards)

SYNOPSIS: The *Liberator* crew, suffering from stress, have retreated to the outer edge of the galaxy's spiral rim. They see a Federation space freighter heading towards a planet protected by a magnetic barrier, and decide to investigate. Blake and Jenna teleport down and are taken prisoner; they learn that this planet, codenamed 'Horizon,' is a Federation colony world. The bulk of the native population have been enslaved, and the ruler, Ro, is a Federation puppet. Blake and Jenna are interrogated and put to work in the mines, as are Vila, Gan and Cally when they teleport down to investigate. However, their words – particularly their report that his father had been murdered by the Federation – have caused Ro to doubt his Federation training. Avon, alone on the ship, considers leaving, but delays to the point where escape is impossible; he teleports down and rescues the others. The Federation Kommissar has Ro's fiancée Selma tortured for information about the crew; this proves the final straw for Ro, who puts on his tribal robes, casts out the Federation and restores native rule.

ANALYSIS: "Horizon" was written by Allan Prior, an award-winning novelist with an extensive track record in television scriptwriting. It was originally planned as the eighth episode of the season, and was put back to fourth when another, "Death Squad", fell through. Although the script has some very good lines, parts of it are artificial and contrived, possibly due to the fact that the rewrite had to be done hastily in order for it to be completed by its new, earlier, recording date.

One of the changes made was the incorporation of Gan, who would already have been dead had this remained the eighth episode.; As a consequence of his late addition, however, he is in this story only fairly perfunctorily; although he draws his gun and lunges, snarling, at some guards in one scene, he is otherwise very much a fifth wheel. The Federation's stated interest in acquiring Monopasium 239 for use in ships intended for intergalactic travel would have also been more significant had the episode remained eighth in transmission order, as an invasion by aliens from another galaxy would have occurred a mere four episodes afterwards; as it is, it is largely a throwaway line.

The script, furthermore, shows signs that it would have benefited from going through another draft. At the beginning, there are three separate reasons given for the crew to go down to Horizon: Blake's curiosity, the fact that Cally thinks the crew need a rest, and Blake's belief (never evidenced before, or afterwards) that they need a base. As the first reason alone would have sufficed, the general impression is that the writer was trying out several possible ideas and not really satisfied with any of them. Vila reacts to adrenaline and soma (the latter being the drug of choice in Aldous Huxley's novel *Brave New World*) like he's never had them before, but a few minutes later, a conversation between Blake and Cally suggests that the crew have been dosing themselves with this combination of drugs regularly. The idea of the crew all going down to the planet one or two at a time is fairly contrived; in particular, Cally (who has apparently undergone a metamorphosis from a guerrilla fighter into Florence Nightingale) appears to have lost her mind, insisting on going down to Horizon, even though she knows that Blake is most likely in trouble, simply in order to give him a sheet of prison records, which would seem fairly useless under most circumstances.

The script is not, however, entirely without good points. The scene in which Cally plays the mystic under interrogation is excellent; although she pretends to be reading the Kommissar's mind, we know that she is incapable of doing this to non-telepaths at this point, and so is simply feeding back the information she obtained from the prison and execution records. She conducts a psychological game similar to the Kommissar's, only in reverse; whereas he claims that mysticism 'belongs to [Ro's] tribal past,' she plays on Ro's beliefs, sending to him telepathically in order to reinforce her message. Once again, the regular characters acquire some new backstory, in this case, the fact of having met one of Ro's friends on board the *London*. Federation Central Control, mentioned in the previous episode, also crops up here. Avon and Blake are well-characterised; Blake is concerned about his crew, and shows an interest in non-Earth people's oppression, indicating that the old Blake is still present to some degree. Avon's primary interest is still in Blake; although he suggests to Cally that they run off together, there is no sense of a sexual connection between them, and it is similar to the offer that he made to Jenna in the first season. When talking about not needing the rest of the crew, he refers to them as 'Blake and the others.' Avon is still thinking about running away, but then electing to stay behind in the crisis.

Ro and the Kommissar are also well-written and well-portrayed. Darien Angadi has a frail, 'translucent' quality that adds to the vulnerability of Ro's character, and stands in sharp contrast to the burly William Squire. The Kommissar manipulates Ro, making it look as if Ro has a choice when in fact he is slanting the decision in favour of the Federation's interests. He urges Ro to act like a ruler rather than a savage when Ro starts extolling the virtues of the pre-Federation culture, and praises him whenever he makes the right decision – i.e. the decision that the Kommissar wants. He allows Ro to bring Selma back from the mines, but remarks paternally that he will regret the choice. The fact that Ro's father is dead means that the Kommissar, his former teacher, can assume a kind of father-figure status (although the relationship is purely instrumental from the Kommissar's point of view). In the scene in which the Kommissar describes resistance as a genetic aberration, he is plainly lying; within the Federation that we have seen up until now, it has been acknowledged as a psychological 'condition,' and Blake and his followers all have different reasons for engaging in terrorist activity. The lie, however, makes the *Liberator* crew seem that much more freakish to Ro, and therefore much more deserving of execution, as it then becomes simply the elimination of deviants for the good of society. (The Kommissar's continual references to 'training,' furthermore, recall the Soviet and Chinese euphemism 're-education'.) What the Kommissar says in front of Ro and what he actually thinks are two different things. Equally noteworthy is the fact that the Federation have not simply imposed an artificial hierarchy on the planet. Ro refers to the enslaved population as consisting mostly of 'primitives,' and Selma, even in the mines, says: 'I'm not one of *these* people.' The 'primitives' hang back to allow her to eat, and it takes Blake to introduce democracy into the system. Horizon, prior to contact, was thus a class society.

The situation on Horizon is, in fact, very much an allegory of the British Empire: not just in Uganda (which may have been the original inspiration for the story – a planning document suggests that it concerns Blake getting captured in a "Ugandan-like society') but also in India, South-East Asia and elsewhere. The Empire's agents would tend to infiltrate local infrastructures rather than impose new ones; and by encouraging the ruling group to send their children to British schools (much as, in this story, Ro is a product of the Federation's Central Education Facility), they would – or so they thought – ensure that the next generation were loyal to British values. The fact that the Kommissar and Assistant Kommissar are visibly feathering their own nests also recalls the behaviour of East India Company officials, whose involvement in the British colonial endeavour was largely for personal gain. The idea of the natives being worked to death in the mines recalls the Spanish treatment of North and South American Indians in the sixteenth and seventeenth centuries. The production of the episode also refers to these antecedents. Ro and Selma are played by Asian actors; Horizon's architecture and native costumes are decidedly Aztec-inspired, with the 'primitives' wearing dreadlocks; and the Federation officials and Ro each wear a Nehru jacket – an item of clothing that was also adopted by the East India Company officials. It is rather unfortunate that none of this attention to design spilled over to the costuming of the regulars, who look universally ridiculous. (Cally's outfit is particularly risible, and Sally Knyvette appears to have a grimy handmark in the middle of her cleavage in the scenes set in the mines.) The ending of the story redeems a number of its problems. The indication that the population, bereft of Federation aid, will now revert to a low level of technology highlights the fact that technological and educational superiority may not be everyone's idea of social advancement. The final scene, in which Ro says that his people will continue to refer to the planet by its Federation codename, is an echo of the compromises and acknowledgements of past oppression that come out of post-colonial situations. The ending also has an air of ambiguity, as the length of Horizon's current state of independence is likely to depend on how badly the Federation want Monopasium 239.

B5: PRESSURE POINT

UK TRANSMISSION: Tuesday 6 February 1979: 8.10pm – 9.00pm
DURATION: 49:25
VIEWING FIGURE: 6.6m
CHART POSITION: 100
WRITER: Terry Nation
DIRECTOR: George Spenton-Foster

CREDITED CAST: Jane Sherwin (Kasabi); Yolande Palfrey (Veron); Alan Halley (Arle); Martin Connor (Berg); Sue Bishop (Mutoid)

UNCREDITED CAST: Sally Sinclair, Maggie Pilleau (Mutoids); Ridgewell Hawkes, James Muir, Mark Holmes, Patsy Peters, Barbara Hampshire, Barry Summerford (Kasabi's Rebels)

SYNOPSIS: Blake's crew have returned to Earth Sector, where Blake plans to stage a raid on Federation Central Control. He has contacted a woman named Kasabi, the leader of a local resistance group, for assistance in keeping the security forces at bay. Servalan, however, attacks Kasabi's group and takes Kasabi and her daughter Veron prisoner. Kasabi dies under interrogation but not before revealing the coordinates and recognition signal that she was to have used with Blake, allowing Servalan and Travis to send a fake signal. Once down, Blake and Gan encounter Veron in the crypt of a ruined church; she tells them that the group was attacked and she is the sole survivor. Blake decides to go ahead with the plan, and sends Avon and Vila to assess the defence zone around the location of Control before meeting them back in the crypt. As they plan the raid, Veron uses sona gas to knock them out, then steals their teleport bracelets and bars the crypt door. It transpires that Servalan has persuaded her to set Blake and his crew up, offering her mother's life in exchange; after completing her half of the bargain, however, Veron learns that her mother is dead. Gan batters down the crypt door and the crew negotiate the defence zone and other security features of the installation, only to discover that Control is an empty room, a diversion, and that the real communications centre is elsewhere. Jenna teleports down, rescues Veron, takes Servalan prisoner, and supplies the crew with bracelets; the crew escape, but Gan is killed when Travis hurls a strontium grenade, trapping himself and Servalan in the process.

ANALYSIS: "Pressure Point", originally to have been called "Storm Mountain", is a crucial story, involving as it does the death of Gan and the raid on Control. From the start, it was intended to be the big mid-season climax; however, as it turns out, it is the first episode in the series to suffer from major plot problems. As Nation was generally very good at plotting it seems odd that the transmitted story should fall down so badly.

The story was commissioned from Nation in April 1977, and the absence of Orac from the "Storm Mountain" draft suggests that it was written before the decision was made to include him as a regular character. "Storm Mountain" was originally to have been the sixth episode of the second season, but was moved back to fifth when "Death Squad" was dropped at a late stage and "Killer" was moved to eighth (meaning that David Jackson would now be required to appear in only five episodes).

The story is not without redeeming features. The characterisation of the *Liberator* crew is excellent. Blake presenting his followers with a *fait accompli* is something that we have seen several times before; but the crew do voice their objections and state conditions, indicating that this is still a democratic group. The fact that Blake then starts usurping the democratic process by giving the others limited information once he gets to the rendezvous is also a logical progression with regard to the more obsessive character that Blake (who later runs into the computer room shouting 'I've done it!') has taken on. Blake has discussed his plans only with Cally (who is a fanatic), and even then has not told her everything. Even more significantly, in this episode an agreement is reached between Blake and Avon about the future. Avon is not surprised by Blake's plan; having thought through its intended results, he demands the *Liberator* in exchange for his co-operation. Blake, for his part, is equally unsurprised by Avon's request, and agrees to it. The consequences of this agreement will be felt in future episodes over the next couple of years.

The story's villains are well portrayed. Travis objects to killing Kasabi (originally to have been a male character named Kasabian) because she was once part of the Service, even if she has now left it. Travis orders that Kasabi be tied up but has the mutoids do it, and ultimately it is Servalan who kills her. We also learn that, as a cadet, Servalan was a spoilt, idle, vicious bitch with connections, who was willing to inform on her own teacher; Kasabi's last words to Servalan are, 'I'm sorry… I should have tried, in the beginning… to *help* you,' implying that she believes Servalan to have a personality disorder.

The realisation of the story, however, is more of a problem. One corridor is rather too obviously used to represent several corridors through being lit differently in different shots. Vila appears to wear a dissected traffic cone; Servalan sports, at various points, a white boater and a dress with a large silver lizard apparently affixed to her nipples; and Jenna takes her handbag along with her on terrorist raids. There is some poor direction (the scene in which Kasabi's people fail to notice Servalan standing in plain view and are then gunned down without resistance doesn't say much for the revolution), and Veron is played a little too young. However, the main flaws of the episode lie not with the production values, but with the plot.

Approximately half an hour into the episode, it begins to fall apart. Veron is revealed to be a spy and, after gassing the *Liberator* crew into unconsciousness, steals their teleport bracelets but – bizarrely – not their guns. The narrative reason for this is so that they can later shoot a path through the sensor mesh that surrounds Control, but it severely damages the sequence's credibility and makes a mockery of the fact that they then use Gan to break down the crypt door rather than simply blasting it open. Later, after Blake, Avon, Vila and Gan have entered the control complex, we see that Servalan is forced to contact the High Council to have the defence mechanisms switched off so that Travis can follow. However, if Control is a trap in itself, then surely there must be another hidden entrance to the complex (possibly leading from the thatched cottage seen nearby) so that the trap can be fully sprung? In fact, if this is the case, why does Travis bother with the whole Veron routine at all? Next we have the appearance of Jenna out of nowhere, accompanied by a repentant Veron and with Servalan as hostage. None of them appears to be sweating or even out of breath, and yet for them to have arrived at that precise moment would have required all three of them to have run from the cottage to the door of the empty room at full tilt. Lastly, at the end of the story, Blake agrees to leave Veron to continue the fight against the Federation hundreds of feet below ground and surrounded by the defence zone (which no-one tells Blake has been switched off). It is ironic that, in a story concerning diversion and visual trickery, the authors seem to be disguising the failings of the plot by using bangs, flashes, and running down corridors.

Perhaps the biggest problem with the story, however, concerns Gan. It is usual, in similar series such as *Doctor Who* and *Star Trek,* for a main character's swansong episode to focus heavily on that character; where this doesn't happen, it is generally because their departure has had to be written in hastily. However, although it had been decided at a very early stage that Gan would be killed off in this episode, and although David Jackson ultimately gives a very good, poignant death scene performance (enhanced as the presence of the church echoing the religious themes of earlier Gan sequences), Gan gets virtually nothing else to do in "Pressure Point".

The idea of killing off Gan seems to have been in Nation's mind for quite some time. Nation described Gan in interviews as resembling Lenny from Steinbeck's novel *Of Mice and Men*; a gentle but retarded giant who kills a young woman when he suddenly loses control of his impulses, and is then killed by his best friend on the grounds that he is a danger. We see a suggestion of this in the Gan episodes of the first season. The early Gan would have lent himself nicely to a scenario in which he remains in the deconsecrated crypt with Veron, his limiter fails and he loses control and kills her, and is then himself killed by Blake. Hints of the Gan-as-Lenny scenario – a potentially dangerous strong man, a vulnerable young woman, a dramatic death followed by remorse – appear to have made it into the final version. One way or another, however, its full incorporation was abandoned in the light of the new portrayal of the character, or in response to other pressures.

Sources relating to the series give at least two other scenarios that were mooted for the killing of a regular in "Pressure Point", before the final version was decided upon. One, mentioned in interviews with members of the production team, was the idea of killing off Vila, instead of Gan; this was vetoed by Boucher and Maloney on the grounds that Vila was a more popular character (see the Introduction to Season B). Another, mentioned in Marvel's *Blake's 7 Winter Special,* did involve the death of Gan, but at the hands of a traitor, who would then join Blake's crew as a secret Federation spy; this was also scotched, as it was felt that five human characters plus Zen and Orac were quite enough to write for. Boucher remembers that once during a script read-through: 'David Jackson passed me this little note with a four on it, and I said, "Four?" and he said, "That's the number of lines I have in this episode".' The decision not to use either of the two possible scenarios – the Steinbeck-influenced scenario or the Federation traitor scenario – in which Gan could have been killed off in a fitting and appropriate manner left the writers with a large narrative gap to fill. This they attempted to do with the exposure of Veron as a spy, the addition of action-filled set-pieces, and the removal of a secret-entrance subplot, resulting in Travis being forced to engage in a lengthy pursuit of his adversaries down the corridors. Jenna's appearance at the end of the story may have been left over from the earlier storyline, in which it was envisaged that one of the crew would discover the secret entrance and arrive to save the day. (It is also likely that this was originally to have involved one of the expedition party, probably Avon, and that Jenna was a late substitution in response to the actress's complaints about lack of screen time.) If Veron had been killed by Gan, furthermore, or if the 'traitor character' had joined the crew, the story would not have been stuck with the untidy ending in which Veron is left underground. This rewriting of earlier scenarios resulted in a story that is inconsistent and full of loose ends, rather than a poignant and fitting swansong for a regular character.

Although Gan's death as it stands in "Pressure Point" is fairly incompatible with his earlier character, it is not totally inappropriate. "Pressure Point" is preceded by two stories that feature Gan as very much a reformed character, acting as the ship's 'conscience'; according to Boucher, the final version of Gan's death was based on a popular song called *Big John*, about a strong man who saves his friends in a mining disaster by holding up the roof. What we now have, therefore, is a situation in which a former murderer is killed heroically saving his friends at virtually the moment he reforms – saying 'I'm not worth dying for' – and thus the earlier subtext melts away, leaving the viewer with the memory of a heroic sacrifice.

The repeated changes in the way in which Gan's death was planned to be presented mean that what could have been a thrilling mid-season climax – with the discovery of the empty room and the killing of a regular character – comes across as inconsistent, full of plot holes, and weaker than it should have been.

B6: TRIAL

UK TRANSMISSION: Tuesday 13 February 1979: 7.15pm – 8.10pm
DURATION: 51:20
VIEWING FIGURE: 7.5m
CHART POSITION: 82
WRITER: Chris Boucher
DIRECTOR: Derek Martinus

CREDITED CAST: John Savident (Samor); John Bryans (Bercol); Peter Miles (Rontane); Victoria Fairbrother (Thania); Claire Lewis (Zil); Kevin Lloyd (Par); Graham Sinclair (Lye); Colin Dunn (Guard Commander)

UNCREDITED CAST: Peter Tuddenham (Tannoy Voices); Harry Fielder, Derek Southern (Guards); Brian Moorehead, Michael Finbarr (Officers)

SYNOPSIS: Consumed with guilt over the events of "Pressure Point", Blake retreats to a jungle planet to think things over, but keeps his actual location a secret from the rest of the *Liberator's* crew. In a message, he explains to them that he has left a homing beacon that will activate in thirteen hours; should he decide not to return, or the crew decide that they are better off without him, either can choose to ignore the signal. Encountering one of the natives, Zil, Blake learns that the planet itself is a living entity that consumes the creatures on its surface at intervals; to survive, the natives live as solitary individuals. Travis, meanwhile, stands trial for having ordered a massacre on the planet Zircaster; as the evidence is firm and the penalty is execution, this will prevent him from presenting evidence at an inquiry into Servalan's handling of the Blake affair. The crew rescue Blake just prior to his being consumed by the planet. They decide, in order to restore their legend, to strike at Space Command Headquarters, which they do just as Travis is sentenced. Travis escapes in the confusion and forces Servalan to give him a ship, going off to pursue his vendetta against Blake as an outlaw.

ANALYSIS: "Trial", unusually for *Blake's 7*, shows very few changes from the original draft of the story to the final version; the plotting problems with the previous episode clearly had no knock-on impact on the overarching plot development of the series. The story is a clever one, with two strong plots running simultaneously and intersecting briefly at the end, both exploring the relationship of individual to society. This results in one of the strongest episodes in the series' history, in terms of scripting, performances and the themes that it explores.

The scenes regarding Blake's crisis of confidence, for instance, focus on the issue of responsibility. Blake leaves his crew because he feels that he has not met his responsibility toward them, but then he realises that he has to go back to be truly responsible; as his conversation with Avon at the beginning of the story (in which Avon seemingly takes the role of prosecutor, voicing Blake's own doubts as well as the crew's) demonstrates, the crew have a responsibility to follow, but he has a responsibility not to get them killed. The scenes on the planet, furthermore, demonstrate how fine the line is between individual and society. Zil is an individual: she does not merely live, but has a 'waking,' or consciousness. However, the 'host' into which Zil fears absorption is itself an individual, and she notes that although she herself may 'lose oneness' to the host, her society will continue in the form of the eggs. Zil also protects a child (in that this is how she perceives her actions *vis-à-vis* Blake) but urges the child to be alone, exploring the questions of individual versus collective responsibility.

The catalyst for all this is the death of Gan. Significantly, in order to overcome his guilt over the demise of a man who was obsessed with not being alone and needed to be in a group to survive, Blake teleports down to a planet where the inhabitants are obsessed with being alone, and need to be physically alone to survive, lest their host should become aware of their presence in large numbers. Blake's reaction to the death of Gan is much more extreme than his response to Cally's apparent death in "Seek-Locate-Destroy"; however, Gan's death serves a different narrative function, as it is intended to reinforce the fallibility and mortality of the crew for the viewer rather than to set up a dramatic scenario in which the crew falsely believe one of their number to have been killed. Vila's remarks about Gan being a simple, direct soul, incidentally, are not part of Nation's later rethinking of the character; Vila saw Gan as such from the start.

At the end of the story, Blake reaches his own balance with regard to the question of individual versus society: he, who has fled the Federation and says that he is 'not ready to surrender anything,' is reabsorbed into the society of the *Liberator*. Travis, however, who has been absorbed into the society of the Federation's military, rejects it to go off and be alone, highlighting the similarities and differences between the characters.

The courtroom scenes with Travis are, if anything, even more powerful than those with Blake on the jungle planet. Brian Croucher gives his best performance yet in the role; although it was written before Croucher was cast, this is a story that plays very much to Croucher's strengths as an actor rather than Greif's, and he gives a chillingly brilliant portrayal of a man on the edge. Unlike Greif, Croucher saw Travis as having started in the ranks and worked for his commission, making the Service's betrayal of him that much harder. The other performances in this sequence are also excellent: Servalan has an edge of flirtation in her voice when she talks with Thania (Travis's defence counsel) about Travis, but not at any other point in their conversations, suggesting that she is once again engaging in her flirtation with the defeated man, this time by proxy. The scene in which Trooper Par brings Travis a drink in his cell is a little more tricky to unravel: Thania gives Par the drink to give to Travis in the hope that it will loosen his tongue and she will find out why he seems not to be paying attention to the court proceedings. Par's motivations in going along with this are precisely as stated: Travis was a good officer, now he's going to die, and he deserves a drink at least. Travis, however, is cleverer than this – and not the psychotic that Rontane believes him to be – making Par drink first to ensure that it is not poisoned. When Thania comes in, he confronts her with the fact that he has worked out her game, and tells her nothing.

The Travis storyline is well-scripted, providing strong parallels between Travis here and Blake in "The Way Back", both undergoing a trial rigged by a system that wants them eliminated, and both fighting back in their own way. Rontane and Bercol return, reinforcing the links to the first season as well as providing a Greek chorus. There are a number of good lines: Thania's reference to Samor's 'highly polished flagship' is an oblique and faintly vulgar insult. The point at which the massacre occurs is also significant. The Zircaster incident for which Travis is being tried took place three years earlier; Blake's trial in "The Way Back" is stated in "Voice from the Past" to have taken place two years previously, and Blake's original trial took place four years prior to "The Way Back". When we first encounter Travis in "Seek-Locate-Destroy", he has been suspended from duty pending an inquiry into a massacre on the planet Auros, which appears to have been a recent event, as an inquiry has not yet happened and Rai speaks of it as if it is of present concern. As Servalan seems unaware of the facts of Blake's original trial, it is clear that it happened under an earlier regime, and she has presumably been in office for around two to three years. The implication is thus that, in having Travis tried for the Zircaster rather than the Auros incident, she is setting Travis up for an event that did not occur on her watch, further maintaining her political credibility.

As with the Blake plot, there is a strong theme of individual *vis-à-vis* society. For an individual to be responsible to society, society has to be responsible to the individual; as Par, Travis's former soldier, notes, the service looks after its own. But here the society is betraying the individual. Travis's defence (in a sequence in which he usurps Thania's place in court, taking both her and Servalan by surprise) is not, as it might seem on a superficial reading, a Nuremberg-style complaint that he was only following orders: he states outright that it was he who *gave* the orders (as Par says, when Thania asks if he believes Travis to be guilty, 'No doubt about it, Major, we just did the shooting'). What Travis is saying is that those orders were a result of his training; therefore the military, not he himself, is responsible for the deaths. This disturbs the arbiters, as he implies that he is not a lone psychopath, but that the military produces such individuals; Par's lack of hypocrisy is evidenced in that he recognises this fact and accepts it as a natural outgrowth of the culture of the Federation's military forces. Chris Boucher has said that the message of Travis's defence is that we get the armed forces we deserve; if they are brutal, it is a reflection on the society that produced them. Travis as an individual is being held up for a collective crime. At the end, significantly, he cannot kill Servalan, as she is the Supreme Commander; he is still part of the collective, even after it rejects him.

This, then, brings us back to the *Liberator* crew to pose the question: whether or not Blake is really solely responsible for the tragedy at Central Control. The entire crew agreed to go along with Blake's plan; even when Blake started withholding information, they could easily have refused to continue until they had got full disclosure. So in a sense, here, society is as responsible for the tragedy as the individual who caused it.

"Trial", like Boucher's earlier stories, explores the nature of the universe in which both Blake and Travis exist, in this case through comparing and contrasting the two characters and their situations.

B7: KILLER

UK TRANSMISSION: Tuesday 20 February 1979: 7.20pm – 8.10pm
DURATION: 51:11
VIEWING FIGURE: 7.0m
CHART POSITION: 95
WRITER: Robert Holmes
DIRECTOR: Vere Lorrimer

CREDITED CAST: Paul Daneman (Bellfriar); Ronald Lacey (Tynus); Colin Farrell (Gambrill); Colin Higgins (Tak); Michael Gaunt (Bax); Morris Barry (Wiler)

UNCREDITED CAST: Colin Higgins, Michael Gaunt (Voices of Boarding Party); David Charles, Gordon Somers, David Pople, Mark Alan, Adrian Varcoe (Boarding Party/Guards/Firefighters); David Glen, Ray Chaney (Medicos Frell and Joson); Bobby James, Mark Kirby, Robert Van Kaphengst (Men in Dust Suits/Firefighter); Tony O'Leary (Wardin)

SYNOPSIS: Avon and Vila teleport down to the Federation-run Q Base on the planet Fosforon, in order to obtain, with the help of Avon's former accomplice Tynus, a T-P Crystal that will allow the crew to decipher the Federation's new pulse code. Meanwhile, K47, a ship that disappeared seven hundred years earlier, reappears over Fosforon; the scientists on the base mount an expedition to retrieve it, but on the *Liberator*, Cally senses life on the ship. Blake decides to warn Q Base, teleporting down and meeting the scientist in charge, Dr Bellfriar. A corpse is discovered on board K47 and prepared for autopsy, but then seemingly comes to life and strangles the pathologist; shortly thereafter, two technicians come down with a mysterious virus, which spreads throughout the base. Meanwhile, Avon and Tynus initiate their plan – which involves, under cover of a deliberately-set fire, faking a malfunction in the crystal, which will necessitate acquiring a replacement – but Vila discovers that Tynus has informed Servalan of their whereabouts and is stalling them to buy her time to get to Fosforon. Avon and Vila steal the crystal and kill Tynus, setting a fire to disguise the damage; Dr Bellfriar learns that the disease is a plague designed to attack only humans who have ventured into space, but dies before he can tell Blake the cure. Against Avon's misgivings, Blake warns the Federation of the nature of the planet's contamination.

ANALYSIS: "Killer", the first script for *Blake's 7* from veteran television script writer and ex-policeman Robert Holmes, is one of the best episodes of the season, with characterisation, plot and ideas all hanging together well. The few problems that the story has actually stem from the fact that it was originally intended to be transmitted fourth in the season, before "Pressure Point".

The reason for the story's postponement remains unknown; however, the fact that Gan seems to have been written out of "Killer" with very little effort may have been a factor. This story was also clearly written before the decision was made to take Orac on as a regular character; the little he does in this episode could easily have been done by Zen, and the code-breaking for which the crew need the TP Crystal, is normally Orac's function. The relationship between Avon and Blake – with Avon criticising Blake behind his back and remarking that he won't always be in command – is more pre-"Pressure Point", whereas Avon's attitude in "Horizon" – in which he considers taking the *Liberator*, which Blake promised him in "Pressure Point" – seems to be more characteristic of later stories. Also, in an earlier draft, Blake refers to both Servalan and Travis coming to the planet to investigate.

Although there are few references to series continuity, the overall feel of the story is such that it would have fitted in better in its originally intended position. "Trial" sees the crew having just committed a highly visible act of destruction, and the Federation would naturally be looking for them, and in "Horizon", the *Liberator* has been pursued to the edge of the galaxy. Thematically, this is where "Killer" would have fit best.

Holmes's plotting, although clever in its own right, incorporates elements from "Seek-Locate-Destroy" (Tynus's and Avon's plans to steal the communications device; also Jenna's remark that the Federation know about the teleport), "Time Squad" (a small, primitive three-man ship with a deadly cargo) and "Mission to Destiny" (Blake's suggestion that Bellfriar shut down the air conditioning to avoid spreading the plague). It is also an inversion of "Breakdown", in which a 'neutral' group were shown to be, in practice, not terribly apolitical. Here we see the human side of the Federation, with a station full of kind and funny as well as unscrupulous and nest-feathering people, displaying different attitudes towards Blake's cause, engaging in social relations, and more interested in securing their pensions than in being the first person to meet an alien. This is encapsulated in the unusual and touching scene in which we see a guard suffering from smoke inhalation; here, for the first time, we see the guard as a human being in distress, not as an antagonist or tool of the system.

The characterisation of the secondary figures, and portrayal of their society, is excellent. Tynus and Bellfriar are particularly worthy of note, and even the more minor characters Tak, Wiler and Gambrill are well done. The base has a real sense of being a small research or academic community, with Tynus and Bellfriar sniping at one another behind each other's backs, Bellfriar and Wiler openly criticising each other, and the different sections of the base engaged in constant one-upmanship. At the end, Tynus, helpless and afraid when confronted with a foe he doesn't understand, orders Bellfriar to 'do something' about the epidemic; Bellfriar, knowing all the variables, remains calm in the face of death. This characterisation is boosted by some superb performances; Ronald Lacey is a wonderful villain, and Paul Daneman is dignified and sympathetic as Bellfriar, lending a strong sense of pathos and irony to the character's death.

Blake's characterisation is in line with his more sympathetic side; his actions are not driven or selfish, although he is still given to presenting his crew with *faits-accomplis*, teleporting down to Fosforon against Jenna's misgivings. Significantly for the post-"Pressure Point" period, he starts to argue with Jenna over his plan and then apologises to her; given that the scene as written does not necessarily invite this interpretation, it seems that Gareth Thomas (and/or Vere Lorrimer) was keeping an eye on character development. Blake risks his own neck to help Federation people, even Servalan; Avon complains that Blake is too altruistic, and that his bleeding heart will get them all killed. Blake's anecdotal knowledge of history (which may be a holdover from the initial idea of having him be a schoolteacher) also builds on earlier information about the character; he has shown evidence of this before, explaining to Gan about churches in "Pressure Point" and admitting to having a knowledge of natural history in "Bounty". In fact, if the definition of 'natural' includes germs, this may be where he learned the story about the plague blankets.

Holmes also excels at conveying background information unobtrusively through dialogue or unspoken implication, as when Tynus explains to Avon about the function of the T-P Crystal, not realising that Avon already knows about it. Elsewhere, Avon and Vila clearly refuse a food parcel from Tynus because they suspect him of wanting to poison them. Holmes even introduces a couple of subtexts. We learn that the existence of Blake's teleport system is classified information as, although Tynus states that Fosforon receives a lot of 'Federation gossip,' Bellfriar does not know about the teleport on the *Liberator*. In addition, we can see that Blake is wrong when he speculates that the virus is airborne: Gambrill suffers no ill effects after going into the mortuary, but the two technicians who touched the corpse do; Gambrill dies only after he touches Tak and a number of other panicking technicians. Wiler is in the mortuary with the corpse for quite some time before beginning the autopsy (during which he is wearing gloves), and also shows no sign of disease. The virus doesn't spread into Tynus's section until after the technicians and medics panic and break out, also suggesting that it is spread by contact. This explains why Blake, Vila and Avon unaffected – although Tynus' section is contaminated by the end of the story and Vila comes quite close to the infected Tak. It is unknown how Dr Bellfriar gets the virus in the end; however, we see very little of what he does when analysing the virus, and it is possible that he could have touched infected tissue in that time.

Finally, a word on the technology of "Killer". This story is noteworthy in that the technobabble is less obtrusive and nonsensical here than elsewhere; we may also note the unusual fact – from a 21st-century perspective – that Bellfriar does not have a computer of his own. The 'Darkling Zone' into which spaceships vanish, is more referencing of 18th-century nautical conditions, in which areas like the Sargasso Sea and the Bermuda Triangle became notorious for ships disappearing with no apparent reason, and occasionally reappearing much later.

Rather than simply rehashing earlier episodes, Holmes builds upon and develops ideas that were presented in certain first-season stories to construct a complex narrative that stands up well to analysis.

B8: HOSTAGE

UK TRANSMISSION: Tuesday 27 February 1979: 7.15pm – 8.10pm
DURATION: 51:04
VIEWING FIGURE: 7.8m
CHART POSITION: 65
WRITER: Allan Prior
DIRECTOR: Vere Lorrimer

CREDITED CAST: John Abineri (Ushton); Judy Buxton (Inga); Kevin Stoney (Joban); Andrew Robertson (Space Commander); Judith Porter (Mutoid); James Coyle (Molok)

UNCREDITED CAST: Cliff Diggins, Del Baker, Dinny Powell, Rocky Taylor (Stuntmen/Crimos); Margaret Pilleau, Barbara Hampshire (Mutoids); Walter Turner, David Roy Paul, Robert Smythe, David Glen (Crimos)

SYNOPSIS: Blake receives a message from Travis asserting that, as he is now also a fugitive from the Federation, they should pool their resources; he is holding Blake's cousin, Inga, hostage on the planet Exbar, and will kill her if Blake does not agree. Blake goes to Exbar and meets Inga's father, Ushton, who betrays him to Travis. Avon suspects a trap and teleports down with Vila, only for the two of them to be captured by Travis's team of 'Crimos' (criminal psychopaths). Travis announces that he wants the *Liberator* for himself; when Blake will not agree, he traps Blake and Avon in an airlock and has the air pumped out of it. He gives Vila's teleport bracelet to one of the Crimos, Molok, and browbeats Vila into giving the signal for Jenna and Cally to bring him up. Jenna and Cally are taken prisoner, but overcome Molok and teleport him into space. Meanwhile Ushton tells Travis that Inga has escaped, and Travis sends the Crimos after her; Ushton overcomes Travis, releases Blake, Avon, and Vila (who has been placed in the airlock with the others) and sets off after Travis and the Crimos with Blake and Avon. The Crimos are killed, and Travis left behind; Servalan, who has been alerted to Travis's presence by a message from Avon, arrives and offers Travis unofficial support in his pursuit of Blake.

ANALYSIS: "Hostage", as stories go, is a real mess, on a par with (even, arguably, worse than) "Pressure Point" and "Bounty". It first appeared in a season breakdown dated July 1978 – the month before it was formally commissioned – as the eleventh episode. It seems also to have featured, at some point, a 'substitute Blake' character, which was first mentioned in a proposed Nation storyline for the tenth episode. The problems with the story are not confined to the scripting but extend to the production too. "Hostage" faced difficulties well into production; most notably, the original actor cast as Ushton, Duncan Lamont, died three weeks after completion of the location filming, necessitating a partial remount. The second choice, Ronald Lewis, proved to have severe health problems that made him unsuitable for the part, and so the role was recast again with John Abineri.

The story is peppered with a series of loosely connected set-pieces, which gradually get weaker and weaker as the episode progresses. The first ten minutes serve only to reinforce Servalan's (somewhat irrational) belief that Travis is the only man capable of tracking down Blake, although it has to be said that the Space Commander played by Andrew Robertson sports a very nice uniform. (Actually, barring the mutoids and the Crimos, the costumes in this story are quite well done, without the camp flavour of some other second season episodes.) Similarly, a scene with Councillor Joban contributes little to the story, being primarily a retread of the Bercol and Rontane scene from "Seek-Locate-Destroy"; the one interesting point comes when Joban states that sympathy with Blake is now being found among the service grades as well as the higher grades, suggesting that his legend has now spread to the proletariat, and therefore is a source of immediate concern. The fight sequences are poor, with bear-traps and nets being used against the crew; the battle at the end of the story is particularly badly done, with one Crimo apparently undergoing a resurrection part-way through.

The Crimos are themselves problematic. Everyone seems to know what they are – everyone bar the audience, that is. They appear out of nowhere and are never mentioned again; we do not know where Travis acquired four of them, or where his three mutoids (who were previously mentioned in "Trial" and whose functions the Crimos seem to adopt for just this single episode) have disappeared to. The Crimos' presence may have something to do with the abandoned script "Death Squad", which would have dealt with the Federation conducting experiments to modify criminal psychopaths into highly aggressive killers (the Crimos wear what appear to be colour-coded uniforms, which would suggest a military connection), and which was pulled from the schedule a mere three weeks before filming was due to begin. A direct connection, or indirect influence, from this script might explain why characters along these lines appear in "Hostage"; out of the blue like this, however, it seems awkward and strange.

There are a few moments of good characterization in the story. Avon is the one who presents the *fait-accompli* this time, calling in Servalan without telling anyone else. Blake suggests that he himself should go down to Exbar on his own rather than involving the others, although, admittedly, he is not proposing attacking the Federation but acting for personal reasons. Jenna shows signs of jealousy over Inga. Travis mentions feeling shame, presumably as a result of his rejection by the Service. His sadism-by-proxy reappears; he doesn't beat up Inga himself but has Molok (whose name recalls the Biblical deity to whom children were said to have been sacrificed) do it instead, and pries information that he must surely already have (who the weakest member of the Seven is) out of Ushton by having his daughter tortured. This sequence also draws parallels between "Hostage" and "Pressure Point", in which Veron betrays Blake's crew in order, she believes, to save her mother.

Otherwise, however, the story contains a number of character and plot inconsistencies. Although the fact that Servalan comes out to Exbar to make a deal with Travis sets up the idea of them working together in secret, which forms the basis for subsequent stories, the notion comes across as somewhat improbable, to say nothing of contrived. Molok, who claims to have a high intelligence quotient, does not demonstrate it here: by telling the lie that Blake, Avon and Vila are dead, he is forced to take Cally back down to Exbar in order to get Jenna to cooperate, rather than simply threatening to kill her friends. Although his dialogue implies that he is taking bracelets down for the rest of Travis's force, he does not in fact do so. It is never explained why a communications station possesses an airlock. Ushton's tough-guy performance at the end of the story begs the question of why he meekly goes along with Travis at the beginning, even faking a limp for Blake's benefit. Blake kisses his own cousin, who appears to be much younger than he is (the actress, whatever her real age, is playing the character as someone not much older than 20), which makes one rather wonder how old she was when Blake visited Ushton 'as a boy': as she must have been about three or four, the fact that he says, with a romantic overtone, 'she meant a lot to me once,' lends a (surely unintentional) highly suspect character to their relationship. At the end of the story, Ushton rushes over to announce to Travis that Inga has run off, begging the question of how she managed to evade the Crimos, as well as why Ushton would inform Travis of his own daughter's escape, and why Travis would believe it. Vila does not join the others in the final fight sequence, leaving him very much surplus to requirements. The ending, with Inga announcing that she intends to devote herself to feeding the starving and Ushton remarking, inexplicably, 'It's too late for me,' has a peculiarly tacked-on feel.

It is tempting to speculate that, as with "Pressure Point", the problems are largely the result of rewriting. However, although at least one rewrite has clearly taken place on "Hostage" (due to the abandonment of the 'substitute Blake' storyline), it is unlikely that this is the source of the main problems. Although Prior is capable of producing excellent stories, he has also produced two, "Horizon" and "Animals", that suffer from awkward scenes and character inconsistencies in a similar way to "Hostage". It seems more likely that, on this occasion, Prior effectively wrote himself into a corner, devising a hostage scenario in which all of the heroes are captured or otherwise incapacitated, and consequently necessitating some contrived scenes to resolve the issue.

Although Chris Boucher has improved the story to some extent by adding entertaining dialogue, "Hostage" remains a story shot through with inconsistent characterisation and poor plotting and with a farcical resolution.

B9: COUNTDOWN

UK TRANSMISSION: Tuesday 6 March 1979: 7.15pm – 8.10pm
DURATION: 51:05
VIEWING FIGURE: 6.9m
CHART POSITION: 72
WRITER: Terry Nation
DIRECTOR: Vere Lorrimer

CREDITED CAST: Tom Chadbon (Del Grant); Paul Shelley (Provine); James Kerry (Cauder); Lindy Alexander (Ralli); Robert Arnold (Selson); Geoffrey Snell (Tronos); Sidney Kean (Vetnor); Nigel Gregory (Arrian)

UNCREDITED CAST: Rocky Taylor, Cliff Diggins (Stuntment / Albians / Guards); Peter Roy, Toby Byrne (Albians); Derek Suthern, Peter Caton, Tony Snell, Robert Smythe, Ray Knight, Ernie Goodyear, Peter Roy (Albians / Guards)

SYNOPSIS: On the planet Albian, a revolt erupts under the direction of a hired mercenary, Del Grant, and the rebels take possession of the Federation command centre. The commander, Space Major Provine, orders that the countdown be started for a bomb that will kill the population but leave the buildings intact, and flees; however, the way to his escape rocket is blocked. Meanwhile, Blake, Avon and Vila teleport down to Albian in search of Provine, who they believe can tell them the true location of Central Control. Avon and Vila set out to help the

Albians defuse the bomb, only to discover that it is actually located in the planet's arctic regions; Avon teleports to this site along with Grant, who holds Avon responsible for the death of a woman named Anna, who was involved with Avon's bank fraud and appears to have been his lover. Meanwhile Blake searches for Provine, who has disguised himself as a rebel; finding him, he persuades him to reveal that the location of Control, now called Star One, is known only to a cybersurgeon named Docholli. Avon and Grant defuse the bomb at the last minute and reconcile their differences; we learn that Anna was Grant's sister.

ANALYSIS: "Countdown" is a solid story, standing in sharp contrast to the same writer's "Pressure Point" and further highlighting how much that episode's limitations were due to external circumstances.

The idea of Nation doing a single space adventure for the season's tenth episode (later moved back to ninth) had been suggested as early as January/February 1978, as part of the five stories he was intending to do for Season B (of which only three were completed). The fact that Orac is barely featured (indeed, he does not physically appear at all), having no lines and doing a job that Zen (who is not mentioned) could have done, suggests again that most of this story was written before it was decided to take Orac on as a regular character. The storyline, which would have originally been set before "Hostage", was at one point to have introduced a 'substitute Blake' character (who may have been removed in some rewrites suggested by Chris Boucher on 26th July 1978, as "Gambit", which also does not involve a 'substitute Blake,' was commissioned just over a week later). It seems more than possible that this character later became Grant, a charismatic, rogue-with-a-heart-of-gold figure, who has a history with Avon and incurs a combination of respect and animosity from him. Also, Grant was Anna's brother, making him another sibling-figure for Avon.

The story as it stands (which is very much focused on Avon, Blake and Vila at the expense of Cally and Jenna) is clearly inspired by WWII spy dramas, and in particular by the television series *Secret Army,* which had made its debut in 1977. In fact, Paul Shelley had appeared in the latter series as the ruthless British agent Major

Bradley (later to become a semi-regular character) in the episode "Lucky Piece", transmitted on 11ᵗʰ October 1978, about six weeks before filming started on "Countdown", making it more than likely that his casting as Provine was based on his *Secret Army* appearance. Avon's description of the city he lived in on Earth recalls Nazi-occupied Europe rather than the dome seen in "The Way Back", with people willing to take in a gunshot-wounded man rather than to call the authorities. The name 'Albian' recalls 'Albion,' a poetic name for Britain, and thus suggests the 'Britain under the Nazis' story genre as well as the Robin Hood legend. (Note that here, as in "Pressure Point", the rebels wear green.) Checking identity papers is further in keeping with the WWII theme, as is the appearance of Ralli; her posh accent suggests the upper-class women of the 1940s who joined the army as secretaries, drivers, switchboard operators and so forth (although this is probably again due to Lorrimer picking up on the implications of the storyline). The episode also has antecedents in the detective/police story genre, with Blake figuring out Provine's location from the evidence available (Selson's corpse, the tunnel collapse, and the presence of a rocket that can only take off, go into orbit, and then return).

The concept of the bomb revisits another of Nation's interests: the thermonuclear threat. We have a device (the design of which, with rods slotting automatically into tubes, recalls that of nuclear reactors) that kills people but leaves cities intact (a concept that also appeared in the abandoned first season story "Locate and Destroy", and earlier in the *Doctor Who* story in which Nation first introduced the Daleks), causing a Cold-War-style stalemate in that the rebels cannot move against the Federation. It also, incidentally, recalls Gan's limiter in being a device in place to prevent hostile action, and its shifting location similarly evokes the revelations about Control in "Pressure Point". The action of Provine's deputy in activating the bomb countdown as he dies appears to be one of revenge in keeping with the nuclear theme. The resistance are, once again, middle-class, or at any rate its leaders are; Provine briefly adopts a Cockney accent when masquerading as a rebel foot soldier (and is ordered about by a man with a received pronunciation accent). The two Federation officers also seem cool and detached in the face of chaos, as if they feel that they are in a class apart.

This scenario allows for the development of the Federation

personnel as characters. Sergeant Selson's references to the Federation troops making a 'valiant effort' against the rebels seem to be less, as Provine assumes, mindless patriotism, and more an attempt to delay setting off the bomb; he is reluctant to carry out this act, and his last words to Provine are not to tell him to find an alternative route to the spaceship but to urge him to stop the detonation. Later, Provine (who is not only killing millions of Albians through his actions, but all his own men) tries to persuade Arrian to help him to escape, saying that although Albian is doomed, they two can survive by working together; the rebel retorts that he couldn't live knowing that his family and friends were dead, and that he had helped the man who destroyed a world. Finally, when Provine lies dying, he refuses to give Blake information until Blake offers him medical facilities, at which point he tells him about Star One and Docholli. Provine is loyal not to the Federation, but only to himself.

Grant, the other strong figure of this story, interacts well with the regulars. Blake is willing to trust Grant and is friendly with him, but threatens that if anything happens to Avon, he will come looking for Grant. Avon, for his part, saves Grant from being crushed to death, and takes off his own bracelet to prevent himself from being teleported to safety before he has finished defusing the bomb; however, it is worth noting that here he has something to prove to Grant. This story reveals that a woman was involved with Avon's attempted fraud; however, it still does not explain his sometimes aggressive attitude towards the female sex.

Finally, a word on production. The story is very well directed, especially the fight sequences, but the tense scenes with Avon and Grant trying to defuse the bomb as the ice melts around them are also noteworthy. Darrow in particular shows us Avon's more emotional side, sounding nothing like he does normally. The costumes of the regulars are still well done (as they tend to be in the second half of this season), with Cally in particular clad in a flattering green suede tunic. The casting is variable; although Shelley and Chadbon are both excellent, the other guest actors range from average to poor.

"Countdown", coming as it does between "Hostage" and "Voice from the Past", is an island of comparative sanity in between two convoluted and poorly written episodes.

B10: VOICE FROM THE PAST

UK TRANSMISSION: Tuesday 13 March 1979: 7.20pm – 8.10pm
DURATION: 48:36
VIEWING FIGURE: 7.0m
CHART POSITION: 80
WRITER: Roger Parkes
DIRECTOR: George Spenton-Foster

CREDITED CAST: Frieda Knorr (Governor Le Grand); Richard Bebb (Ven Glynd); Martin Read (Nagu)

UNCREDITED CAST: Harry Fielder, Reg Turner, Robert Smythe, Pat Gorman (Guards); Ian Munro, Reg Woods, Alva Shelley, Jules Walter, Barry Summerford, Judy Cowne, Karen Cooper, Count Prince Miller, Joe MacKlaine (Glynd's Rebels)

SYNOPSIS: Blake, complaining of a high-pitched oscillating tone that none of the rest of the crew can hear, diverts the *Liberator* from its planned course, to the planet Del-Ten, to one leading to the asteroid P-K118. Avon and Cally, supported by Orac, suspect his actions to be related to his conditioning following his trial on Earth; they restrain him, restore the course of the ship, and plan a programme of therapy for Blake. However, Blake persuades Vila that Avon and Cally are working against him; Vila releases Blake, who resets the coordinates and locks Avon, Cally and Jenna in a recreation room. When they arrive at P-K118, Blake teleports down and encounters a group of rebels, including Ven Glynd, who has now defected from the

Federation, and a heavily bandaged man called Shivan. They have a plan to act in concert with the Governor of Outer-Gal, Le Grand, to expose the corrupt nature of the Terran Administration and Space Command by releasing damning evidence – including some concerning Blake's trial – at a meeting of planetary governors. The now-released crew are suspicious, but Blake agrees to the plan and he, Jenna and Vila go to the conference. This, however, proves to have been a trap set by Servalan. On board the *Liberator*, Shivan is revealed to be Travis, who teleports down and kills Glynd. Blake and his crew escape, and Avon destroys the device that Glynd was using to control Blake.

ANALYSIS: "Voice from the Past" is another story that seems to have undergone some significant rewriting; however, as with "Hostage", the problems with it appear to have less to do with the rewrites, and more to do with deficiencies in the basic storyline.

The episode was commissioned on 3rd April 1978 from Roger Parkes, a former *Out of the Unknown* story editor who had written scripts for, among others, *The Prisoner* and *Survivors,* and who had also been editor of the periodical *Farming Express*. The story was then moved up and down the transmission order before finally being settled in the number ten spot. A draft submitted on 5th May contains references not only to "Storm Mountain", but to Blake having made a failed alliance with aliens (possibly a rejected storyline); Gan is also still present. At one point it was positioned as the ninth episode, following "Horizon" (before the latter was moved back to fourth), which explains why the crew are more interested in going to the Del-Ten recreational planet than in finding Docholli.

The premise of the story is inherently flawed. Le Grand's and Glynd's proposal to present evidence indicting the Terran Administration and Space Command to the planetary governors seems lamentably naïve for a pair of seasoned politicians. The Federation a totalitarian regime, and it is difficult enough to blow the whistle even in democratic societies; people, especially politicians, tend to follow the most powerful group, rather than necessarily the group with justice on its side. If Le Grand is the only sane member of the planetary governors, as Avon says, then one shudders to think what the rest of them must be like. This is not assisted in any way by Frieda Knorr's appalling performance; she pronounces every word emphatically and appears not to blink at all when talking to Blake, turning a story that has, up until this point been increasingly bad into one that is decidedly dire.

Throughout the episode, Blake's two trials are conflated. It is implied that Blake was sent to Cygnus Alpha for political dissidence, rather than for kidnap and paedophilia. The details of the case given here contradict what we have seen earlier: Blake's hallucinations have Glynd sentencing him to Cygnus Alpha, despite the fact that he was not the arbiter in this case, and they also have Glynd, rather than Dr Havant, being the one conditioning him (and, to be honest, repeating 'renounce, renounce the Freedom Party' appears a little unsubtle when compared with the scene in which Dr Havant engages Blake in a tricky discussion on truth and perception in "The Way Back"). It seems likely that all these problems stem from the fact that the story was originally to have featured clips from "The Way Back", an idea dropped when Robert James proved unable to reprise the role of Glynd. However, with regard to the changed accusations against Blake, it must be noted that there was a definite toning-down of the series' darker themes in the second season – as can be seen in the apparent disappearance of Gan's limiter – and Maloney has also stated that he felt that revisiting the child-molestation theme in this episode would have been distasteful.

The story contains a number of other continuity references, for instance to Orac's barrier against telepathic interference. Not all of them are accurate, however; Servalan is said to have attempted to cheat the Federation out of a hundred million credits to pay for Orac, whereas we know that this was not the case. This is the first and last time we hear of Blake's now-defunct political group being called the Freedom Party (although that's not a problem in and of itself, as we've had other bits of backstory added this season). Glynd is stated to have been an 'Arbiter General'; he is still a pretty shifty character, using Blake's conditioning to force him to support his cause.

The script in general, although it contains a few good lines (mostly given to Servalan) is quite clunky for the most part, with Glynd's group and Le Grand coming up with such dialogue gems as 'Did not the Arbiter General explain? For years now, the Arbiter

General and I have prepared for this moment. He gathering evidence of the Administration's infamies, while I lobbied the support of my fellow governors.' Jenna and Cally do get rather more to do than usual, but Blake has an extreme reaction to his conditioning at the end of the story, which, although it may add drama to the scene, makes no sense whatsoever in plot terms.

The Shivan plotline is also a problem. Although Travis was featured in "Voice from the Past" from its initial date of commissioning, his behaviour at the end of the story is ludicrous. Given that when last seen he wanted the *Liberator*, why does he not just kill Cally and Avon and take it over, rather than teleporting down to the planet, standing around not doing anything, and then having a fight with Glynd (whom he shoots only after Glynd attempts to throttle him)? The Shivan plotline does not appear to have been a late addition, as the presence of a traitor in the ranks recalls "The Way Back", Nagu's fate recalls Chevner's in "Project Avalon", and, finally, Servalan's remark that she has had Le Grand under surveillance for some time might well refer to Shivan, either as a deliberate traitor or as someone acting under conditioning. Whether Shivan was always intended to be Travis, or was originally a separate character, is, however, unknown; one way or another, though, it seems that the *Liberator* crew must be singularly dim not to be suspicious of a heavily bandaged 'rebel leader' with an injured left eye and concealed left arm.

The production is very much on par with the script. The bandages and artificial eye on 'Shivan' are particularly dire, even worse than the grey bathrobes worn by Glynd's group. Blake's spacesuit, which is similarly dreadful, appears to have no oxygen tank. On P-K118, he is seen superimposed against a badly painted alien landscape, apparently featuring a planet on a trapeze; we can only assume that the miners were fond of painting murals, as it is unlikely that this is the actual surface of the asteroid. Although the model shots are quite effective, the shuttle landing goes on far too long. There is, however, an impressive interior shot pulling back from the *Liberator* window to reveal Avon, Cally and Jenna; and it is also of note that, where the previous year saw no ethnic-minority extras among the rebels, Glynd's group includes two Black men and an Asian-looking woman. It also has to be said that Gareth Thomas gives a wonderful performance: the sequence where he persuades

Vila to release him and put the *Liberator* back on course for the asteroid (in an echo of Gan's persuasion of Cally in "Breakdown") is particularly good; note that Blake, even when he is claiming to Vila that the other crewmembers have betrayed him, is inclined to be lenient with Jenna, saying that she was 'probably duped by the other two.' Unfortunately, however, none of this makes up for the story's shortcomings.

"Voice from the Past" is easily the worst story this season, and, in spite of stiff competition, arguably of the entire series.

B11: GAMBIT

UK TRANSMISSION: Tuesday 20 March 1979: 7.20pm – 8.10pm
DURATION: 51:48
VIEWING FIGURE: 6.6m
CHART POSITION: 90
WRITER: Robert Holmes
DIRECTOR: George Spenton-Foster

CREDITED CAST: Aubrey Woods (Krantor); Denis Carey (Docholli); Nicolette Roeg (Chenie); Sylvia Coleridge (Croupier); Paul Grist (Cevedic); John Leeson (Toise); Harry Jones (Jarriere); Michael Halsey (Zee); Deep Roy (Klute)

UNCREDITED CAST: Norman Bacon, John Cannon (Cevedic's Heavies); Barry Summerford (Thrylce); Mike Mungarvan, Pat Gorman, Jan Murzynowski, Joe Kaye, Bill Gray, Robert Smythe, Derek Southern, Steve Kelly, John Holland, Ronald Horn, Ridgewell Hawkes, Stephen Kane, Karen Cooper, Karen Apted, Fay Hillier, Donna Scarfe, Arnold Lee, Willow, Shenoo Rethna, Ohjah Maharaja, Steve Margo, Tawny Sands, Mark Kirby, Dave Holland, Gita Santana (Runner/Trantinian/Customers/Bouncer/Gamblers)

SYNOPSIS: Blake, Jenna and Cally teleport down to a neutral world called Freedom City in search of Docholli. Travis is also there, acting as Docholli's unofficial bodyguard, as is Servalan, who has hatched a scheme to destroy Travis, Docholli, and Krantor (the owner of Freedom City). Servalan asks Krantor to bring her Travis alive and Docholli dead or alive, knowing that

Krantor will be intrigued, will have Docholli interrogated and will send her the corpse; the fact that he will have learned the location of Star One will place Krantor on the Federation's death list. Krantor sends Servalan the unconscious Travis, on whom he has placed a listening device; realising this, Servalan places a bomb in Travis's artificial arm, saying that she intends that he will go looking for Docholli to repair the arm and that the bomb will detonate when Docholli tries to do so, killing them both. This information is in fact intended to cause Krantor to redouble his efforts to find Docholli and to kill Travis before he reaches Docholli; the bomb is not primed. Krantor, stalling for time, lies and tells Servalan that he has Docholli prisoner, but she is suspicious when he will not let her see him. Meanwhile, the bartender Chenie helps Docholli to gain passage off-world. Blake, Jenna and Cally locate Docholli, as do Travis and Krantor's men, whom Travis then kills. As Docholli operates on Travis's arm, he reveals that he does not in fact know the location of Star One, but that he made a copy of the brain-print of one of the men who did, Lurgen; this brain-print is said to be on a thong around the neck of a tribal chieftain on the planet Goth. Blake passes up the opportunity to kill Travis. Meanwhile, Avon and Vila have teleported down to Freedom City in order to make a fortune in the casinos with the assistance of Orac. Krantor, suspicious at the size of their win, manipulates Vila into playing a game of 'Speed Chess' against a sinister chess champion, the Klute. If Vila wins or draws, he will double his winnings, but if he loses, he will be electrocuted. With Orac's help, Vila achieves a draw, and the trio are back on the *Liberator* before the others realise that they are gone.

ANALYSIS: "Gambit" (originally to have been entitled "Doc Holliday") is a convoluted tale drawing, as many of Robert Holmes's scripts do, on a variety of external influences.

To begin with, the story is heavily indebted to Jacobean drama. Not only do the Byzantine plotting and dramatic costuming recall the works of Middleton and Shakespeare, but the violence taking place off-screen and being heralded mostly through dialogue, the A and B plot connected by a single character, Krantor's seeming asides-to-camera, and the (literally) upstairs-downstairs world of the opulent Big Wheel casino versus the seedy bars of the Rink, are all standard elements of the drama of the time. Middleton, furthermore, used chess games as political and social metaphors in two of his plays, *Women Beware Women* and *A Game At Chesse*. Holmes also explicitly intended to reference Westerns, with Docholli's name being derived from Doc Holliday's; this is further recalled in Chenie's barmaid outfit and Travis's gunfighter act. In particular, there are superficial resemblances to the Fritz Lang Western *Rancho Notorious*, which featured an ageing showgirl (played by Marlene Dietrich, to whom the Croupier's costume is an explicit homage) opening a ranch on the proceeds of a gambling game. If this were a Western, though, Travis would be the hero: the scarred stranger who comes out of nowhere looking for someone, and saves a man's life in the first few minutes; this recalls the hero/villain reversals involving Travis in "Seek-Locate-Destroy" and "Trial".

A less direct, but no less significant, influence is the Weimar Republic: the explicitly homoerotic relationship between Krantor and Toise; the Croupier, whose appearance and behaviour reference both *Cabaret* and *The Blue Angel*; and the atmosphere of decadence overlying a seamy underside (with Servalan declaring her Hitler-like intentions to restore order), all recall this period. Servalan refuses Krantor's repeated offers of 'diversions' not because she is a hypocrite, but because to accept would be to give him a hold over her; her speeches about the degeneracy of Freedom City are also visibly motivated from political ambitions rather than from her particularly caring what happens to the place.

One of the clearest influences on "Gambit" is, however, the BBC series *Gangsters*, whose second batch of six episodes was shown in January/February 1978, some months before Holmes started work on "Gambit". Not only do the early episodes of *Gangsters* take place around a nightclub, with a comedian providing a Greek chorus as the Croupier does here, it also has a protagonist named 'Kline' and contains a number of cowboy-film references. Krantor explicitly recalls Rafiq in the *Gangsters* series, a bisexual Indian crime lord who has a diminutive, camp underling and a kind of lust-hate relationship with the beautiful Triad leader Lily-Lee Tang. Furthermore, *Gangsters* was noted for using postmodern techniques such as ironic asides to camera.

Servalan's scheme is particularly well planned, to the point where certain aspects of it do require explanation. When Servalan fits Travis with a bomb and sends him to find Docholli, in order to set Krantor's men to kill Travis as well as to redouble their efforts to find Docholli, the one thing that can go wrong is that Travis evades Krantor's men, finds Docholli and kills them both. Hence the reason why the bomb is not primed; this means that, even if Travis finds Docholli first, Krantor's men will still be able to track them down and take Docholli prisoner. However, the plan's convolution causes it to fall down due to unforeseen circumstances; Servalan could not have predicted that Krantor's henchman Cevedic would tell Travis about the bomb, and that Travis would be sufficiently self-destructive by this point to decide to use it to blow them all up. Had the bomb been primed, ironically, Servalan would have achieved a more valuable end than destroying Krantor and Freedom City, in that she would have killed Blake and half his crew along with Docholli and Travis, due to a chance meeting that, again, she could not have foreseen.

The degeneration of Travis is well portrayed, and this story is much more in keeping with what Travis would do after leaving Space Command than is "Voice from the Past"; note that he is no longer wearing his uniform. Travis is, by this point, at his lowest ebb; an early scene cut for time reasons would have shown a number of sleeping derelicts along the Rink, with one revealed to be Travis. Although Travis was in fact standing guard on Docholli, the association of Travis with derelicts would have been made. Blake's refusal to kill Travis, although it may seem odd, is thus an act of cruelty, along the lines of not killing a wounded animal. Travis's relationship with Docholli is ambiguous; although Travis finds Docholli useful, he also seems to feel a kind of sympathy for him, suggesting that utility and affection are becoming blurred in his increasingly insane perceptions.

Avon and Vila are also well-characterised (apart from the brief moment in which Avon calls Vila 'dummy'). Holmes directly references "Shadow", with explicit mentions of Space City and deserts hot enough to fry one's eyeballs. (In the original draft of the script, the word used was 'gonads'; understandably, this was later changed.) The most significant point with regard to Avon is the fact that he is willing to gamble with Vila's life – unnecessarily and uselessly, as the *Liberator* contains vast amounts of wealth, and they won't be able to boast about their feat afterwards. Avon's urging of Vila to play the game (which means, of course, literally playing chess with death) when he hears that ten million credits are involved recalls his attempt to defraud the Federation of five million credits before the series begins. In light of this, Avon's remark about how, for gamblers, playing for your life becomes the ultimate thrill, is deeply significant; here he gambles with Vila's life, not out of necessity, but just for the sheer hell of it.

Jenna and Cally, however, are back to doing almost nothing; their bitch-fight scene is embarrassing, although the part where Cevedic assumes them to be prostitutes tells us a lot about both him and the culture of Freedom City. It is worth noting that references to prostitution are never explicit in the script. There are also a few late rewrites; the references to Goth at the end were added only after it was known what the next script would involve and who would be writing it, as "The Keeper" and "Star One" were written late in the day. The fact that the situation at the beginning of the next story had to be grafted onto the end of "Gambit" means Docholli's explanation contains some logical inconsistencies: if knowing the location of Star One carries an automatic death sentence, how is it that the location of Lurgen's brain-print is the subject of casual gossip? Also, who precisely told Docholli where it was, and, if the information is so freely available, how is it the Federation have not also found it out? Travis, furthermore, seems to disappear from the story at this point, inexplicably and without trace, presumably as a side effect of the rewrite.

The direction on this episode is variable; the cast are good, and include two actors with Scottish accents. (Chenie also briefly develops an East London accent at the end, although it is unclear whether this is due to the actress's natural accent showing through, or to a dispute between the director and the actor over whether the character should use received pronunciation or not). The costuming is fantastic (including, in the Big Wheel, every sort of outfit from a man dressed as a nun to Jacobean dandies to Pierrot suits), echoing the Jacobean, 19th century and Weimar influences of the story. The fact that there is no incidental music in this episode also contributes toward it having a very unusual feel. (The only pieces of music heard are 'ambient' pieces integral to the action, all of which were composed by Elizabeth Parker.)

On the other hand, however, one does get a few dreadful moments such as the abrupt cut from Travis's 'Thanks for the drink' to Travis's 'What's this all about?' and the scene in which Krantor asks which gambler is winning, when his viewscreen is fixed on Vila in maximum close-up. Servalan's reference to having booked "Room 100 at the Terminal" is a somewhat tasteless joke about the 12 October 1978 stabbing to death of Nancy Spungen in Room 100 at the Chelsea Hotel. Another minor script quibble is that Travis's injury now affects his entire arm rather than just his hand.

"Gambit" is, overall, one of the cleverest stories we have seen so far in *Blake's 7*, making it one of the highlights of a variable season.

B12: THE KEEPER

UK TRANSMISSION: Tuesday 27 March 1979: 7.15pm – 8.10pm
DURATION: 51:17
VIEWING FIGURE: 7.0m
CHART POSITION: 70
WRITER: Allan Prior
DIRECTOR: Derek Martinus

CREDITED CAST: Bruce Purchase (Gola); Freda Jackson (Tara); Shaun Curry (Rod); Cengiz Saner (Fool); Arthur Hewlett (Old Man); Ron Tarr (Patrol Leader)

UNCREDITED CAST: Nosher Powell (Stuntman/Goth Warrior/Double in fight); Stuart Fell, Dinny Powell, Paul Weston (Stuntmen/Goth Warriors); Steve Kelly, Jan Murzynowski, Jeff Howard, Eric Franch, Ridgewell Hawkes, Paul Taras (Goth Guards); Eileen Brady (Harpist)

SYNOPSIS: Following Docholli's revelations, Blake, Jenna and Vila teleport down to the planet Goth in search of Lurgen's brain-print. There they are ambushed by the natives. The *Liberator* has meanwhile moved out of orbit to destroy Travis's pursuit ship. By the time it returns, Vila and Jenna have been captured, so only Blake is able to teleport up. Jenna and Vila are taken to Gola – the Charl, or ruler, of the Goths – and learn that Servalan and Travis are there as his guests. Gola takes a liking to Jenna and asks her to pair-bond with him; she agrees. Blake, meanwhile, has returned to search for the other two, and forms

185

an alliance with Gola's brother, Rod. Travis suggests to Servalan that he should take her pursuit ship and warn the nearest Federation fleet; Avon and Cally let the ship go, as to stop it would mean moving out of teleport range again. Jenna learns that neither Gola nor his sister, Tara, possess the brain-print. Blake and Rod arrive and the brothers fight a duel in which Rod (who also proves not to have the brain-print) is killed. Tara poisons Gola and takes the throne. The crew discover that the brain-print was in the possession of the siblings' father, whom they have imprisoned in the dungeon; however, Travis has taken the print and is now en route to Star One. The old man's dying words to Blake, however, cause the court Fool to repeat Star One's co-ordinates, and the crew set off to find it.

ANALYSIS: "The Keeper" – commissioned in September 1978 as a last-minute replacement for the first instalment of Terry Nation's proposed concluding two-parter, which he failed to deliver – is a good episode and hangs together well. Although it may not be as clever as "Gambit", it too has antecedents in Jacobean drama and is firmly plotted.

The production on this episode is fantastic, with Derek Martinus's direction being easily some of the best of the second season. The lighting is unusually good, as are the sets, and the only poor aspect is the bad blue-screen effects as Jenna and Vila approach the tents of Goth. The tents are quite attractive both inside and out, recalling Mongolian designs as well as Viking architecture. The tunnel sets have bubbles of cooled lava at the top, which is a nice touch. The locations are also well-shot, and lit in yellow to indicate a sulphurous atmosphere. The exploding pursuit ship is great, and would look good in a big-budget film even now. Servalan and Jenna are both well-costumed (Jenna looks particularly striking in her red-and-gold Goth dress), and Travis is still out of uniform. The Goths' outfits, bar the guards' uniforms with their medieval gas-masks, are less good, being all furs and leathers and big medallions, and the duel sequence involves the well-worn cliché, seen in virtually every medieval- or fantasy-set film or television programme, of having the fighting pair knocking the food off a banqueting table.

The story itself is heavily indebted to *King Lear*, involving as it does three siblings, two of whom are fighting for possession of the kingdom, and their deposed father, who has gone mad and whose only supporter is his Fool. The difference is that, in this version, the third sibling is a witch who takes possession of the kingdom herself when everyone else is dead, rather than a virtuous woman who is killed at the end. Travis's presence recalls that of the treacherous Edmund. There are also echoes of *Hamlet* in the deliberately-arranged duel with a poisoned cup for the victor, and of *Macbeth* in Tara's prophecy that if Gola pair-bonds with Jenna, he will die. The script also reflects the Jacobean fondness for clever ripostes and physical comedy, in particular in the scenes in which a guard slings Vila over his shoulder and, later, picks up the Fool by one arm and leg. Another apparent influence is C S Lewis's *The Silver Chair*, which features an underground city and a queen who keeps her captives passive with drugged vapours.

Tara's prophecies seem, for the most part, to be either shrewd psychology (as Jenna remarks, it doesn't take magic to tell that Gola desires her) or secret advance planning (as she herself has called in Rod before prophesying his arrival). The one exception is her prediction of the arrival of Jenna and Vila, which she could not have known about; she also appears at one point to stop Jenna's hand with the power of her mind alone. It is worth noting that, if the Goths insist on marrying within their bloodline, the siblings must all be fantastically inbred. The Fool's character (as well as his portrayal) is very effective, combining humour and pathos; his rivalry with Vila is particularly well played. Prior also has a bit of fun with the character Rod, giving him a line – 'That is the difference between us' – lifted directly from the scene in "Hostage" in which Blake claims the moral high ground over Travis. This might make the audience think that Rod is actually the good guy in the Goth royal family, when in fact he proves no better than his brother.

The plot does have a few weak points. The biggest one is the lack of any plausible explanation as to how Docholli heard that Lurgen was on Goth, even down to the specific detail of the brain-print being worn as a necklace by a member of the royal family. Lurgen would not have wanted that sort of information to get around, particularly as the location of Star One is supposed to be a secret, and Goth doesn't appear to be the sort of place that gets regular traffic. It also seems that Travis must have been hiding somewhere in the docking cradles at the end of "Gambit", in order to have heard what Docholli said to Blake. In addition, there is evidence of a long gap between the end of "Gambit" and the beginning of "The Keeper"; somehow Travis and Servalan have made up their differences, formed an alliance, gone to Goth and got into the Charl's good graces well ahead of the *Liberator*'s crew, despite the fact that the *Liberator* is much faster than any Federation ship. It further appears that Travis must have arrived long before Servalan, as he has had enough time to work out where the brain-print was and to steal it – Servalan would, presumably, have learned of Goth's significance through the listening device she planted on Travis in "Gambit". This episode also sees the return of the cliché of the *Liberator* going out of teleport range just as it's needed; however, it also subverts it through having Cally refuse to do the same again (producing the spectacular irony that Avon and Cally have passed up an opportunity to kill Travis, having unwittingly missed him the first time).

The Travis-Servalan scene early on, in which Travis persuades Servalan to let him borrow her ship, has some good psychological development for Travis, despite being slightly clumsy and containing a large info-dump in the middle. Having discovered that the *Liberator* has destroyed his transportation, Pursuit Ship 4 (which we first heard of in "Trial"; Travis also appears to have had at least one mutoid left, to fly the ship), he starts talking to Servalan about the value of Star One in order to gain access to her ship; when he speaks of 'my ambition,' he is really appealing to Servalan's ambition. Once he has what he wants, he runs off to Star One; he must, however, have made good on his promise to contact the Federation, as a fleet of pursuit ships are bearing down on the *Liberator* at the end of the story.

Jenna, for her part, actually gets something interesting to do for a change; she also shows a degree of intelligence, telling Tara that she knows that the old woman regards her as a political threat, and offering to depart and leave her to her power games in exchange for the brain-print. Sally Knyvette apparently got on well with Bruce Purchase, who encouraged her to take up her studies again, which she did after leaving the series, ultimately doing an MA. Cally also gets some action, quarrelling – and winning the argument – with

Avon over whether or not to pursue the Federation ships. (Their romance seems to have been called off in this season; and while Blake and Jenna manage a few moments of affection and/or jealousy in "Killer" and "Hostage", theirs also seems to be in a bit of a slump.) Servalan shines in her brief appearances, with Jacqueline Pearce giving an outstanding performance: her headshake in response to Gola's order to come to him is nothing short of inspired.

Although "The Keeper" is not the best story of the season, there is little with which to find fault here, and it goes some way towards redeeming Prior's reputation after the problematic "Horizon" and the execrable "Hostage".

B13: STAR ONE

UK TRANSMISSION: Tuesday 3 April 1979: 7.20pm – 8.10pm
DURATION: 48:22
VIEWING FIGURE: 8.2m
CHART POSITION: 30
WRITER: Chris Boucher
DIRECTOR: David Maloney (uncredited)

CREDITED CAST: Jenny Twigge (Lurena); David Webb (Stot); Gareth Armstrong (Parton); John Bown (Durkim); Paul Toothill (Marcol); Michael Mayard (Leeth)

UNCREDITED CAST: Jim Dowdall (Stuntman/Double for Travis); Derek Broome, David Cann, Mark Allington, Giles Melville, Bobby James, Christopher Holmes, Geoffrey Whiteson, Mike Finbar (Searchers); Michael Spice (Voice of Pilot/Other Voices); Hugh Dickson (Voice of Keldon Controller/Other Voices); David Glen, William Wyatt (Bodyguards); Giles Melville, Bobby James (Corpses)

SYNOPSIS: Having located Star One on a distant planet, Blake teleports down with Cally and Avon, armed with bombs, in order to blow the installation up. Unknown to them, however, Star One has already been showing signs of severe malfunction, and Servalan has seized the opportunity to establish herself as President of the Federation. Blake and Cally are welcomed by the technicians at Star One, but it transpires that this is because they believe Blake to be Travis. Avon takes Travis prisoner, and learns

191

that the technicians have been replaced by shape-shifting aliens from the Andromeda Galaxy. They have done a deal with Travis, and he is there to switch off Star One's anti-matter defence zone, allowing their battle-fleet through. Travis evades Avon, wounds Blake and switches off a portion of the defence zone; Avon, aided by Cally, the injured Blake, and an unreplaced technician, Lurena, takes control of the installation, killing Travis. The *Liberator* crew send a message warning the Federation of the alien invasion, but, as the nearest Federation ships are over an hour away, they must stand as its first line of defence.

ANALYSIS: "Star One" was written at the very last minute, which makes the fact that few significant changes were required between the first and final drafts very impressive. The concept of the story, however, dates back to early 1978, when one of the first documents defining the structure of the season included a outline of a two-part finale by Terry Nation, which would have introduced the idea of an alien invasion at Star One and ended with Blake siding with the Federation against the aliens. On 23rd June 1978, it was indicated that Vila and Jenna might be killed in part one. On 23rd November 1978, the two-part story fell through, although it was still hoped that Nation would write the final episode; in late December, Chris Boucher agreed to write it from Nation's original outline (omitting the deaths of Vila and Jenna), leaving Nation free to concentrate on the opening of the following season.

Appropriately, the story as transmitted recalls earlier episodes in the series. In particular, it reads like "Mission to Destiny", involving a quarrelling group that bands together when faced with an external threat and featuring a secret traitor, writ large. As in many earlier stories, we see the human side of the Federation: Lurena sacrifices herself to save humanity, both figuratively in accepting work at Star One and literally in blowing herself up at the end. Appropriately also for the final story of the season, the production is exceptionally good, with the sets, location filming and costumes all being well done; the alien noise that follows the 'technicians' wherever they go is a nice touch; and the explosions done on location at Lightmoor Colliery in Cinderford, Gloucestershire, were so violent that they actually brought the emergency services rushing to the scene.

David Maloney directed the episode after Vere Lorrimer dropped out at the last minute, but he remained uncredited, as it was frowned upon at the time for someone to produce and direct the same programme. The aliens (described in the script as looking like 'a cross between a large spider and the entrails of a horse' – which, albeit with the spider bit removed, is arguably close to what we see on-screen) are also well realised. The idea of an anti-matter minefield defending the 'route' between the Andromeda Galaxy and the Milky Way seems highly implausible on the face of it. (The defence zone clearly does not involve a sphere around the entire galaxy, as then the quantity of mines would be measured in numbers considerably larger than thousands.) However, it is in keeping with the nautical metaphors used throughout the series; the operation of the defence system clearly recalls the practice of planting mines in particular bodies of water.

The Star One installation itself must be fairly recent, as Lurena hasn't changed much since the photo Servalan has of her was taken; it may have been moved from Earth 30 years ago (as observed in "Pressure Point"), but it seems to have had other locations than its present one in the interim. Lurena herself is well-played; the script, at the beginning, suggests that she could, in fact, be insane, and only gradually do we discover the truth. In the script, too, Parton was supposed to be older and senior to Stot, making the fact that Stot commands the aliens seem out of place; as it stands, however, the fact that Stot is clearly older than Parton makes it harder to spot what is wrong with the situation until much later. Why the aliens have left Lurena alive is never directly stated; it is likely, given their curiosity about human motivations, that they have been studying her.

Blake here is very self-centred: he speaks in 'I' rather than 'we' terms of the destruction of Star One, and treats the crew very much in line with his 'This ship is a democracy… [but in the end] we do it my way' remark cut from "Time Squad". (The crew, for their part, ultimately accept being handed over to Avon's leadership, despite their protests.) This Blake is also condemning untold millions of innocents to death quite casually, in contrast to the Blake of "Space Fall", who gives up control of the *London* in order to save the lives of the other prisoners. Even at this point, however, Blake is not without ethics; when he realises the true nature of the situation, he insists on saving Star One, as: 'Humanity is going to need all the resources it can get.' It is also worth noting that Jenna alerts the Federation to the alien threat despite thinking that Blake would object to this.

Avon, for his part, announces his intention, as stated before in "Pressure Point", of taking over the *Liberator* once Blake has what he wants. He again shows aggression towards women in his treatment of Lurena, although this was somewhat toned-down on recording: the camera script has him hitting her when she emerges from Room M, rather than simply tussling with her. Another example of violent content being toned down is that, whereas in the first draft script Avon shoots Travis as he lies dying on the floor, in the final version he does so while Travis is hauling himself up for a second shot at Blake. Blake's remark 'You really do hate me, don't you?' is correct: it has now become apparent (particularly in the second season) that Blake has his own agenda, to which Avon is only peripheral, so Avon, although he still appears to be drawn to Blake, is feeling a sense of betrayal paralleling that of Travis. Blake's agreement to give him the *Liberator*, effectively an attempt to buy him off, is not enough to make amends. Although Avon says at the end of the story that he intends to stay and fight off the aliens because, 'I gave him [i.e. Blake] my word,' Chris Boucher argues that the underlying reason is self-serving: 'Avon had no choice but to try and hold off the aliens, because they were intent on eradicating the human race, and he was as much at risk as anyone. If Avon had just run away, he wouldn't have lasted long, and he knew it.' Avon's reference to having given his word to Blake is therefore a calculated move to keep the crew – who have already voiced their doubts about his potential as a leader – on his side, by attributing the decision to fight to a figure that he knows they will follow.

It is left unclear when Travis made his deal with the aliens; certainly this must have happened before "The Keeper" and possibly before "Gambit", as it is there that he first expresses an interest in Star One. We don't know how he found them, or they found him, or even what the deal precisely involved, but it has evidently taken place in one of the between-episode gaps that have become particularly common over the course of this season. Chris Boucher, asked about Travis's motivations for betraying humanity, has said that in scripting terms, the production team needed someone who was established in the series and 'sufficiently damaged' to commit such an act. (Conveniently, with Gareth Thomas leaving the series, Travis also had to be written out, to maintain a balance.) In character terms, however, Travis has been betrayed by the institution that was everything to him, and he is now going to destroy it utterly, expanding the self-destructive urge we've seen in him from the beginning of the series to include everyone else. (Note that Durkim's name recalls that of Emil Durkheim, the well-known sociologist of the early 20th century whose best-known work was on suicide.) In the original script, the dying Travis says to Avon that he should have killed him earlier, and that Blake has made him soft. He wears his uniform for the first time since "Hostage", and deactivates the defence zone – itself a purely symbolic act – with his artificial hand. Travis is not so much destroying humanity as a substitute for Blake, as he is destroying Blake, the Federation and himself along with the rest of the human race.

Servalan, for her part, is now in charge, meaning that Boucher had (as he has often stated in jest) anticipated Margaret Thatcher's election as British Prime Minister by some months. The coup also recalls similar events in the Soviet Union, with the state turning on its own members in a crisis; Servalan's line about the technicians' sacrifice being 'inspiring' also recollects Soviet propaganda about revolutionary martyrs. A line in an earlier draft, in which Servalan states that the civil administration was negligent, ignorant and corrupt, was removed, making her achievement in taking over an apparently robust, functional state that much more dramatic. The irony of this part of the story is that, had Blake succeeded in blowing up Star One ahead of the alien attack, he would only have ensured that Servalan became President, suggesting that the use of violence and terrorism never produces its intended results.

At the end of the story, we see its other major irony: that Travis, who has spent most of his life defending the Federation, is now on the verge of destroying it, while Blake, who has been working to bring it down, now finds himself cast in the role of its defender. Blake's final line, 'Avon, for what it is worth, I have always trusted you, from the very beginning,' is ambiguous. Is he telling the truth? Is he lying for psychological reasons? Or has he come to trust Avon, and thus is speaking retroactively? Avon's motivations are enigmatic – emphasised by Paul Darrow's use of an acting technique, employed most notably by Stan Laurel, of keeping his face totally blank, allowing viewers to read any emotion they like into his appearance. What is definite is that this line marks the handing-over of power from Blake to Avon, and with it the reformatting of the series. Avon has taken over from Blake, the Blake/Travis antagonism has ended, and Servalan is now President. The final scene of the episode, recalling Lord Thomas Babbington MacCauley's poem *Horatio at the Bridge*, is a wonderful cliffhanger; even if we know (as the production team did by this point) that a third season will follow, the presence of the alien invasion makes it very unclear as to what this future will hold.

SEASON C (1980)

SEASON C - CREDITS

Series Creator: Terry Nation
Script Editor: Chris Boucher
Producer: David Maloney

Title Music: Dudley Simpson

Cast:
Paul Darrow – Kerr Avon
Jan Chappell – Cally
Michael Keating – Vila Restal
Jacqueline Pearce – Servalan (C1 – 3, C5, C7, C8, C11 – C13)
Steven Pacey – Del Tarrant
Josette Simon – Dayna Mellanby
Peter Tuddenham (voice) – Zen/Orac

Stunt Co-ordinator:
Stuart Fell (C1, C3, C5, C6, C8, C11 – C13)
Max Faulkner (C2)
Tex Fuller (C10)

Production Assistant:
John Harris (C1, C6)
Edwina Craze (C2, C3, C8, C9)
Roselyn Parker (C4, C7)
Michael Owen Morris (C5)
Catherine Page (C10, C11)
Ann Faggetter (C12)
Pauline Smithson (C13)

Production Unit Manager:
Sheelagh Rees

Director's Assistant:
Christine Fawcett (C1, C5, C6, C12)
Shuna Young (C2, C7, C10, C11)
Hermione Stewart (C3, C4)
Eileen Staff (C8, C9)
Joy Sinclair (C13)

Assistant Floor Manager:
Anthony Root (C2 – C4, C8, C9, C13)
Riitta Lynn (C1, C5, C6, C10 – C12)
Jenny Osborn (C7)

Film Cameraman:
Peter Chapman
Anthony Mayne (C1)

Film Recordist:
Ian Sansam
Stan Nightingale (C9)

Film Editor:
Sheila S Tomlinson

Visual Effects Designers:
Steve Drewett
Jim Francis

Electronic Effects:
A J Mitchell

Graphic Designer:
Doug Burd

Technical Manager:
Peter Valentine (C2-C3 (both uncredited), C4, C5, C6 (uncredited),
C8 – C12)

Peter Granger (C1 (uncredited), C7)
Brendan Carr (C13)

Senior Cameraman:
Bob Baxter (C1 – C3 (uncredited), C4)
Dave White (C5 – C13)

Vision Mixer:
John Barclay (C1 (uncredited))
Nigel Finnis (C2 – C3 (both uncredited), C4, C8, C11)
Shirley Coward (C5, C13)
Paul del Bravo (C6, C7, C9, C10, C12)

Vision Supervisor:
Bryn Edwards

Principal Series Videotape Editors:
Sam Upton
Malcolm Banthorpe

Studio Lighting:
Brian Clemett

Studio Sound:
Malcolm Johnson (C1 – C7, C13)
Richard Partridge (C8 – C12)

Special Sound:
Elizabeth Parker (C1 – C13)

Costume Designer:
Dee Robson (C1 – C4, C6, C7)
Nicholas Rocker (C5, C8 – C13)

Make Up Artist:
Sheelagh J Wells (C1 – C9, C10 (uncredited), C11 – C13)

Incidental Music:
Dudley Simpson

Dayna's Song:
Tanith Lee (C9)

Designer:
Don Taylor (C1, C6)
Gerry Scott (C1 – C4, C6, C7)
Ken Ledsham (C5, C8 – C12)
Ray London (C7)
Paul Munting (C8)
Jan Spoczynski (C10, C11)
Jim Clay (C13)

SEASON C: INTRODUCTION

The shaping of the third season began on 24th November 1978, before the second season was even transmitted. Although the initial ideas for its direction were very much in line with what had gone before, the finished product was a strong departure from the mood and structure of the first two seasons.

The idea of recasting Blake after Gareth Thomas left was apparently considered, but when Sally Knyvette also expressed a wish to leave, it was decided that this would involve recasting too many major characters, and so new ones were introduced instead. Chris Boucher, in a press document, defended the decision to keep the title *Blake's 7*, despite the absence of Blake and the fact that there are only five crewmembers, by pointing out that there have never been exactly seven crewmembers on the ship (the 'seven,' he argued, originally referred to Blake's seven assets: his five followers, the *Liberator* and Zen) and that Blake is still out there somewhere in the universe, even if he is absent from the episodes themselves.

The original plan was to develop ongoing storylines like those of the first two seasons; Terry Nation was again given an option to write several scripts (he would ultimately write three) as well as to decide the story threads for the year. The first half of the season was initially planned to be taken up with the search for Blake (who would have gone missing during the intergalactic war, and become something of a legend), with the crew apparently finding his grave around the sixth episode. The other running storyline was to have been one revolving around a new character, the Captain (first mentioned on 19th December 1978). An older male character conceived as a Blake replacement, he was to have been a Federation captain who joined the crew after the war with the Andromedans. His main interest would have been to turn in the *Liberator* for the sake of his own profit, and – following the usual Nation trope – he would have been revealed as a traitor in the end. Nation, Boucher and Maloney all agreed that there should be a 'darker feel' to the season: an idea welcomed by the cast, who felt that it would make for more character development.

Ultimately, however, the problems encountered with co-ordinating scripts in the second season led the production team to make a conscious decision to shelve the idea of continuing storylines after the initial two-part season opener. 'We were trapped in a serial pattern,' recalls Maloney, 'and we needed to break free of that. A series format allowed us to juxtapose episodes and this made everything much easier.'

There were also some more specific problems with the two running plotlines that had been suggested. The searching-for-Blake story thread might, for instance, have wound up becoming like the search for Greg Preston in the third season of Nation's earlier creation *Survivors*, which built up the absent Preston to the detriment of other, equally interesting, characters. Furthermore, Paul Darrow was unhappy with the proposed searching-for-Blake storyline, pointing out that Avon had spent a long time trying to get the *Liberator* for himself, and thus was unlikely to want to seek out its previous owner.

David Maloney expressed concerns that it might be difficult to get an older, established actor to play the Captain; he suggested instead a younger man who would make for maximum contrast with Avon. Darrow had raised objections to Maloney's initial idea of having Avon become a conventionally moralistic hero, arguing that it was Avon's antihero qualities that made him popular. Consequently, the Captain became Tarrant, a much younger and more moralistic character. (Early scripts featuring a ruthless Tarrant were toned down as it was felt that Avon seemed too pleasant in comparison.) This effectively short-circuited the plan to have the Captain/Tarrant turn out to be a traitor.

With the idea of having continuing story threads dropped, continuity was not done away with entirely, but references to earlier stories were kept to a minimum and most third season episodes can be viewed as single, self-contained playlets.

Several actors were considered for the role of Tarrant, and a tape still exists showing David Maloney conducting auditions with Duncan Preston, Paul Seed and Steven Pacey, with Paul Darrow assisting. The role eventually went to Pacey, who tried for the part when he heard about it from Chris Boucher in the BBC bar.

The other new character introduced in this season, as a replacement for Jenna, was Dayna. Contenders for this role included Kirstie Pooley, Lindsey Duncan, Floella Benjamin (best knows as a children's TV presenter) and Marina Sirtis (who had previously gone up for the role of Cally, and was later to find fame as one of the regulars in *Star Trek: The Next Generation*.). The part eventually went to Josette Simon, who later in her career would be presented with the MBE for services to acting, but at the time was a student actress from the Central School of Speech and Drama and did not even yet have an Equity card – the union membership card without which, in the 1970s, it was virtually impossible to work as an actor. Maloney, having seen her interviews and screen tests with Paul Darrow, was convinced that Simon was worth taking on. Simon had not seen *Blake's 7* at all before accepting the part; Pacey had, but admitted to having been unimpressed. The changes in the series also meant that Servalan's role was made more substantial than in earlier seasons. 'I was very pleased with the decision,' says Jacqueline Pearce. 'Servalan was now a major part of the show. It was a very happy time for me.'

Reflecting developments in the wider world of British television, the third season saw some changes in the approach taken toward casting other roles in the series. For the first time, working-class and regional accents start to become a regular feature of the guest cast. We also see more non-White actors in important roles; and, more significantly, these roles are for characters whose ethnicity is not suggested by the script, whereas previously non-White actors were confined to the roles of sinister foreigners or oppressed natives. Notably, the fact that Dayna is Black is only ever referred to three times within the series; and the production team's only stipulation about her appearance when casting the role had been that she should not be a brunette, in order to provide maximum contrast with Cally. The casting of a Black British actress with a received pronunciation accent as Dayna was particularly inspired, as most Black actresses in Britain at the time had Caribbean or American accents, reinforcing the erroneous notion that Black and British identities are somehow mutually exclusive.

The change in format also made for some changes in approach to scripting. We begin to see stories that test the limits of the series format, ranging from conventional space-operas (e.g. "Volcano") to comedies (e.g. "City at the Edge of the World") to surrealist fantasies (e.g. "Sarcophagus"). However, there are also a number of stories that revisit the themes of earlier episodes in the new format, from experienced as well as new writers: besides "Aftermath" and "Terminal", both of which consciously reference key episodes from the earlier seasons, "Ultraworld" is clearly based on "Redemption", "City at the Edge of the World" on "Deliverance", "Children of Auron" on "Killer", and "Sarcophagus" on "Time Squad". Perhaps ironically, considering the lesser focus on continuity, romantic undercurrents between the regulars once again become a feature of the series, particularly with regard to Avon and Cally. However, largely as the production team were anxious to avoid any scenes that might be deemed unsuitable for family viewing, these never become the focus of the story.

Production development was much smoother than in the previous season. Two scripts did fall through at a very late stage – Robert Holmes's "Sweetly Dreaming ... Slowly Dying", for reasons still unclear, and an unnamed John Fletcher story involving 'space-age Hells' Angels' and a spaceship chase sequence, which was abandoned after shooting had actually begun on that recording block. However, the lack of ongoing links meant that finding replacements for these scripts was not difficult. One of the substitute stories, "Death-Watch", would in fact prove to be a highlight of the season.

The series was again afforded a bigger production budget, which allowed for more location work and the introduction of a new ship for Servalan. Jim Francis and Steve Drewett from the BBC's Visual Effects Department took over the series' visual effects work from Mat Irvine, Peter Pegrum and Andy Lazell at this point, making for subtle changes in the series' overall look. A new title sequence, featuring the *Liberator* and a squadron of pursuit ships, was designed by Doug Burd to replace Bob Blagden's original and reflect the new Blake-less set-up. Of the directors, the only one to return to the series was, again, the staff director, Vere Lorrimer. This year, *Blake's 7* was able to avoid the usual trade union strike action that crippled many studio productions of the time, as the team were engaged in location filming when it occurred. The episodes were still made on a very tight recording and post-production schedule, but by now any problems with this seem to have been ironed out.

The series was restored to its successful Monday night slot for this season, opposite *Coronation Street* on ITV. The soap proved to be less tough competition than *Charlie's Angels*, and viewing figures increased by about two million on average, most episodes hovering around the 9.0 million mark, with both "Children of Auron" and "Moloch" taking the highest figure, 10.4 million, and "City at the Edge of the World" taking the lowest, 8.8 million. This made for a decided improvement on previous seasons.

It seemed, however, that this would be the last season. During the recording of "The Harvest of Kairos", Jan Chappell expressed a wish to leave the series, and Maloney was also keen to move on to something new. (He ultimately revived, for a fourth and final season, *When the Boat Comes In,* the popular North East-set drama starring James Bolam, which had initially finished in December 1977.) A number of the cast and crew felt that the series that had gained them all such positive exposure should end while it was still on a high. After talks with Gareth Thomas, it was agreed to bring back Blake for a final episode, and to destroy the *Liberator* for an additional sense of poignant finality; Thomas's stage commitments meant that he was not available for studio recording, and so his scenes were shot on film in a specially constructed set in a village hall at Parton Hill.

The changes in the series, particularly those to do with casting and attitude to continuity, meant that *Blake's 7* was essentially reformatted in its third season, while still retaining the essential concept of earlier years.

C1: AFTERMATH

UK TRANSMISSION: Monday 7 January 1980: 7.15pm – 8.10pm
DURATION: 5:46
VIEWING FIGURE: 9.5m
CHART POSITION: 43
WRITER: Terry Nation
DIRECTOR: Vere Lorrimer

CREDITED CAST: Cy Grant (Hal Mellanby); Alan Lake (Chel); Sally Harrison (Lauren); Richard Franklin, Michael Melia (Troopers)

UNCREDITED CAST: Kevin White (Voice in Space); Alan Mechen, David Christian, Bobby Webber, Jason West, Brian Montana (Sarrans); Gareth Milne (Sarran/Stuntman)

SYNOPSIS: The battle against the aliens is won by the Federation forces, although Star One is destroyed in the process along with over eighty percent of the fleet. The *Liberator* is severely damaged, and the crew escape via its life capsules. Avon crashes on the planet Sarren, where he encounters now-President Servalan as well as a beautiful weapons designer named Dayna, her father, Hal Mellanby, and her stepsister Lauren. The Mellanbys are exiles from the Federation, and agree to give shelter both to Avon and to Servalan. After Avon rejects her offer of co-rulership, Servalan steals Orac and kills Hal Mellanby; Dayna and Avon go after her, discovering in the process that Lauren has been killed by the planet's natives. The natives also have Servalan captive; Avon and Dayna rescue her

209

and retrieve Orac. Before Dayna can kill Servalan, they are teleported back to the *Liberator*, where they discover that a Federation force has taken possession of the ship.

ANALYSIS: "Aftermath", the first story of the season, is one that recalls pivotal episodes from earlier in the series. We get references to "The Way Back" (Mellanby's story), "Orac" (a scientist and his child hiding out on a primitive planet) and "Cygnus Alpha" (primitives who crucify their enemies), as well as more obvious continuity references to "Star One". All these flag up the fact that the series is about to undergo a subtle reformatting.

This reformatting principally involves a change of character for Avon. Although he is still violent with women, selfish and corruptible (note that he shows little sympathy towards Dayna with regard to her bereavement, being more interested in obtaining Orac), for the first time he shows a real interest in the welfare of his fellow crewmembers other than Blake. This is presumably because of their shared experiences. He tells Zen to prioritise Vila's and Cally's safety above his own, and not to destroy the ship approaching the *Liberator*, despite the unspecified threat it poses, because either of them might be on board. He has not changed all that much, however. Although he tells Dayna not to kill the unconscious Sarran, his motivation is not simple altruism, as to kill him would be to deliberately make enemies of his family and friends. Also, it is notable that he does not put Orac in the bedroom with him, despite the fact that he must know that Servalan will try to steal Orac; as Mellanby is in the living room with Orac (and, quite likely, intending to sleep on the couch, if Avon has taken his bed), he would rather put Mellanby in the line of fire than himself. The character is being reformatted to fit his new role as leader; however, as with Gan and Blake in the previous season, this is not a gross distortion of his personality, merely a change in emphasis to one of its elements.

The scenes between Servalan and Avon also indicate a change. Although they have, up to this point, met only twice (and then fairly briefly), they seem quite familiar with each other. This flags up further reformatting: with the Blake-Travis and Travis-Servalan dynamics gone, the new driving force behind the action will be the tension between Avon and Servalan. Avon plays along with

Servalan, although he cannot be naïve enough to believe that she is truly offering him co-rulership of the galaxy; however, when they kiss, he grabs her by the throat and flings her to the floor, again turning violent towards a woman who tries to manipulate him and who offers him sex. If he had played along with her, ironically, she would have had no motivation to steal Orac, believing that she had Avon under her control. It is also worth noting that Servalan (who, when her ship was shot down, was in the area simply to gain a bit of kudos in the aftermath of the battle) treats Avon very differently than she treated Travis, Rai and Carnell, and does not switch off the flirtation after Avon rejects her. Is she taunting Avon? Or are there other motivations to her behaviour, which have not fully been revealed?

Dayna's relationship with Avon changes over the course of the episode. She kisses him at the beginning in a homage to *The Blue Lagoon*; her situation also recalls that of Miranda in *The Tempest*, who grows up alone with her father on a remote island (or, in Dayna's case, under the ocean, making Shakespeare's phrase 'full fathom five thy father lies' very appropriate), and who falls in love with the first outsider she sees. (There are planning notes still in existence that refer to this episode as being based on *The Tempest*.) However, after her father dies Avon seems to become, for a time, a father-substitute; the scene in which he tells her not to kill Servalan parallels the earlier scene in which Mellanby tells her not to kill or seriously injure the natives. Dayna has a violent streak (which Boucher describes as 'the ruthlessness of the very young'), enjoying taking pot-shots at the natives; but her own father's and stepsister's deaths affect her differently.

Dayna's attitude towards the natives seems to derive from that of her father. Hal Mellanby, like a colonial official, is patronising and slightly hypocritical towards the Sarrans; as Dayna remarks, what is the point in making guns if not to use them? Mellanby's belief that if they hurt the Sarrans when they approach the door, the Sarrans will learn, in a Pavlovian response, to associate the door with pain, classifies the natives as being on the level of animals. This plan does not work because, of course, the natives are not animals; Chal may understand little of physics and space travel, but he is a leader of men who keeps finding strangers landing in his territory and zapping his warriors with pain and/or death rays. Dayna's indignant exclamation that she is not a Sarran, saying 'Do I look like them?', flags up the racism inherent in colonialism. (Since Dayna is herself played by a Black British woman, a minority that has experienced such oppression, this further highlights the arbitrary nature of prejudice.) Lauren's presence is ambiguous; we never learn whether she was abandoned by her tribe, or deliberately kidnapped as a playmate for Dayna. The Sarrans kill her because she has been contaminated by contact with the oppressors, and acquiesced to their colonialist attitudes. There is also an irony in Mellanby's death. If the house were not filled with guns, Servalan would simply have bided her time, and tried to steal Orac by subterfuge. But finding the gun in Dayna's (and, presumably, Lauren's) bedroom has given her a means of arming herself; she steals Orac, presumably with the intention of hiding him and using this to bargain with Avon, but is surprised by Mellanby and kills him, meaning that she then has to flee with Orac.

The situation *vis-à-vis* Hal Mellanby is intriguing, recalling in a way aspects of Kurosawa's cinematic masterpiece *Rashomon*. Mellanby (played by Cy Grant, whose performance is hampered only by the – even then – rather dated Blaxploitation-film costume he wears) tells three stories over the course of "Aftermath", none of which contains the entire truth, but all of which, taken together, give enough information for us to tease out the real story. The first version that Mellanby gives is to try to ingratiate himself with Avon, telling him that he is a fugitive from the Federation with a price on his head; later he tells him that he was supplying weapons to resistance groups, but that the Federation caught him and destroyed his optic nerves in 'persuading [him] to talk'. (Notice that the phrase implies that he did, in fact, turn informer.) He does not explain how he got the image amplifier before he left – which he must have done, or else he would have been unable to fly the ship.

Dayna's conversation with Servalan provides another version. Servalan skilfully manipulates the innocent Dayna into giving her the information she desires; before beginning, she even remarks that she finds 'unsophisticated people,' by which she clearly means Dayna, 'obvious,' flagging up her intentions. Dayna's responses indicate that her father has told her that they live on Sarren because he wanted independence and the Federation would not allow him to travel. (Note that as Dayna doesn't answer Servalan's question about whom they supply weapons to, it's open to interpretation as to whether or not he is still trading arms.) But, as Servalan observes, hiding away for twenty years in a backwater seems something of an overreaction. Evidently Mellanby has given Dayna a very different version of the story than he did Avon.

Later, when Servalan confronts Mellanby, we get yet another version, which Servalan teases out of him through using ambiguous phrases, never directly accusing him of anything. Mellanby says that he led a revolt in which everyone bar him died, including his wife, his friends and their children. When Servalan asks if being the sole survivor makes him feel guilty, he says, tellingly: 'I had a chance of saving Dayna. I took it.' This narrative is ambiguous; his references to the deaths of the families of the rebels (as well as Servalan's revelation that the revolt took over three weeks to suppress) suggest the Federation rounding up the families of political dissidents rather than troopers opening fire on an uprising. The fact that Mellanby witnessed the killing and lived is significant: the only other person who we know has survived a massacre of this sort (twice, in fact) is Blake; however, on both occasions, the reason Blake survived was that the regime had a use for him.

Mellanby thus seems to be the anti-Blake, as it were. Piecing the story together, it appears that he was a gun-runner and rebel leader who was captured and tortured; he agreed to turn in the others in exchange for his life and that of his daughter, and was given an image amplifier and a chance to escape. When Servalan says, 'They branded you a coward. Your name was universally despised,' Mellanby replies: 'Might have been true. I've never been sure.' He tells Avon a story calculated to ingratiate, and Dayna another designed to keep her from asking too many awkward questions. We have seen before that Mellanby is a hypocrite; his omissions and lies confirm that he is not the kindly figure he seems to be. Avon appears to pick up on this, hence his lack of regret over Mellanby's death. Here, then, we have a Blake-like figure who proves to be a hypocrite, and dies, thereby symbolically allowing Avon to become the leader.

"Aftermath" therefore marks a turning point in the series, allowing Avon to take the leadership role and flagging up the fact that the social and political dynamics of the series are going to be quite different from here on in.

C2: POWERPLAY

UK TRANSMISSION: Monday 14 January 1980: 7.15pm – 8.10pm
DURATION: 50:34
VIEWING FIGURE: 9.4m
CHART POSITION: 37
WRITER: Terry Nation
DIRECTOR: David Maloney (uncredited)

CREDITED CAST: Michael Sheard (Klegg); Doyne Bird (Harmon); John Hollis (Lom); Michael Crane (Mall); Primi Townsend (Zee); Julia Vidler (Barr); Catherine Chase (Nurse); Helen Batch (Receptionist)

UNCREDITED CAST: Max Faulkner (Federation Guard/ Stuntman); Bobby James, Bruce Guest, Pat Gorman (Federation Guards); Sarah Tarr-Byrne, Judy Towne, Val Clover (Patients in Hospital Ship); Nikki Bunsford, Sheila West, Melinda Hall, Nicola Kimber, Michael Gordon Browne, Laurie Goode, Tony Christopher, Alan Humphreys, Perry Phillips, Christopher Holmes, Ian Ellis (Federation Survivors); Lara Shaw (Hitech Assistant)

SYNOPSIS: Avon and Dayna discover that a Federation force, led by Captain Del Tarrant and Section Leader Klegg, have taken over the *Liberator*. They suspect Avon and Dayna of being members of its crew; Avon dissembles, lying about his identity, and Tarrant knocks him out before Klegg can check his voice-print. Meanwhile, Cally encounters Servalan on a hospital ship, and Vila is rescued by two primitives; they are seemingly attacked, but their assailants turn out to be beautiful women who tell Vila that they are here to help him. On board the *Liberator*, a recovered Avon and Dayna hide in the inspection channels and try to take back the ship, aided by the fact that someone among the Federation crew is killing the others. Dayna is captured by Klegg, and Avon discovers that the traitor in the ranks is Tarrant. The two of them rescue Dayna from Klegg and kill him and his men. Vila and Cally, reunited, learn from Servalan that their 'rescuers' are in fact intending to kill them and use their organs in spare-part surgery; they are teleported up at the absolute last second. Avon instructs Zen to accept voice commands from Dayna and Tarrant.

ANALYSIS: "Powerplay" follows directly on from "Aftermath", and, like "Deliverance", contains three strong storylines running simultaneously. This episode completes the establishment of the new series format, and sets the stage for what is to come.

As with the previous story, there are echoes of earlier *Blake's 7* episodes. Avon recycles Sara's plan from "Mission to Destiny", firing off the life capsule to make it look as if he and Dayna have escaped; he also pretends to turn traitor in order to gain control of the situation, like Jenna in "Bounty". The relationship between Tarrant (whose name we last saw in "The Way Back") and Klegg is an echo of that between Leylan and Raiker from "Space Fall": an (apparently) antagonistic relationship between a strait-laced officer and a vile NCO, which is in fact a cover for something totally different. Tarrant's and Klegg's threats to report each other further recall similar tactics used by Leylan and Raiker. The *Liberator* being boarded but failing to respond to the boarding party's commands also recalls the end of "Space Fall". The description of Klegg's men as a 'death squad' with 'a record of brutality hard to match,' sounds like an echo of the abandoned Pip and Jane Baker story "Death Squad". Finally, WWII history again gets a reference: the idea of civilian as well as military ships being used against the Andromedans recalls the famous rescue of British troops at Dunkirk.

In production terms, however, there are notable differences between this episode and its antecedents: there has been a budget increase since last season and, as a result, there is an unusually large amount of location filming both here and in the previous story, and some very believable sets. The model work is also excellent; although the planet on which the hospital ship finds Servalan looks nothing like Sarren, the model shot is so good that we can forgive the slight discontinuity.

"Powerplay" was recorded before "Aftermath", in order to give the new regulars time to settle in to their roles before giving what would be their debut performances on transmission; David Maloney also persuaded Graeme McDonald, the new Head of Series, to allow him to direct the episode, so that Pacey and Simon would initially be guided by a person very familiar with the series.

Avon once again shows leadership qualities, although we may note that the first crew member he asks Zen about is Blake. He has also adopted one of Blake's less admirable traits in that he presents Dayna with a *fait-accompli*, not telling her what he plans, just asking her to do what he says. He is also still a pretty ruthless sort; he and Tarrant watch dispassionately as Dayna throttles Klegg. Dayna, for her part, seems to be settling in well, with Josette Simon giving a stellar performance. Several other characters are also established as ruthless, with Tarrant murdering his way through a squad of Federation soldiers. Servalan is particularly vicious, telling Vila and Cally the truth about their 'rescuers'' plans to kill them and harvest their organs as they lie paralysed.

This episode establishes Tarrant as a regular character. The image we get of him here is not a very nice one. The story he tells Avon is overly convoluted and sounds untrue in places: he claims that he was present for 'the first salvo' from the Andromedans, yet the nearest ships were at least an hour away at the end of "Star One", and, significantly, they were Federation. He then gives an account of his own ship being destroyed, and claims to have been picked up by a Federation ship from which, despite being in the heat of battle, he apparently acquired a Federation uniform, which just happened to be a captain's. Later, he admits to having trained as a Federation Space Captain, which would seem a bit of a coincidence. He then claims that this second ship was destroyed, and that he made his way by life capsule to the *Liberator*, where he met up with Klegg and his men. This all seems to involve a lot of lucky coincidences. In his initial story to Avon, he says: 'I've been on the Federation wanted list for quite a while. I had my own ship. I was running contraband, getting myself mixed up in other people's wars…. Naturally I heard something of what Blake and the rest of you were doing.' This sounds like the sort of ingratiating fabrication we have recently heard from Mellanby, painting a portrait of himself as a neutral mercenary with no love for the Federation and some sympathy for Blake (in an echo, perhaps, of his namesake Del Grant). Significantly, however, he never says which side he joined when mixed up in 'other people's wars,' or how he felt about Blake's activities. Also, although Klegg does not seem that pleasant, we have only Tarrant's word for it that he leads a 'death squad,' and indeed his men seem little different from the other Federation personnel we have encountered up till now. Finally, it is particularly interesting that Nation decided to make the new regular character the killer in the murder-mystery plot; for a viewer unaware that Tarrant is a) the murderer and b) going to join the crew, the twist-upon-twist nature of the final minutes is nothing short of fascinating.

The main reason for this portrait of Tarrant as a decidedly shifty individual is that this script was written with the (ultimately abandoned) character of the Captain in mind, rather than the Tarrant who later became established. The fact that he gives a complicated story that has the ring of untruth (and that he shares the name of the Federation agent in "The Way Back") would have tied in with the planned later revelation that the Captain was a traitor who intended to turn over the *Liberator* for the bounty money. Even with this storyline having been abandoned, however, it is not inconceivable that Tarrant's association with the Federation is more recent than he claims, and that he is being evasive in order to ingratiate himself with Avon; the image we get is of a Federation captain who switches sides when he discovers, after the war with the Andromedans, that the Federation military may no longer hold good career prospects.

The Tarrant we see here, in a very strong performance from Steven Pacey, is visibly a sharp character. He realises who Avon is from the outset; and whenever Klegg starts to question Avon about his identity, he breaks in and changes the subject. He works out the ruse with the inspection channels instantly. It is also safe to assume that he is telling the truth when he says that he didn't believe the trick with the life capsule either. Naturally, tension emerges from the outset between him and Avon; he remarks that 'it was an even bet' as to whether his prisoner was Avon or Vila, in what seems like a deliberate swipe at Avon (who has just said that he considers himself more intelligent than Vila). It appears a little odd under the circumstances for Avon to allow this intelligent and shady character to have voice access to the ship at the end of the story; however, Tarrant did trust Avon in the final scheme to take the *Liberator* back from Klegg, and one has to start somewhere.

Vila's role, meanwhile, is re-defined as one consisting entirely of comic relief; any edge that the character might once have had is now gone. His situation with Barr and Zee, two beautiful girls who chase after men in order to send them to their deaths, is like a twisted version of the famous closing sequences to *The Benny Hill Show*, and is played up almost to the point of farce, with Vila thanking his 'rescuers' effusively while they are evasive about the 'contribution' he will make to their society. The conflict between the primitives and the hi-techs also recalls the 1970s concern over the simple versus the technological life. The primitives, in echoes of the contemporary Richard Briers and Felicity Kendall sitcom *The Good Life* and the self-sufficiency fashion trend, are not unaware of technology, but simply choose not to use it.

There is possibly a new continuity point established in the scene in which Vila uses his communicator bracelet to hail the *Liberator*, despite the fact that the ship is out of orbit and thus (as seen in numerous earlier episodes) ostensibly out of communicator range. In "Aftermath", Avon had to use Orac to contact Zen, and here, Cally, while on the hospital ship, is unable to reach the *Liberator* at all. Blake and Jenna are also currently incommunicado, their earlier communications having presumably been when they were within range of either the damaged *Liberator* or their life capsules. Unlike the rest of them, however, Vila is close to his life capsule when he uses his communicator; it is thus implied that the life capsule boosts the communicator's signal, allowing crew-members stranded a long way off to contact the ship.

Finally, although Blake and Jenna are no longer present, their lives do appear to be continuing off-screen. In "Aftermath", Jenna was said to be on a hospital ship, destination unknown; here she is reported to be aboard a neutral cargo carrier *en route* to Morphenniel. It is therefore likely, especially as her injuries are mentioned again here, that she was treated and transferred to the cargo ship. Blake, similarly, now has a definite location, being *en route* to Epheron.

"Powerplay" concludes the establishment of the new scenario for the third season; with the present situation in terms of the *Liberator* crew and Federation politics now firmly in place, the series can continue.

C3: VOLCANO

UK TRANSMISSION: Monday 21 January 1980: 7.15pm – 8.10pm
DURATION: 51:32
VIEWING FIGURE: 9.0m
CHART POSITION: 41
WRITER: Allan Prior
DIRECTOR: Desmond McCarthy

CREDITED CAST: Michael Gough (Hower); Malcolm Bullivant (Bershar); Ben Howard (Mori); Alan Bowerman (Battle Fleet Commander); Judy Matheson (Mutoid); Russell Denton (Milus)

UNCREDITED CAST: Guy Hassan (Robi – Mechanical Man); Graham Jarvis, Karen Burch, Barbie Denham, Eric Harrison, Keith Adam (Pyroans); David Theakston, Mark Uttley, Ian Bleasdale, Barry Summerford, Guy Standeven, Rodney Cardiff (Kommandos); Tim Hindle (Natin); Karen Cooper, Jean Havilland, Sue Barkshire (Mutoids)

SYNOPSIS: Tarrant and Dayna teleport down to the planet Obsidian in the hope of making an arrangement with its natives, the Pyroans, to use it as a base. The Pyroans' leader, Hower, refuses their offer, as Pyroan society is based on pacifism and they will not ally themselves with any warlike faction. Unknown to him, however, his son, Bershar, has made an arrangement with Servalan, who is interested in both the *Liberator* and the strategic possibilities of Obsidian; Bershar leads Tarrant and Dayna into a Federation ambush, and the Kommandos teleport up to the *Liberator*, which is simultaneously attacked by pursuit ships. Avon holds off the attackers and regains control of the *Liberator*, but two of the Kommandos teleport down to the planet with Cally and Orac to await recovery. Bershar is killed as a rogue element, Tarrant and Dayna rescue Cally and Orac, and Hower activates a thermonuclear device, destroying the planet before Servalan can launch an attack and take control.

ANALYSIS: "Volcano", despite one or two minor problems, is a very strong story, even though as originally devised it was to have featured Blake and Jenna rather than Tarrant and Dayna.

This episode fully shows us the reformatting of the Federation that has been hinted at in the previous two episodes. This is visibly no longer the galactic empire of earlier seasons – despite the fact that the series' budget increase has allowed for it to be given a more polished depiction (with a new starcruiser, redesigned mutoids and nice sets). Servalan's officers are scruffy and unshaven, not like the well-groomed young men we have seen before. Mori, who takes on Travis's role in the new organisation (and dies in a similar way, falling into the heart of the volcano), has a London accent, and the Battle Fleet Commander is South African (which, in the context of 1970s TV drama, suggests that he is a mercenary; note that the word 'Kommandos' is given an Afrikaans spelling in the script). Avon speaks of 'Servalan's people' rather than of 'the Federation.' Servalan is out on the front line herself, which would seem unusual for an autocratic ruler; her interest in the *Liberator* is strategic rather than to impress anyone or eliminate a threat. There is a strong implication that, in the time that has elapsed between the previous story and this one (which would appear to have been several months at least), the Federation has broken into warring factions, of which Servalan's group is only one, each laying claim to the Federation's heritage: Mori refers to a drawn-out 'Galactic War,' which cannot mean the events of "Star One"/"Aftermath", because that was an intergalactic conflict and was over within hours.

The new crew dynamic on the *Liberator* has also been established. Avon, while nominally the leader, continues to put his own life above those of the others; although he does not trust the situation on Obsidian, he allows Dayna and Tarrant to teleport down, effectively putting them in the firing line. He seems concerned when he asks after Cally's fate, but is more subtle than Blake in "Seek-Locate-Destroy", giving Tarrant the option to try to save both her and Orac (knowing that Tarrant will take the bait), rather than ordering the others to stage a rescue. He also says, tellingly, that if Tarrant and Dayna do not return within the hour, he will abandon all of them. Finally, Avon is now giving up on the idea of finding Blake, saying that they cannot spend the rest of their lives pursuing rumours of his presence.

Avon also explicitly does not trust Tarrant. Although Dayna has cause for going down to Obsidian (Hower is an old school friend of her father's), there is no reason why Tarrant should be the one to accompany her. The implication is that Avon has deliberately allowed the less cautious Tarrant to put himself into the line of fire. He also clearly views Tarrant as expendable when he manipulates him into going after Cally. Elsewhere, Vila plays upon Avon's concerns by flagging up the clumsy nature of Tarrant's backstory:

VILA: Oh, yes, Tarrant says he was a space captain, but then he says a lot of things, and you don't have to believe it all, do you?

AVON: I'd be more inclined to believe that he was a captain than that you could have been.

VILA: Well, never mind about me. But it's Tarrant you should be worried about.

Although the scene in which Avon sends Tarrant after Cally does suggest that he's giving him a means of proving himself, there is a clear implication that Avon is not convinced of Tarrant's trustworthiness.

Tarrant himself has now abandoned his convoluted narrative about being a mercenary. He again admits to having been a Federation captain; the only indication that this employment isn't recent comes when he says this was 'some time ago'; and, as Avon notes, that's a meaningless phrase. Hower remarks that Tarrant still speaks like a Federation captain.

Orac also shows his selfish side here; he needs people, but he doesn't particularly care which people, and he is willing to help out Mori as well as the *Liberator* crew.

Vila, finally, briefly regains his edge: as well as trying to play on Avon's concerns about Tarrant, he is really rather nasty with Cally. If Vila hadn't put the teleport bracelet on her, the Kommandos (who, in their haste, had not checked whether she was wearing one) would have teleported down to Obsidian, and she would have been left safely on the *Liberator*. Vila thus complies with them simply in order to avoid personal risk; he then goes and, effectively, gets drunk on scriptwriter Allan Prior's old favourite, adrenaline and soma.

At the end of the story, Avon speaks of the destruction of Obsidian in strategic terms, saying that no one can now use the planet; Cally speaks in almost fanatical terms, describing the people of Obsidian as victors, because they chose death over slavery to any group, whether themselves or the Federation; and Vila glumly observes that he would prefer slavery to death.

Tarrant's proposal that Hower provide recruits and a base for the crew is another common theme in Prior's writing for the series. This is no more credible here than in "Horizon", as there is no real need for either of these if the crew still have the *Liberator*. However, it is interesting that Tarrant offers the natives spoils in return, rather than (as Blake did in "Horizon") political freedom. One might also ask what exactly the *Liberator* crew need the base for, as the mention of 'spoils' suggests piracy rather than liberating the oppressed (and, if the Federation is no longer a political force, who would they fight?). As Servalan's discussion with the mutoid highlights, without Blake, the crew are little more than common criminals with no political interests.

Finally, we come to Obsidian. The planet's name (obsidian volcanic glass), and that of the society it houses (Pyroans = pyros = Greek for 'fire'), both recall the volcano that is its key feature. The Pyroans have a small-scale, leisure-based society – the only flaw in the depiction of which lies in the design of the robot seen in the indoor sequences, with its regrettably-placed lights blinking away at groin level. There are echoes of Fritz Lang's 1926 film *Metropolis*, both in the plotline of the son of a political leader fomenting rebellion behind his father's back, and in the theme of a society that has achieved leisure through a dreadful cost: in *Metropolis*, the oppression of workers, and here, the deliberate mental manipulation of the populace, as well as a thermonuclear device that the Pyroans are prepared to set off if they feel threatened by outsiders.

The theme of mental manipulation again recalls that of limiters from earlier in the series. Hower says: 'We have taught them peace from the cradle, and we have blocked, usually with a minute electric shock, every tendency towards an aggressive act. Plus, of course, daily psychological propaganda.' Even the leaders appear to undergo such conditioning; it is the robot, not Hower, that kills Bershar, and it does so without a direct command from Hower. (Hower's destruction of the planet is not murder, but a suicide to which the population has socially consented.) His son, however, overcame this conditioning. Hower welcomed this on the grounds that he felt he needed 'one man who could think aggressively like [his] enemies'; however, this turns out to have had too high a cost. The scenario of a society of people conditioned into pacifism coming under subjugation from a few elements who have escaped or thrown off psychological conditioning is one that Nation mentions in an early draft of "Time Squad", and that forms the basis for Damon Knight's seminal short story *In the Country of the Kind* (first published in 1956). Hower also never explains why the Pyroans are dying of the effects of radiation, raising the possibility that they live as the remnant of a world ravaged by some form of conflict, desperately trying – and, ultimately, failing – to build a peaceful society.

"Volcano" plays out themes from earlier in the series – war and social conditioning – in the new post-Federation scenario, thus reinforcing the new direction of the series.

C4: DAWN OF THE GODS

UK TRANSMISSION: Monday 28 January 1980: 7.15pm – 8.10pm
DURATION: 50:54
VIEWING FIGURE: 8.9m
CHART POSITION: 39
WRITER: James Follett
DIRECTOR: Desmond McCarthy

CREDITED CAST: Sam Dastor (The Caliph); Terry Scully (Groff); Marcus Powell (The Thaarn)

UNCREDITED CAST: Steve Ismay, Ridgewell Hawkes (Guards); Kevin O'Brien, Michael Leader, Bruce Guest, David Melbourne, Bob Hargreaves (Technicians); Rory O'Connor, Keith Norrish (Salvage Men); Jimmy Muir, Barry Summerford, Brian Massey (Monsters)

SYNOPSIS: The *Liberator* is drawn off course towards what seems to be a black hole, which Orac has not told the crew about as he wishes to study its unusual features. The ship goes through the black hole without any significant ill effects, winding up in an underground chamber. Cally, meanwhile, is contacted telepathically by the Thaarn, whom she recognises as an Auronar mythological figure. Leaving the ship, they meet a man calling himself the Caliph, who explains that they are on the artificial planet Crandor, and that the Thaarn wishes to extract the metal herculanium from the *Liberator*'s hull (as he has done with other spaceships) to further his plans to conquer the universe using a gravity generator. Tarrant and Avon are put to work solving

227

dynamic flux equations, Dayna and Vila are locked in a cell, and Cally is brought to the Thaarn. The *Liberator*'s defence mechanisms kill the crew sent to break it up; Cally, by a ruse, gets the Thaarn to switch off the energy isolators that prevent weapons from working, allowing Avon and Tarrant to kill their guards, and a fellow-captive named Groff to throw the gravity generator into reverse, causing Crandor to disintegrate. The crew escape to the *Liberator* and flee, coming back through the black hole into the normal universe.

ANALYSIS: "Dawn of the Gods", by well known radio scriptwriter and novelist James Follett, is one of the weaker stories of the season, although it must be said that it follows three very strong episodes, and perhaps seems, in comparison, worse than it actually is.

As with other writers new to the series, Follett (who wrote the script in a week) explicitly borrows from earlier stories, notably "Redemption" (Orac putting the crew in danger; the black hole is also in the Twelfth Sector, where Spaceworld was), "The Web" (a shrunken dwarf from Auronar mythology with a team of slave-workers) and "Shadow" (Cally being contacted by a malevolent presence; Space City is mentioned in the board game sequence). The *Liberator*'s defences from "Space Fall" make a brief return. Follett also draws on research he was doing at the time for his own forthcoming radio series, *Earthsearch*. (For instance, there is mention of the time-distortion effect of faster-than-light travel, which contradicts the way in which space travel is normally treated in *Blake's 7*.) Erich von Däniken's *Chariots of the Gods* is referenced in the implication that the Auronar 'gods' are in fact space aliens; at one point the Thaarn is explicitly said to have a chariot. The Thaarn's ambitions are rather James-Bond-villainesque, and the machine used to round up slaves recalls the 'Dragon' vehicle that appears in *Dr No*, complete with lights for eyes and painted-on teeth. (Vila is afraid of it, which, the dialogue in the story implies, means that he has a primitive and superstitious mind.) Finally, the earliest available draft of the script not only refers to Tarrant as 'Captain,' but features Jenna (whose role was later taken over by Dayna).

"Dawn of the Gods" also contains a lot of backstory on the Auronar. This tends to be in line with the version given in the later story "Children of Auron", which had been written by this point; for the first time, Cally admits that not all Auronar (called 'Aurons' here) are telepathic. An exchange between Cally and Tarrant about what Cally may have done to offend the Auronar before she left is consistent with her previous backstory about not wanting to return because she'd failed, though it does add to it somewhat. The Auron myth we hear is a cross between the Biblical Garden of Eden and the Norse legend about Loki killing his fellow-deity Baldur, although the idea of it being written in the 'Book of Auron' is a little naff. It is also never explained *why* the *Liberator* is flying to Auron, as the crew have no reason to go there at this point.

Avon and Tarrant are now in an open rivalry for control of the ship. Tarrant has a thrust at Avon's professional pride – 'Just because you don't know how to build a high-energy traction beam doesn't mean that no-one else knows how to build one' – which Avon counters by suggesting that Tarrant is stupid enough to use brute force against something he doesn't understand. Avon then says, 'Once we understand how the force is operating we may be some way toward defeating it,' looking right at Tarrant as he does so, suggesting that he either means, 'I understand you,' or, 'You will never understand me.' Avon again is self-interested – he actually says 'I look upon self-interest as my great strength,' at one point – putting on a space suit in order to save himself when the *Liberator* enters the black hole (the fact that Orac is not going to do anything to put himself in danger having suggested to him that the situation must be survivable). He also orders the crew to leave without looking for Cally. By contrast, Tarrant is becoming the more moral character; here, he is the one who insists on going to Zarana to tell Groff's family what happened to him, and he castigates Avon when he selfishly tries to get into the only spacesuit on the flight deck.

Orac gets something interesting to do for a change. Again he is following his own concerns rather than the crew's; he wants to study the black hole, but knows that they will not agree to his request to look at it, so he prevaricates. He can also be petty and sulky, as when he is irritated that the crew interrupt the game they are playing to deal with a drift problem. Ultimately, however, his presence helps save the crew, as it occupies the Caliph and his guards; the scenes in which Tarrant and Dayna tell the truth about Orac while not telling the Caliph where or what he actually is, implying that he is a bald dwarf (rather ironic, when one considers the Thaarn's physical form), is rather good.

Cally's scenes with the Thaarn recall Samson and Delilah, or, perhaps, an inverse of the Greek myth in which Zeus's lover Semele persuades him to reveal himself to her in all his glory, despite Zeus's pleading that the sight would kill her. Cally does not kill the Thaarn, in the end, or tell the others what he looks like, despite the fact that her mythology depicts him as a god of evil, and that he is not really a very nice person in and of himself. This act of mercy is probably motivated by the fact that she pities him; he is the first telepath she has encountered since "Shadow", and he, like her, is alone. This way, also, she preserves the myth, allowing him to be an omnipotent god rather than a pathetic old man.

The script has some rather good lines. A good example is Avon's: 'So, the Lord Thaarn escaped. I suspect we have made another enemy. A pity.' Another is the sequence where Tarrant explains why a finger is better suited for pushing buttons than holding writing implements. Unfortunately, however, the episode also contains lines like: 'The universe… and the great universal force that controls the universe.' There are some blatant info-dumps as well, such as Orac's and Avon's discussion of black holes, to say nothing of Avon's and Tarrant's exchange about Newton's laws, which seems to come from a children's science programme, and Cally's appallingly contrived explanation of the Thaarn being a mythological figure.

There are other problems with the story. The relatively low level of budget allocated to this particular episode is fairly obvious, and the sequence where Cally lies on a sheepskin in front of a row of cinema screens looks dreadful, as does the representation of a black hole by a large black dot in the middle of a dense starscape. One might also ask why the Caliph is dressed like the Mad Hatter, or why Groff wears the clothes of a Victorian bookkeeper. There is no explanation for why Vila and Dayna are left in the cell rather than being put to work, and, although it is nice to see the crew playing a board game (called 'Cosmos' in the script), it is a shame that it has to be a blatant analogue of Monopoly. The story's title also seems rather meaningless, referencing the Norse myth of the Twilight of the Gods but bearing no further relation to it. That having been said, Follett avoids potential consistency problems by not bothering to explain the physics of Crandor, and it is rather nice to have a character (Groff) with a Dutch accent, as well as a visible alien among the slave-workers.

In summary, then, "Dawn of the Gods" is far from the best *Blake's 7* story, but it is also, despite its problems, not the worst.

C5: THE HARVEST OF KAIROS

UK TRANSMISSION: Monday 4 February 1980: 7.15pm – 8.10pm
DURATION: 51:27
VIEWING FIGURE: 9.4m
CHART POSITION: 31
WRITER: Ben Steed
DIRECTOR: Gerald Blake

CREDITED CAST: Andrew Burt (Jarvik); Frank Gatliff (Dastor); Anthony Gardner (Shad); Sam Davies (Carlon); Charles Jamieson (Guard)

UNCREDITED CAST: Jean Havilland, Sue Berkshire (Mutoids); Haywel David (Voice of Interceptor Captain and Leader Two); Christopher Douglas (Voice of Leaders One and Three); Reg Turner, Pat Gorman, Peter Caton, Richard Sheekey (Guards); Stuart Fell (Labourer/Stuntman); Tony O'Leary, Ian Sheridan, Alf Mangan, Michael Bryden, Salo Gardner, Malcolm Ross, Michael Joseph, Les Shannon, James Haswell, John Cannon, Peter Dukes, Tom Gandl (Kairos Guards and Labourers); Mike Kelt (Insect)

SYNOPSIS: Tarrant hatches a plan to steal the annual harvest of Kairopan, a valuable mineral found on the planet Kairos; Avon, however, has become fascinated by a specimen of Sopron rock and takes little interest in the scheme. Meanwhile, Servalan finds her authority challenged by Jarvik, a former Federation Captain turned construction worker, who claims he can take the *Liberator* with three pursuit ships. He succeeds in doing this by concealing guards in the crates that supposedly hold the Kairopan harvest. Avon agrees to hand the *Liberator* over in exchange for the crew being teleported down to the nearest Earth-like planet; Servalan, however, teleports them down to Kairos, which possesses unknown dangers all year except for the week of the harvest, and the crew find themselves under attack from the native fauna. Servalan asks Jarvik to go down to Kairos and retrieve the crew's teleport bracelets; he does, but Dayna fights him and he is forced to teleport up to the *Liberator* with her. Meanwhile Avon wires an analogue of Sopron into the systems of a landing module that the crew have found. Sopron, it transpires, is a life-form that defends itself by making other creatures think that it is something analogous to, but slightly more powerful than, themselves; when the *Liberator* is confronted with the module, Zen is convinced that it is a larger and better-armed ship and counsels surrender. Servalan abandons the *Liberator*, and Jarvik is accidentally killed by one of her guards.

ANALYSIS: "The Harvest of Kairos" is a very strange story, almost not like *Blake's 7* at all. Most of this seems to be down to the fact that Ben Steed – a prolific short story and TV writer – was unfamiliar with the series, but there are other problems that cannot be explained in this way.

To begin with, Tarrant has, for some unknown reason, become the crewmember that Servalan is most worried about, running rings around the Federation. This may be a remnant of the earlier concept of the Captain, but since so much effort has gone into establishing Avon as the one to watch out for in earlier episodes, it seems odd. Steed was under instruction from David Maloney to come up with a script focusing on Tarrant, but the story seems to take this to extremes. It is also peculiar that Servalan would care what a construction worker thinks about her leadership skills. (The pubs must be full of people convinced that they can run the Federation better than her, after all.) For that matter, it seems odd that Dastor (whose rank is never explained) cares enough about the criticisms to repeat them. It is also never stated why Kairopan is so valuable, which is at variance with the usual pattern for the series. Servalan (with the normally assured Jacqueline Pearce giving, this time, an over-the-top performance, at one point even flinging her arms wide and holding the pose for ten seconds) is unusually dim, bragging to Jarvik about her strategising ability just before her plan falls through altogether.

Jarvik, with his hypermasculinity complex and tendency to emphasise the word 'man' every time he says it, has given this episode an undeserved reputation for sexism. In fact, the story seems to be a very anti-sexist one; Jarvik's attitude may allow him to win in the short-term, but not in the long-term. For all his posturing about not wanting to be under Servalan's command, he goes down to Kairos for no reason other than that she tells him to; he then gets his backside thoroughly kicked by Dayna (and if Cally had joined in, he would have been beaten on short order). Although Jarvik is right about men being physically stronger than women, it is how one uses one's strength that matters; similarly, it is not whether one uses battle computers or not, but how one uses them, that wins the fight. Servalan uses her computers to predict what Tarrant will do, whereas Tarrant uses his to work out what she expects him to do, and does the opposite. Servalan's 'I should like you to do it again' is also significant, because that phrase takes the kiss on the flight deck (seemingly forced upon her by Jarvik) and places it firmly in the consensual sphere; nobody kisses Servalan unless she wants it. In the end, it is Jarvik's sense of chivalry that gets him shot, whereas Dayna keeps her cool and survives. After Jarvik's death, when Tarrant starts to pontificate about him, Avon cuts Tarrant off, saying, 'Spare us the eulogy, he was a Federation thug,' thus confirming the message that waxing romantic about masculinity and honour is self-delusion.

This anti-sexist message is also mirrored by Avon's and Tarrant's relationship in the story. In the end, it is not Tarrant's macho posturing that saves the day (indeed, it is what gets them caught in the first place) but Avon's experiments with the Sopron rock. Avon's perpetually blasé attitude undermines Tarrant's cheering about his own achievements. (He remarks that Tarrant has the fastest and strongest ship in the galaxy, implying that he cannot help but win under such conditions.) Avon flits in and out of the action casually, with the fight sequences barely impinging upon him; he outthinks Servalan by quickly adding a condition to the deal giving her control over the *Liberator* (although she trumps him in the end by putting the crew down on Kairos). The scene in which

Avon comes in and casually guns down the ambushing guards, remarking, 'They were an obvious possibility, Tarrant,' again establishes that he considers Tarrant his inferior.

The episode does have some rather good lines, as well as some of the better comedy moments in the series: the scene in which Avon putters away at testing the Sopron rock, apparently oblivious to the fact that the rest of the crew are preparing to seize the Kairopan transporter (casually remarking '…sorry,' as he accidentally causes a minor explosion) is hilarious, as is Jarvik's: 'Woman, you're beautiful.' The scene in which a guard scornfully tells the workers that they will have to stay on Kairos and die, and then finds the ship has taken off without him, is also richly ironic. There is an Irishman among the workers, and Shad is a real RAF type, with a seriously over-the-top accent. We also get some more character development: Tarrant, we learn, was a lieutenant a few years previously, confirming that he isn't very long out of the Federation. He is also the one suggesting that the crew engage in piracy. We learn that Cally's parents are dead, and that Tarrant assumes that she and Avon are having a relationship. Servalan here, as in "Powerplay", gives her full title as 'President and Supreme Commander of the Terran Federation,' which demonstrates that she has gained control of both the civil administration and the military. Finally, the Sopron rock is a great idea, particularly in the very psychological moment in which Cally looks into it and sees her parents – like her but, to her mind, still authority figures.

The production, however, has more unfortunate than brilliant aspects. While the webs on Kairos are good, Servalan commits a crime of fashion in her prom dress with a single white ruffle, and the scene in which she and Jarvik share a post-coital drink is ruined by the presence of curly novelty straws. Jarvik's unzipped shirt is a little too clichéd Seventies macho-man to be credible, and this is one of the camper episodes for guard costumes, with Shad and his men looking like something out of *Flash Gordon*. For some unfathomable reason the sets are the ones for Servalan's starcruiser, but the establishing shot is of Space Command Headquarters. A native giant insect on Kairos is not very good either; although it looks to have been an expensive prop, it inches painfully across the landscape, and it is blatantly obvious that there is only one of them. While the splash of saliva coming out of its mouth is effective, the 'munch, munch, munch' soundtrack dubbed over as it eats, isn't. The spacecraft, leaving aside the question of what it's doing there, is visibly an Apollo-programme lunar module, making it impossible that it could take off and land on a planet with Earth-normal gravity.

"The Harvest of Kairos" is a flawed story, but one with an interestingly subversive message about gender relations, and enough humour, intentional and unintentional, to keep the viewer interested.

C6: CITY AT THE EDGE OF THE WORLD

UK TRANSMISSION: Monday 11 February 1980: 7.15pm – 8.10pm
DURATION: 51:30
VIEWING FIGURE: 8.8m
CHART POSITION: 36
WRITER: Chris Boucher
DIRECTOR: Vere Lorrimer

CREDITED CAST: Carol Hawkins (Kerril); Colin Baker (Bayban); Valentine Dyall (Norl); John J Carney (Sherm)

UNCREDITED CAST: Derry Jordan, Dustin Lord (Vila's Guides); Chris Chivers, Ray Lavender, Tony O'Leary, Ted Lane (Guards in City); Judith Lund, Teresa Critchley (Norl's People at Stockade); Colin Lister, Leo Kane, Mark Uttley (Guards at Stockade); Valentine Dyall (Voice from the Past); Stuart Fell (Guard/Stuntman); Terence Creasey, Michael Brydon, Rebecca Semark, Patricia Clarke (Norl's People in City)

SYNOPSIS: Tarrant has done a deal with the seemingly primitive natives of the planet Keezarn, trading Vila's services as a thief for crystals needed for the *Liberator*'s weapons systems. When the crew receive the alleged box of crystals, however, it turns out to be empty and booby-trapped, and they set off in search of Vila. He, meanwhile, is taken to the instigator of the trick, Bayban the Butcher. Bayban wants Vila to open a door behind which, he believes, is all the wealth of the planet. Vila works out that the door is actually a force-field made to look like a door, and opens it. With one of Bayban's crew, a woman named Kerril, he investigates and discovers a matter-transmitter that takes the two of them to a spacecraft. There they learn that, three thousand years ago, the natives programmed the ship to look for a planet that they could colonise once they had exhausted the resources of this world; the ship has now landed. Vila discovers the crystals he needs on the planet and insists on returning; the people of Keezarn all travel to the new world, as does Kerril, who asks Vila to come with them, but he refuses. Bayban, who cannot believe that there is no treasure hidden behind the reconstituted door, destroys himself and the city in the process of trying to open it using a laser cannon.

ANALYSIS: "City at the Edge of the World" is a deliberately comedic episode, appropriately enough for one that showcases Vila; Boucher apparently wrote it in response to a comment from Michael Keating's daughter that she thought Vila was stupid. Although it is not fantastically complex or significant, it hangs together well and is really very funny.

The first scene of the story previously served as one of the two audition pieces for Tarrant (the other was his backstory speech in "Powerplay"), and, as such, highlights his character. Tarrant comes across here as an arrogant bully, browbeating Vila and allowing his belief that the natives are simple primitives to cloud his judgment. However, to his credit, he does offer to go down to Keezarn himself to make things right, and apologises to Vila at the end. This is very much in keeping with what we have seen thus far: Tarrant is an arrogant man who is more credulous than the rest of the crew, but possessed of a stronger moral sense than Avon.

The Avon-Tarrant rivalry is very much present in the scenes they have together. Tarrant tries to pull off a *fait accompli*, but here it goes wrong: he protests, 'I gave them my word,' and Avon responds, 'You didn't give them mine.' Avon remarks that Vila will trust him over Tarrant, even though Vila knows Avon to be amoral, because Vila knows what Avon thinks of him, and exactly how useful he is to Avon. Dayna, for her part, again shows the ruthlessness of youth, saying that Avon and Cally should have killed Bayban's guards rather than just knock them out. There is a reference to Blake, but the crew seem to have followed Avon's lead and just given up looking for him.

Bayban makes an excellent villain, played in a suitably over the top manner by Colin Baker. The rehearsal script says that 'although he looks very slightly ludicrous, it would be a reckless man who laughed at him.' He is proud of his position close to the top of the Federation's most wanted list, and resents Blake taking 'political shortcuts'; Tarrant describes Bayban as 'the type that gives crime a bad name.' Appropriately for a Vila-focused episode (and mirroring Vila's description of himself: 'A thief isn't what I am, it's who I am'), crime is here presented as a profession and source of pride.

Kerril, for her part, is a slightly problematic character. The warrior Kerril, with her personal hygiene problem and perpetual bickering relationship with her colleague Sherm, works very well, as does the conventionally-feminine Kerril, frightened of cobwebs and skeletons. The challenge is to reconcile the two figures in the same person, which would seem to be an exercise in contradiction; it is not a matter of the performance being at odds with the text, either, as her reaction to the skeletons is scripted. She and Vila also have the world's most chaste sex scene; they hug, then we suddenly cut to a shot zooming in on one of the *Liberator*'s more phallic protuberances, followed later by the sight of the pair of them lying on separate couches, with the postcoital overtones of their subsequent dialogue being the only evidence that they have done more than settle down for a nap. They don't even kiss. This seems to be down to a combination of script and direction; the scene as written is not particularly explicit, but it must be said that it could be played much more suggestively than it is.

The plot of the story is largely a riff on "Deliverance", with Norl taking the Meegat role and mystically predicting the arrival of a saviour to lead his people to another world. We have a hero with a local love-interest whom he disappoints in the end. We have a trap set to ensure that the hero performs. We have Vila more interested in weapons systems for the crew than in living idyllically on the unnamed planet. The idea of a civilised society 'reverting' to the primitive, furthermore, is a theme very much associated with Terry Nation (although it did feature in many other 1970s series; for instance *Quatermass*). In this case, however, the aggressive primitives are, in fact, the technologically-advanced pirate crew, and Norl's tribe are neither stupid nor naïve, shrewdly manipulating Bayban into giving them what they want. The sequence in which Vila appears to take on the authorial role – explaining that the door is an illusion, a combination of the psychological and the physical backing one another up, masking the weak part of the structure, or else making one think that it isn't what it seems to be, in an analogy of the real process of scriptwriting – and is, also, pure Boucher, echoing similar sequences in "Weapon" and, later, his *Doctor Who/Blake's 7* crossover novel *Corpse Marker* (which featured Carnell from "Weapon" as well as characters from his *Doctor Who* story "The Robots of Death").

The story does contain a few awkward conveniences. The normally self-renewing *Liberator* suddenly needs a vital component – crystals to power the main blasters – that it cannot replace by itself, which seems something of a design flaw. There follows a set of unsubtle coincidences, in that Bayban happens to carry one of the crystals as a lucky piece, and Vila then happens to find a whole lot of them on the new planet. It is also surprising that a three-thousand-year-old translator unit can identify Vila's and Kerril's language and speak it. The idea of genetically engineering a racial urge to go looking for a locksmith every thirty-five generations is a little contrived: the concept of 'racial memory' actually has more to do with symbolic archetypes, and what we have here rather resembles the case of salmon swimming to the spawning ground every seven years. These problems stem mostly from the change-over between formatting the series as one made up of story arcs and one made up of standalone episodes: in the latter situation, everything must be explained within a very short time-frame, increasing the risk that the scripting mechanism will show through.

The dialogue is, however, universally brilliant, with many clever lines: Vila's 'All right, you've talked me into it!' to the silent natives, and Bayban's 'Treat every hour as if it were your last. I'll be back in an hour, Vila,' are good examples. Vila's line 'For a little man, I'm a wonderful mover,' is a paraphrase of one used by the Morecambe and Wise comedy duo. There were one or two changes between the script and the transmitted version: for instance, Vila's line 'I don't have to take any rubbish about it from you' originally used the epithet 'crap.' A sequence in which Cally explains that she knocked out the guards with tranquilliser pads was also omitted, implying that the guards are simply physically stunned, and making it seem odd that she is confident that they will sleep through anything. Two different spellings of the planet's name are given in the script: 'Keezarn' and 'Kezaarn.'

The production has many good points: the location filming – done in Ripon, North Yorkshire – stands out, as does the City model, although the fact that the model has a night-time backdrop makes for an awkward jump from the night-set model to the broad-daylight location scene. The voice on the ship (also played by Dyall) is very good. However, the addition of a Gregorian-chant-like piece of music over the sequence in which the natives converge on the City, which is not in the rehearsal script, verges on cliché; and 'Vilaworld' looks more like 'Vila Asteroid' One is also left to question where Dayna has concealed the heat-seeking device. (The script has her taking it out of a pouch, but her costume does not feature a pouch of any sort, let alone one large enough to conceal something the size of a portable CD player.)

This story is not, as Boucher scripts go, particularly deep or clever, but it does have some very good concepts, and sparklingly witty dialogue.

C7: CHILDREN OF AURON

UK TRANSMISSION: Tuesday 19 February 1980: 7.20pm – 8.10pm
DURATION: 48:44
VIEWING FIGURE: 10.4m
CHART POSITION: 25
WRITER: Roger Parkes
DIRECTOR: Andrew Morgan

CREDITED CAST: Sarah Atkinson (Franton); Rio Fanning (Deral); Ric Young (Ginka); Ronald Leigh-Hunt (C A One); Beth Harris (C A Two); Jack McKenzie (Patar); Michael Troughton (Pilot Four-Zero)

UNCREDITED CAST: Jim Haswell, Robert Peters, David Webb, Tony Webb, Jenny Elsden, Jackie Elsden, Noel Flannigan, Chris Flannigan (Auron Technicians); Robert Peters, John Cannon, Harry Fielder (Federation Troopers); Jenny Elsden, Jackie Elsden, Karen Cooper, Jean Havilland (Mutoids); Noel Flannigan, Chris Flannigan (Orderlies); David Glen (Federation Medic); Johanna Briggs (Double for Cally/Zelda)

SYNOPSIS: The *Liberator* is en route to Earth when the crew receive a distress call from Cally's sibling Zelda on the planet Auron, which has been afflicted with a mysterious plague. This has been deliberately spread by Servalan, who pretends to offer help in exchange for access to the Auronar bio-replication plant, which she intends to use to produce a batch of clones of herself. When the crew turn up, she takes Avon, Cally and Tarrant prisoner and sends one of her officers, Deral, to the *Liberator*, where he is himself taken hostage by Dayna and Vila. Avon, Cally and Tarrant then escape with the help of Zelda and Franton, the head of the bio-replication programme; they hide in the bio-replication plant, knowing that Servalan will not destroy it while it holds her clones, and teleport the Auronar gene stock up to the *Liberator*. One of Servalan's officers, Ginka, tricks her into destroying the plant, killing the embryos; the crew take Franton and another survivor, Patar, to an uninhabited planet to build a new Auronar colony.

ANALYSIS: "Children of Auron" (which was scheduled a day late due to the BBC's coverage of the 1980 Winter Olympics) is something of a curate's egg. Although it has some redeeming points, the story itself does not hold together very well.

The episode cleverly paints the backdrop of a postwar galaxy riddled with peculiar phenomena, such as the ionic reefs floating through space and disrupting ships, rather like the electric gas-weapons in Philip George Chadwick's 1939 novel of future war, *The Death Guard*. The references to an 'Intergalactic War' with the aliens further differentiate it from the 'Galactic War' mentioned in Allan Prior's scripts. The Federation plotline ties up with these as well: Servalan's group (the model shots for which now match up with the sets again) still appear to be a small remnant and, although Servalan talks about 'building up the Federation,' there's no evidence that there is any huge system present. Again, Servalan wishes to capture the *Liberator* to increase her group's strength and gain an advantage, rather than as a prize or to impress her superiors. The Auronar (who are referred to here, as in "Dawn of the Gods", as 'Aurons') swallow her story about her ship being an 'ex-Federation' vessel, lending further credibility to this scenario. She also uses a kind of IMIPAK device (see "Weapon") on her officers (although it appears to be rather short-range), pressing a button and killing them instantaneously. This speaks volumes about her methods of ensuring her followers' support, as her crew seems to consist entirely of mutoids and officers under sentence of death, and makes her remarks about loyalty rather ironic.

Ginka is also particularly well-characterised: ambitious to the point of obsession, envious of Deral, and not too intelligent. There is, furthermore, no reason within the story for the character to be

Asian, which makes the casting of an Asian actor for the role rather refreshing. His belief that Deral was promoted over him because of Deral's connections seems to be Ginka's own rationalisation or, perhaps, inability to face the truth; the fact that his ambition overrides his common sense makes him a poorer risk as captain than Deral, and, as Servalan is the one who makes the final decisions about promotion, there is no reason for her to pass over an officer in favour of one with better connections.

We also get more of a backstory for Cally, which confirms that she was not telling the whole truth in "Time Squad". Here, she says that she opposed the Auronar isolationist policy, and went out to Saurian Major to join a group of freedom fighters, but the Auronar punished her for her defiance by exiling her. Her cryptic remark in the earlier story about having failed was thus not the real reason why she cannot return to her people, and Blake's rationalisation that she was feeling survivor guilt was nothing more than that – Blake's rationalisation. The Auronar cloning programme cannot have been active for more than a generation or two as Franton, who appears to be in her thirties and who was born when her father was developing the programme, is vulnerable to the disease, whereas the two older officers, who grew to adulthood before the instigation of the isolationist policy over thirty years ago, are not; bio-replication therefore must postdate the isolation of Auron. Telepathy is said to be a byproduct of the cloning programme, which contradicts the fact that in "The Web", the Auronar 'ancients' are said to have been capable of similar feats. To represent the cloning programme, the director has cast three sets of identical twins among the extras – the female set, Jenny and Jackie Elsden, can be seen in the background in the early scenes in Auron Control, and one of the male sets, David and Tony Webb (best known as regulars in the sitcom *Hi-De-Hi!*), can be briefly seen in the foreground. (Both sets can also be seen later, entering the therapy unit on Servalan's ship.) The other male set, Noel and Chris Flannigan, appear both as technicians and as medical orderlies, implying that there are many more of them. The Auronar, due to their lack of outside contact, do not recognise Servalan, demonstrating that even if you ignore political events, they have a tendency to catch up on you.

Tarrant and Avon have a further clash on moral grounds, with the former asking the latter if he rates a revenge mission over a mission of mercy (which he actually does appear to do). We also get some idea of post-Blake dynamics on the *Liberator*; although Avon is the nominal leader, the crew outvote Avon, and Tarrant says: 'As long as Cally is part of this crew, she has full call on your loyalty and support, no matter what the risks.' Avon and Cally appear to have a bit of a past, as she says: 'Why do you imagine I've never gone back? Affection for him?' This earns a reaction from Avon and an exchange of looks between Tarrant and Vila.

The episode is also one of the series' more violent and hard-hitting, with Servalan plotting to kill an entire people (or possibly species) in order to get the *Liberator* and a bunch of foetuses, and later killing two of her officers, while Ginka tricks her into destroying a placental-unit full of unborn babies. The *Liberator* crew fare no better morally, as Avon – with, significantly, Tarrant's approval – puts a bracelet on Deral and sends him back to certain death on Servalan's starcruiser. Even if Avon doesn't know that Deral has been cooperating with his captors, this is rough justice. The disease is also very graphically portrayed, and Servalan's treatment of the Auronar, luring them into her medical unit with the promise of a cure and then killing them outright, has echoes of the Holocaust. We also get another form of social control, this time through telepathic suppression of the opposition; the Auronar are no more democratic than anyone else. C A One and C A Two are blinded by idealism and do not comprehend Servalan's motivations. It is only when they are minutes away from being shot that they seem to realise that they are dealing with someone who does not think in their terms of reference.

Despite this, however, the episode suffers from a poor characterisation of Servalan, whose sudden interest in reproduction is utterly unprecedented. She has previously shown herself to be an astute politician, making her portrayal here as a megalomaniac, bent on producing a batch of clones of herself, something of a problem. She also appears not to know that Dayna is a permanent crewmember, which directly contradicts "The Harvest of Kairos"; it would make no sense for her to send Deral up to the *Liberator* if she knew that he would be ambushed straight away. The fact that this was the second script of the season to be commissioned (on 10th April 1979), even before "Powerplay", suggests that Parkes did not know that there would be a story between "Aftermath" and "Children of Auron" in which Servalan would encounter Dayna in her new role as a *Liberator* crewmember. (The "Rumours of Death" foreshadowing dialogue was a later addition by Chris Boucher.) Servalan wears black from this episode onwards; Jacqueline Pearce has said that this was to symbolise Servalan's feelings over her 'psychic miscarriage' at the end of the story, although if this is the case, it is peculiar that she is dressed in black before the event in question takes place.

Zelda is also something of a pointless character. She has little to do bar telepathically contact Cally, a plot function that could have easily been taken by a distress signal. She is played by Jan Chappell in an oddly insipid way. She takes off her teleport bracelet to save the embryos in the artificial placenta unit despite the fact that, as the sterile environment has been broken by the crew, they are all doomed anyway, and all she achieves is to kill herself. Finally, it is implied that Cally is not just a twin, but one of a batch of clones – Franton refers to a 'sibling group,' and Dayna facetiously says 'There are plenty more like her on Auron, apparently,' – which raises the question of why Cally is so concerned about that particular clone, as all her sibling group would be dying.

There are also some plot holes in the episode. Servalan says to Vila that if he destroys her ship, he will destroy the only cure for the plague, and thus any hope of his friends' survival. However, she must know that they – and particularly Avon – are not the sort to expose themselves to a disease unless they're sure they can cure it themselves. Vila, for his part, doesn't simply wait until she's back on her ship and blow it up; consequently, she is able to take pot-shots at his friends for several minutes until they reach the bio-replication plant. The episode's conclusion is also rather strange, leaving the viewer with the question of how Patar and Franton expect to raise five thousand children on a planet with no population or infrastructure – planting them in a field, perhaps?

The biggest problem with the story, however, lies in the disease plotline. The Auron medic describes the illness as a 'non-bacterial, non-viral... disease pathogen of alien origins.' This tallies with the intergalactic war plot, as a disease totally unlike any other would do a good job of eradicating humanity. The medic then goes on, however, to say that the older Auronar, who were alive before the isolationist policy came in, are less strongly affected by the disease because they have built up immunities. However, if the disease is alien, introduced very recently, and is neither a bacterium nor a virus, there is no way that they could have built up any sort of resistance to it.

"Children of Auron" has a few good ideas and bits of characterisation, but also contains fatal plot holes, and ends with a contrived belly-laugh totally at odds with the sombre tone of the episode.

C8: RUMOURS OF DEATH

UK TRANSMISSION: Monday 25 February 1980: 7.15pm – 8.10pm
DURATION: 50:58
VIEWING FIGURE: 9.0m
CHART POSITION: 33
WRITER: Chris Boucher
DIRECTOR: Fiona Cumming

CREDITED CAST: Lorna Heilbron (Sula); John Bryans (Shrinker); Donald Douglas (Grenlee); Peter Clay (Chesku); David Haig (Forres); David Gilles (Hob); Philip Bloomfield (Balon)

UNCREDITED CAST: Gareth Milne, Stuart Fell (Stuntmen / Rebels / Troopers); Tony de Cosy, Nigel Mclaughlin (Troopers); Reg Turner, Tony O'Leary, Ian Sheridan, Michael Leader, Peter Roy, Ray Knight, Robert Smythe, Ray Sumby, Terence Creasey, Pat Gorman (Toopers / Rebels)

SYNOPSIS: Avon allows himself to be captured and holds out under torture until he is assigned to Shrinker, the man he believes to have been responsible for the death of his lover Anna Grant. He captures Shrinker and interrogates him, learning first that Shrinker did not kill Anna, and secondly that Central Security's top agent, codenamed Bartolomew, was keeping him under close supervision, as his attempted bank fraud was believed to have been politically motivated; no-one knows who Bartolomew is, apart, possibly, from Servalan's chief advisor Chesku, and Servalan herself. Meanwhile, a revolt breaks out on

Earth under the direction of Chesku's wife, Sula, who kills her husband and takes Servalan prisoner. Avon and the crew teleport down and discover Servalan chained up in the wine cellar of her own residence. As Avon questions her, Sula comes down to the cellar. It transpires that Anna and Sula are one and the same, and furthermore that she is also Bartolomew; Avon kills her and frees Servalan. Servalan is rescued by Federation forces, and Avon returns unwillingly to the *Liberator*.

ANALYSIS: "Rumours of Death" is a disturbing, well-written story that marks a turning point for the characters of both Avon and Servalan.

Although she remains a shadowy figure within the story in terms of her strategies and motivations, 'Anna Grant' appears to have been Bartolomew's real name. While we know that the families of deserters and political criminals are rounded up by the administration (which would thus make Anna's survival seem an implausibly lucky escape), Anna could have survived her brother's defection by virtue of being already a Central Security agent; furthermore, the fact that Del Grant was a known opponent of the regime would give his sister the perfect cover to investigate Avon, as his bank fraud was originally suspected to have been politically motivated. Servalan never addresses her by name, which highlights the fact that 'Sula Chesku' is a false identity, and that her real identity was only ever used with one person present within the episode.

Anna, furthermore, fell in love with Avon, and let him go, leaving his capture to somebody else. Her dying words, 'I was only ever Anna Grant with you,' imply that she felt she could only ever actually be herself with Avon. We learn in "Countdown" that Avon left when he heard that she had been picked up by a patrol; she could have set a trap for him by telling him that she was alive, knowing he would come back for her, but instead she let him think she was dead, allowing him to run. To maintain the mystery, there are differences of hairstyle, appearance and demeanour between 'Anna' and 'Sula,' making it initially difficult to tell that they are in fact the same woman – a deliberate ploy on the part of the production team.

Servalan, for her part, knows Anna's identity. She cannot,

however, know that Bartolomew was involved in an investigation of Avon, or she would not say, 'Tell me why,' when Avon asks who Bartolomew is. At first she suspects Avon of working with 'Sula,' saying: 'I might have known you were behind all this'; however, it becomes clear that this is not the reason for his presence, and when Avon asks about 'Anna,' she realises that Avon does not know that Bartolomew and Anna are one and the same. Whether or not Anna is acting as a security agent in this story is, however, open to speculation; the men she recruits are from the wastelands, but that might be a case of Central Security ensuring that they have plausible deniability.

It seems likely that Avon has, on a subconscious level, suspected the truth about Anna all along; his real underlying motivation appears not to be revenge, but to find out whether or not she betrayed him. The flashback sequences of conversations between Avon and Anna concern trust and identity; before the first of these, when Shrinker asks Avon, 'Who is she?', Avon does not answer. These sequences also show that Avon's feelings for Anna have been complex from the beginning, 'Why do I never know what you're thinking, Avon?', she asks, and he replies that he could never say it: 'Especially not to you,'; but later, when he is expounding on the danger of trusting people and she asks if he trusts her, he says: 'I'm afraid I do.' This probably explains the violent behaviour that he has, throughout the series, exhibited towards women – particularly women who appear to show sexual interest in him and then betray him, as Anna, significantly, does here in the climactic scene. This behaviour has continued after his encounter with Del Grant.

Avon's dangerous state of mind is sharply revealed in a sequence cut from the final version of the story. This was to have come at the end of the first scene with the two Federation functionaries Forres and Grenlee. The original ending had Forres wondering aloud why thousands of men are willing to die for Servalan, and his superior replying:

GRENLEE: Every man needs something to believe in, Forres. There are no exceptions to that. It's a universal rule.

FORRES: If you say so, sir.

GRENLEE: I do say so. Just be grateful you joined the service and you don't have to worry about what to believe in. It's all laid out for you.

FORRES: Oh, I am grateful, sir.

GRENLEE: I mean it. Some men have to find their own faith.

FORRES: Tough.

GRENLEE: It can be, Section Leader. There's only one thing more dangerous than a man looking for something to believe in. And that's a man who thinks he's found something.

The scene would then have cut to one featuring Avon, clearly linking Avon to this hypothetical man who thinks he has found something to believe in, with dangerous consequences. The case of Forres, a man who believes in something without realising what it is, also parallels that of Avon, who is unaware of what is truly motivating him. For Avon, the best outcome would be to find that Anna died under interrogation, as Grant claimed; the worst thing would be for him to find her, as he does, alive and well on Earth, and working as a security agent.

Avon is very much a tough character in this story. When Servalan tells him to go to hell, he says: 'Probably.' He treats the dying Grenlee roughly, and later kills him by letting him drop onto the cellar floor. He also seems to manifest an unconscious death-wish, perhaps due to his conflicted feelings about Anna; he gets himself tortured simply in order to gain access to Shrinker, and, as Tarrant notes, takes a terrible risk in teleporting down to the cave to confront Shrinker while still in a state of exhaustion. At the end of the story, he takes off his teleport bracelet and frees Servalan, which, under the circumstances, is practically suicide.

Avon does not involve the crew in his activities; they join in at the end because they have decided collectively to do so, and are in fact going against Avon's stated wishes. Dayna's line, 'We're as surprised about it as you are,' recalls Avon's similar remark after rescuing Blake in "The Web" – implying that they shouldn't care about him, but do anyway. The fact that Avon trusts Tarrant to rescue him once he has found Shrinker suggests that the lack of faith he had in Tarrant earlier in the season has faded somewhat. In an early scene, Dayna, Vila and Tarrant behave appallingly to Shrinker, to the point where Cally tells them to stop it; Dayna appears to shrug this off, but Tarrant, who has been particularly savage towards him, protests: 'He's an animal.' Cally's riposte, 'Yes, and it's contagious,' appears to shame him, and he is quiet and subdued throughout the rest of this scene.

Cally seems to have moved on from the fanatical idealism she showed in "Time Squad", "Duel" and "Volcano", perhaps affected by the events of "Children of Auron"; Tarrant, for his part, is generally brash and aggressive, but not totally without compassion.

On Earth, Servalan's power is still insecure; note that her title has increased since "The Harvest of Kairos", to 'President of the Terran Federation, Ruler of the High Council, Lord of the Inner and Outer Worlds, High Admiral of the Galactic Fleets, Lord General of the Six Armies, and Defender of the Earth,' rather recalling a tinpot dictator or member of a ruling group whose function is purely symbolic, and highlighting the insecurity of her position. Her sphere of influence now consists of Earth and the Inner Planets (suggesting that at least one portion of her title is exaggerated, or perhaps laying claim to territory she does not yet possess). Not everything has changed, however; Forres and Grenlee (the latter of whom has a Canadian accent) form another case of two Federation functionaries who are really quite likeable types, doing their jobs and making the best of things. There has evidently been a rebellion on Earth not too long ago, perhaps as part of the upheavals following the Intergalactic War; it failed, as the instigators were more bent on revenge than on long-term plans. Shrinker's line about the revolutionaries 'kicking the corpses' recalls "The Web", where the Decimas's first act was to kill their puppet rulers rather than to go for the real power. It is also reflected in the conflict among the insurgents in the story; the men wish to kill Servalan, but Anna argues that to do so would be simply to kill a figurehead, as the Federation, even weakened as it is, is more than just Servalan, and so she is of more value to them alive than dead. Anna's rebellion, furthermore, with its 'people's council,' recalls the use of references to 'the people' to justify totalitarian oppression, as, for instance, in the People's Republic of China. Revolutionary groups also have a tendency to take over the private residences of the gentry for public use. The fact that Shrinker was taken on as a torturer by the rebels suggests that they are not much better than the regime they briefly replaced. Anna's rebellion does, however, present the only contrived part of the whole story, as it is something of a coincidence that Avon should teleport down just as the revolutionaries have secured the palace, again highlighting the difficulties of fitting such a complex narrative into a single episode.

The scene in which Avon asks if Servalan has 'murdered [her] way to the wall of an underground room' is particularly noteworthy. Servalan has been attacked, not on the field of battle, but at the heart of her power, in her own residence; we see her with her head bowed as the rebels break into the room, implying that she has in fact lost her nerve (although she briefly composes herself before they see her). She is in the state of despair of someone who has experienced a great personal blow, and expresses the hope that Avon will also experience this before he dies. Again we see Servalan's use of sexuality as a weapon in her scenes with Avon; the message appears to be that although she may be chained to a wall in a wine cellar, she is not without resources. The scene in which she rubs her gun sensually over Avon's shoulder and cheek is reminiscent of the way in which she used to flirt with Travis whenever she had the upper hand over him; and the way in which Darrow and Pearce interpret the sequence lends it strongly sadomasochistic overtones.

Finally, an explicit parallel is drawn between Avon and Servalan, at the walls of their respective underground rooms. Servalan's question to Avon as he holds Anna's corpse – 'Can you convince yourself that didn't happen?' – recalls Tarrant's remark that in order to set Servalan free, it would be necessary to convince her that the attack on her also 'didn't happen.' Both Avon and Servalan are strongly affected by their experiences, but the results of this will become clear only in future episodes.

C9: SARCOPHAGUS

UK TRANSMISSION: Monday 3 March 1980: 7.15pm – 8.10pm
DURATION: 51:46
VIEWING FIGURE: 9.9m
CHART POSITION: 22
WRITER: Tanith Lee
DIRECTOR: Fiona Cumming

CREDITED CAST: None

UNCREDITED CAST: Jan Chappell (First Apparition/Alien); Michael Keating (Second Apparition); Josette Simon (Third Apparition); Steven Pacey (Fourth Apparition); Paul Darrow (Fifth Apparition); Val Clover, Barbie Denham, Celestine Carroll (Mourners); Sandra Arabian, Karen Cooper, Martine Cherrell, Wendy Smith (Mourners/Corpse)

SYNOPSIS: The crew investigate an alien vessel that appears to be a tomb of some sort; they retrieve an artefact from it, and Cally secretly steals a ring from the corpse. However, only Cally is able to teleport directly back to the *Liberator*; she returns, and rescues Avon and Vila by holding onto their hands as she teleports. When the crew investigate the artefact, Cally falls into a coma, and something starts to drain the power from the ship and disables the computers. A strange being that resembles Cally manifests itself on the flight deck; it is the alien from the tomb, for whom death is only a temporary state, and it is drawing power and substance from Cally and the *Liberator* in order to live again. It offers to employ the crew as its servants. Avon, however, shows no fear of it, and, kissing it, removes the ring from its finger. The alien is destroyed, and both Cally and the ship returned to normal.

ANALYSIS: "Sarcophagus", by fantasy novelist Tanith Lee, is an unusual story for *Blake's 7*, but one that, consequently, shows that the series format can stretch to include things other than traditional space-opera. The Federation, for the first time in the series, is neither mentioned nor represented; and there are no guest actors apart from a few non-speaking artists in the opening scene. Despite this, the story fits within the themes and ongoing narratives of the series, with the writer drawing on "Duel", "Time Squad" and "Shadow", and clearly also having been made aware of the events of "Children of Auron" and "Rumours of Death" by Chris Boucher.

The story is very good from a production point of view: the lighting is great; the direction is stylish; and the opening scene, which could have looked silly (with the crew dressed in leotards and performing mime routines at a funeral), doesn't. The fantasy-sequence costumes are also not bad, although Steven Pacey does not look terribly good in a hooded leotard. The one problem is that the crew costumes for this story, with the exception of Cally's, are generally unflattering; Avon in particular is made to look rather stout.

Perhaps because this was Lee's first time writing for the series (although she had been a professed enthusiast of it for some time, praising in particular its character development), there are a couple of problems with the story. The crew's interest in an asteroid at the beginning of the episode seems odd, as they have all the wealth they want on board the ship, the *Liberator* has not developed a sudden deficiency as in "City at the Edge of the World", and they are a terrorist-cum-pirate organisation rather than an exploratory mission. There is also a massive and rather clunky info-dump at the end of the story where (as in "Shadow") the writer seems to feel obliged to explain what the episode was all about, which rather destroys the magic, turning the mystical into the mundane. Dayna suddenly manifests a musical ability we have never seen before, nor will do again. We also get yet another plural form for Auron people – simply 'the Auron.'

Otherwise, however, there is little to complain about. Cally's references to Auron, as scripted, do not necessarily have to refer to the destruction of its civilisation, but merely to her being an exile, as this story might have wound up running before "Children of Auron". However, the fact that the viewer knows Auron has been destroyed makes the scene that much stronger. We learn that Cally can now read minds 'sometimes,' but then, her powers do seem to have been developing over the course of the series, and we have seen hints of this in earlier episodes. Tarrant refers to Cally's ability to engage in telekinesis when assisted. The Tarrant/Avon rivalry resurfaces, along with another case of the crew outvoting their putative leader; Tarrant overrules Avon with regard to whether or not to investigate the alien ship, but Avon trumps him by assuming control of the situation, saying that he will go across to it with Vila and Cally. The crew (wrongly, as it transpires) blame Zen for the teleport malfunction, assuming it to be Zen's self-protective abilities kicking in as in "Time Squad". This is the first time this function has been mentioned since "Breakdown", although, to be fair, Zen has had little to do of late, due both to its duties being partially usurped by Orac and to *Blake's 7's* shift away from more computer-focused stories.

The ghost and her 'intelligent menials' are interesting in that they follow the Indo-European five-fold social classification system, which includes leaders (Cally/the ghost), warriors (Tarrant/the warrior), priests (Vila/the magician), producers (Dayna/the musician), and 'negative-function' people (Avon/Death). The equation of Avon with destruction, following the manifestation of his death-wish in "Rumours of Death", is particularly good, although it does have to be said that Dayna could equally be the warrior, and Tarrant, being young and handsome, the producer. The ghost, however, seems to be trying to force the crew into stereotypical moulds, to define them by one character trait only – Vila is The Funny One, Tarrant is The Macho One, Dayna is The Creative One – refusing to accept that people have other, even contradictory, sides to their personalities. This may in fact suggest why Dayna suddenly develops a musical talent; the ghost might need a musician and consider Dayna the most suitable candidate, magnifying a single, normally-unseen, aspect of her personality out of all proportion. The ghost also appears to assume that the crew will cooperate in their own servitude; Avon's reference to treating them like 'pets' is singularly apt. Little of this seems to come from Cally herself; although she has been a fanatic in the past, she has been less so in recent episodes, and we have never seen evidence of her forcing the crew into particular moulds. Her feelings for Avon, also, appear to override the ghost's will to live.

Finally, this story develops the relationship between Avon and Cally. It seems quite clear that Cally has feelings for Avon; the ghost says that Cally likes him, and it is Avon kissing the ghost that brings Cally out of it. Whether Avon reciprocates or not is more ambiguous; at the end of the story, when Tarrant says his name, Avon looks around, and Cally catches his eye. She smiles, but he does not and looks away. At the outset of the story, Avon comes into her room and urges her to stop dwelling on the past and to make regret, as he does, a smaller part of her life; but, although he saves her in defeating the ghost, he is also saving his own life and the rest of the crew's in doing so. After they return from the alien vessel, she confronts him and accuses him of going over to it with her because he was suspicious of her motivations, and he does not deny this. While he has shown feelings for Cally earlier, in "Project Avalon" (although she was unconscious at the time), and while in "Children of Auron" Cally jibes at him with the line 'Why do you imagine I've never gone back? Affection for him?', there are three possible interpretations of his behaviour in this episode. First, that he feels affection for her, but does not wish to show it, to the point where he is willing to act as if he is contemptuous of her; secondly, that he feels nothing for her; or thirdly, that he did feel something for her once, but no longer does. The viewer is left to make up his or her own mind as to which might be the correct reading.

Tanith Lee's story is one that explores and develops the crew's relationships, through using plot and theatrical devices unusual for the series. By placing the characters in a scenario in which they are forced by an outsider into two-dimensional roles, Lee is able to demonstrate how they are in fact more than simply collections of stereotypical attributes.

C10: ULTRAWORLD

UK TRANSMISSION: Monday 10 March 1980: 7.20pm – 8.10pm
DURATION: 48:59
VIEWING FIGURE: 9.2m
CHART POSITION: 28
WRITER: Trevor Hoyle
DIRECTOR: Vere Lorrimer

CREDITED CAST: Peter Richards, Stephen Jenn, Ian Barritt (Ultras); Ronald Govey (Relf)

UNCREDITED CAST: Tex Fuller (Stuntman / Menial); Jack Macguire, Tony O'Leary, Glen Hayes, Hugh Cecil, Norman Gay, Stephen Kane, Reg Woods, Ridgewell Hawkes, Charles Rayford (Menials)

SYNOPSIS: The *Liberator* is approaching a mysterious, apparently artificial, planet when Cally, for no discernable reason, teleports down to it. Avon, Dayna and Tarrant follow, and meet a trio of humanoids called the Ultra; the whole planet, Ultraworld, is a giant living computer dedicated to the acquisition of information about the universe. Tarrant and Dayna learn that the Ultra are copying Cally's memory and personal characteristics for inclusion in their database, and that her body will be 'absorbed' into the Core, a giant brain. This the Ultra do to all whom they encounter, apart from a few who, after their minds have been copied, are put to work as menials. Avon is subjected to the mind-copying process, and the Ultra also capture the *Liberator*, influencing Vila with the same wave emissions through which they influenced Cally. Orac destroys the Core, and thus Ultraworld, through feeding Vila's illogical brain-patterns into it; Dayna and Tarrant rescue the other two and the crew escape in the *Liberator*.

ANALYSIS: "Ultraworld" by Trevor Hoyle – a novelist and story writer in many genres, who had by this point written two *Blake's 7* novelisations based on nine episodes from the first season – is really little more than a retread of "Redemption" (also directed by Lorrimer) without the subtext, and "The Web" without the horror; with slight personnel changes, it could just as easily have been an episode of *Star Trek*.

This adventure has a bigger budget than its predecessors – the scene of the giant brain bursting was effective enough to be censored on its first Australian transmission – and the location filming is nice, although the glitter-ball used to represent the hypnotic influence of Ultraworld is not the most sophisticated of special effects. In plot terms, it shows influences from "Bounty" (the crew being lured down by a recording of Cally's voice) and "Star One" (the frozen racks of menials). Perhaps wisely, considering the confusion over the plural form of the name of its dominant species, the planet Auron is not referred to. The Federation gets a brief mention, as does the fact that Servalan is now consolidating her power and expanding it at a disturbing rate. The Ultra say that they have encountered 'millions' of species; although the only space-faring ones whom we have seen apart from humans are the Andromedans, (possibly) the Auronar and the two unnamed alien species in "Dawn of the Gods", it is a big universe.

The characterisation of the crew is, for the most part, in line with what we have seen before. As in "Dawn of the Gods", Avon is willing to abandon Cally if it looks like her rescue will be too much of a risk; Tarrant and Dayna overrule him, insisting on going down to look for her. It is also implied that Tarrant is the sort of person who will rush in with guns blazing rather than gather information about his foe and then act upon his knowledge. Vila, however, is very poorly depicted; where he has been shown in the past to be silly and comic, here he is frankly puerile. Twice he is asked to stay by the teleport, and twice he stays on the flight deck instead. The idea of recording oneself telling jokes is the sort of thing a nine-year-old would find amusing, rather than a grown man. The riddles themselves are also anachronistic – a prime example being: 'Where do space pilots leave their ships.... Parking meteors!' – and how Vila knows about tea, gherkins and tin-tacks (a phrase already old-fashioned in 1980) is incomprehensible, leading one to speculate that the word he is groping for in the limerick beginning 'There was a young man from...' is 'Nantucket.' One riddle – 'Which lock cannot be opened by a key? An airlock!' – makes no sense whatsoever. Of course, the ultimate effect of Vila's jokes on the brain is, apparently, to cause it to go gangrenous and then explode; at the end of the story, there is little to contradict Orac's implication that Vila is a total moron.

Avon's backstory appears to differ slightly from that given in "Space Fall", in that he is said here to have attempted to embezzle five hundred million credits, but in the earlier story the figure was given as five million. The actual reason for the discrepancy appears to be Trevor Hoyle conflating the earlier figure with Avon's boast, also in "Space Fall", that he could easily steal a hundred million credits, but the difference between the accounts does actually make sense in plot terms, due to two later pieces of information. First, the Ultra's description of Tarrant's past resembles the story which he tells Avon in "Powerplay" more closely than do the later accounts of his origins; and secondly, the Ultra state that they have identified Vila's personal characteristics from 'the female Cally's memory traces.' Therefore, their information on the crew is from Cally, and as such is not necessarily accurate. (Avon could easily have been bragging, and Tarrant is more likely to have told her the version of his history that makes him look good than otherwise.) Clearly the Ultra do not obtain their 'considerable information' on Earth from communications transmissions or computers, as otherwise they would know a lot more about sex than they do; the only sources they seem to have are the minds and ships of the people they encounter. As they appear to know next to nothing about sexual activity, this says little for Cally's love-life.

The story does contain some good lines, mostly from Avon. On the subject of learning from the Ultra, he says: 'We certainly have nothing to teach them, except how to remain ignorant.' On Tarrant's calculated risks: 'Calculated on what, your fingers?' And, when the

Ultra fail to understand Tarrant's sarcasm: 'Ignore him, that's what passes for wit on our ship'. There is also a clumsy line, though, when Tarrant examines Relf's memory tube, and says: 'Your thoughts, your memories are contained in this cylinder.' As this fact is strongly implied both in this scene and in the next one, it really doesn't need saying. Tarrant's and Dayna's 'sex scene' is also rather funny; there is a big bang, and Ultraworld moves for everyone. (As Trevor Hoyle used to write for *Men Only*, this scene may well be an inside joke.) The bit where Relf stops in front of Dayna and does not react to her presence at all is quite nicely creepy, and the ending is well-played, leading the viewer to think at first that damage to the computers during Tarrant's and Dayna's fight with the menials has caused the system to seize up, but later revealing that this is the action of Orac on the Core. It has to be said, though, that it is something of a lucky coincidence that Tarrant finds the right memory tubes at the end of the story; Cally could easily have woken up as Relf.

"Ultraworld" is not a bad adventure in and of itself, and has two good antecedents; however, it is less clever and intelligent than either of them, and its treatment of Vila is more than a little unflattering.

C11: MOLOCH

UK TRANSMISSION: Monday 17 March 1980: 7.15pm – 8.10pm
DURATION: 51:26
VIEWING FIGURE: 10.4m
CHART POSITION: 22
WRITER: Ben Steed
DIRECTOR: Vere Lorrimer

CREDITED CAST: Davyd Harries (Doran); John Hartley (Grose); Mark Sheridan (Lector); Deep Roy (Moloch); Debbi Blythe (Poola); Sabina Franklyn (Chesil)

UNCREDITED CAST: Stuart Fell (Stuntman/ Federation Guard); Peter Hannon, Keith Norrish, Tony de Cosy (Federation Guards); Nikki Dunsford (Servalan's Mutoid Aide); Mary Eveleigh (Gila, Servant Girl); Stephen Ismay, Keith Guest, Buddy Prince, Len Gilbey, John Clamp, Mort Jackson (Convicts/Troopers); Tommy Reilly (Harmonica-Playing Convict)

SYNOPSIS: The *Liberator* follows Servalan's starcruiser into an uncharted region of space near a penal colony, Kalkos. There, the crew encounter the planet Sardos, the stratosphere of which is comprised of two energy fields, which make the planet invisible and refract medium-pulse emissions, rendering normal teleportation impossible. Vila and Tarrant teleport across to a troop transport ship bringing a consignment of convicts from the penal colony to Sardos; Vila is discovered, but assumed to be a stowaway. Servalan finds the remnants of the Federation's Fifth

Legion on Sardos, led by the sadistic Section Leader Grose; they have discovered machines that, given a computer pattern, can replicate anything from weapons to food, although copies of living beings always come out dead. They plan to equip convicts with guns and ships, and use them as an army; they have copied Tarrant's brain-pattern with a view to programming his knowledge into the ships' computers and thus avoiding the need for training the convicts in space-flight techniques, and have lured Servalan there in order to gain possession of her ship. They take Servalan captive and give her to the convicts; with the aid of Vila, however, she escapes, leaving Vila alone to find Tarrant. Avon and Dayna teleport down to the planet using an omicron-pulse-based technique; together with Vila, Tarrant and one of the convicts they kill Grose and some of his men, and discover that at the heart of the master computer is a wizened, one-eyed creature named Moloch, which was accidentally brought into being by the Fifth Legion based on a computer projection of the future evolution of the natives. Moloch steals a teleport bracelet and, imitating Tarrant's voice, instructs Cally to bring him up to the *Liberator*, but dies due to his mistaken assumption that the teleport will recognise his life-support system as an integral part of himself.

ANALYSIS: "Moloch", which was written as a possible replacement for Robert Holmes's abandoned story "Sweetly Dreaming … Slowly Dying", is very much a black comedy: it has some funny scenes, but the elements of rape, torture and murder mean that it is hardly what one would call light amusement.

Once again, it is worth considering whether or not this story could be deemed sexist. Certainly it is much more brutal than Steed's earlier contribution to the series, featuring as it does allusions to the casual gang-raping of native women, as well as the misogynous character Doran. Vila also gets a quite nasty and insensitive line when he remarks that the presence of a gang of murderous criminals on Sardos might do the natives 'a bit of good.' Poola's and Chesil's dialogue is singularly appalling, and Dayna is unusually thick, wondering why she can't see the T.16 troop carrier on a recorded image of the astrodome. However, Moloch, Lector, Grose and the faintly psychopathic Doran are not in the slightest bit sympathetic, which means that misogyny is shown to be an attribute of criminals and unpleasant characters rather than an admirable or normal trait. Servalan is also excellently characterised, with Pearce's body language and range of facial expressions speaking volumes, particularly in the scenes in which she desperately tries to direct Vila and ultimately gives it up as a lost cause. She shows no sympathy for the native women nor distaste at the Fifth Legion's tactics, suggesting that these are primarily issues of power rather than of sexism. Ultimately, she takes charge of the situation, and the scene in which Vila comes across the trail of dead she has left behind is one of the best in the story.

Servalan's reconstituted Federation returns stronger than before, although still weak enough to require her to go chasing off into uncharted space after a missing legion. The legion in question has now become another remnant of the Federation, having broken off from it during the Intergalactic War. At the end of the episode, Servalan has very much won the day; she has returned with reinforcements to take the replication machines away from the few criminals still on the planet, meaning that she has not only triumphed over the Fifth Legion and the *Liberator* crew, but, with the ability instantly to manufacture weapons and ships, over any possible rival. As her official title is given as "President and Supreme Commander of the Terran Federation," this may suggest that "Moloch" was to come earlier in the series order.

Tarrant's relationship with Avon has also progressed. Tarrant is becoming even more arrogant, and Avon is undermining him at every possible opportunity. Tarrant insists on going down to the planet, but is forestalled when Avon casually wonders aloud what the energy fields will do to the teleport beam. (Pacey, in a nice bit of acting, freezes in the doorway.) Tarrant then suggests taking the ship into the atmosphere again, which Avon just as casually thwarts by asking Zen if they were monitored on their last pass through. Tarrant is also very bullying towards Vila, who rebuts by pointing out that he was issued a uniform and was going to become a starship captain, implying that there is no need for Tarrant to give himself airs.

Steed's script, which apparently required extensive rewriting, is – perhaps as a consequence – more in line with earlier *Blake's 7* stories than his previous one. The character Doran, a killer ('Went off in my hand' he says as he guns down two unarmed guards) who is sentenced to a penal planet and has a morbid obsession with women, is, curiously, very much in the mould of Nation's first-season depiction of Gan. He does not, however, have a limiter, suggesting that Gan was a harder (or perhaps more insane) case. He also bonds with one of the crew, in this case Vila (with whom Gan also had a friendly relationship), and dies. Doran sounds rather psychopathic in places, being utterly obsessed with Vila and apparently getting confused about their relationship. (By the time he meets Chesil, he's calling him 'my pal from Kalkos,' even though they never met there.) Although his scenes with Chesil are not as nasty as they would most likely be in reality with a man of this sort, there is enough violence in the dialogue to belie the toned-down performance.

There also appear to be elements of "Death Squad" in the subplot about training up criminals as soldiers. The most likely reason seems to be that the strongest influence on this story is "Hostage", in which Travis had secretly recruited a team of criminal psychopaths, and in which the torture of a woman and a *Liberator* crewmember also featured. The name "Moloch" is common to both, in this case referring not to the sacrifice of children, but to feeding living beings into a machine which then kills them. "Horizon" is also something of an influence on the concept of a distant, hidden planet with natives being brutally subjugated in order to gain control of a valuable resource. Moloch appears to foreshadow the Links of "Terminal"; however, there is no known explanation for this, apart, perhaps, from coincidence.

There are some weak aspects to the episode. The ending is very abrupt and slightly rushed, with all the guest stars conveniently dying in the last five minutes. Federation terminology seems to be an uncomfortable mix between military and naval, with 'legions' having 'flagships.' We encounter yet another uncharted region of space, and the reconfiguring of the teleport mechanism is a slight *deus-ex-machina*, but both are excusable within the context of the story. Moloch, finally, despite the fact that he is supposedly a highly evolved being who lives at the heart of a supercomputer, shows a disturbing lack of foresight, failing to consider the possibility that his life-support system might not be brought up with him when he teleports. Even if he *could* bring it up with him, one might ask how exactly he plans to take over the ship: staring at Cally until she bends to his will, perhaps?

The story's greatest strength lies in its sense of black comedy. Some of the better scenes include Tarrant being stuck behind a bulkhead, Servalan's abovementioned gun rampage, Grose's and Lecter's rather casual discussion of how all the officers above the rank of Section Leader met with mysterious accidents, and Avon's silently making the connection between the dead mouse and what might have happened had he instructed the machine to copy Tarrant. There are some very good lines, such as the following from Avon (which Darrow delivers at the speed of an express train): 'Well now, there is technology and there is technology. Anyone who can transmute mass and energy on a planetary scale is not going to upset himself too much over my little sidearm. Or a neutron blaster, come to that.' Another good example is the blunt exchange between Vila and Doran: 'Ahh, my problem was always women.' 'You like them?' 'No.' The 'Convicts' Freedom March,' which the prisoners sing *ad nauseum*, was written for the episode by Vere Lorrimer. Thomas Harris's novel *Red Dragon* was not published until 1981, so the resemblance of Lector's name to that of Harris's famous fictitious cannibal is, unfortunately, mere coincidence; the name 'Grose' (pronounced 'gross'), however, is clearly a character reference; and Colonel Astrid has a very feminine name. It is fairly unsurprising that a colony of three hundred people who refuse to breed with any outsiders would evolve into a one-eyed chinless hook-nosed dwarf whose ears stick out; the only question is why it would take them as long as two million years to reach this point.

"Moloch" is more in line with the series as a whole than Steed's earlier script; while it still retains the comedy elements of "The Harvest of Kairos", it is both better characterised and more vicious than the earlier story.

C12: DEATH-WATCH

UK TRANSMISSION: Monday 24 March 1980: 7.15pm – 8.10pm
DURATION: 51:02
VIEWING FIGURE: 8.9m
CHART POSITION: 29
WRITER: Chris Boucher
DIRECTOR: Gerald Blake

CREDITED CAST: Mark Elliott (Vinni); Stewart Bevan (Max); David Sibley (Commentator); Katherine Iddon (Karla)

UNCREDITED CAST: Stuart Fell (Stuntman/Gunman); Steven Pacey (Deeta Tarrant); Mark Elliott (Voice of Teal Control/Voice of Director); Stewart Bevan (Voice of Teal Star Captain); Jean Hastings (Female Voice on Teal Star); Philip Webb, Roy Seely (Arbiters); David Bartlett (Medical Orderly)

SYNOPSIS: Vila suggests that the crew take a break, and that they all go to watch the war between the planetary confederacies Teal and Vandor. According to the Teal-Vandor Convention, wars are settled by combat between champions, which is scrutinised by arbiters, but also experienced, vicariously, by observers through mental links with the champions. The crew learn that Tarrant's older brother Deeta is the First Champion of Teal, and that Servalan is one of the arbiters. Avon suspects that Servalan may try to arrange a violation of the Convention, so that an all-out war will take place between the systems and her forces can move in, ostensibly to restore order. Deeta is killed in the combat, but his opponent, Vinni, proves to be an android; before Servalan can request a medical examination of the victor, however, Tarrant claims a blood-feud against the android, and destroys it.

ANALYSIS: "Death-Watch", Chris Boucher's professed favourite of his own *Blake's 7* scripts, is, despite being a last-minute replacement for an abandoned John Fletcher story, very cleverly done, incorporating a skilful allegory of the greatest strengths and worst excesses of the contemporary media.

Production-wise, the episode is quite good, with some inspired direction from Gerald Blake, for instance in the gunfight scene, and in the shot of Avon seen through the centre of Orac. Although the re-use of the set for the *Teal Star* at the end seems a bit cheap (Chris Boucher's original script reads, deadpan: 'Since all deep-space liners are the same basic design, this gallery is identical to that of the 'Teal Star''), it is dramatically fitting that the story begins and ends in the same setting, with Pacey playing a different role in each scene. The only real production quibble one can raise is that

Avon's outfit features two huge shoulderpads, making him look like a matador. Although this story again features the device of an actor playing his/her own sibling, Pacey does a much better job than Chappell, and seems almost like a different person; Pacey has remarked on occasion that he found Deeta a much more interesting character to play than Del. Finally, this story features a huge coincidence, with the *Liberator* turning up to witness a fight that just happens to feature Tarrant's brother, leading one to ask why Boucher did not simply have Tarrant learn about the combat and urge the crew to go to support Deeta. However, if this were the case, we would not have had the build-up of suspense as the crew figure out what is going on; also, Tarrant would have known all about the Teal-Vandor Convention, the discs used by observers to establish a mental link with the champions and so forth, shattering any element of discovery.

The story also features a number of good lines. Vila in particular shines, saying: 'Are you sure you can't redesign [Orac] as something useful, like a drinks dispenser? Or an empty space. I think he'd look really good as an empty space'; and, 'For my next trick, I shall swallow my other foot.' (The scene in which Dayna rejects his offer of a drink was originally to have had her pouring it in his lap, making it even more plain that she is also refusing his romantic advances.) Deeta, after the diplomat Max has remarked on how professional killers make him nervous, comments: 'Have you ever thought you might be in the wrong business, Max?' Avon, however, has the best – and most appropriate – line in the story: 'I presume you have no tedious scruples about cheating and lying?' The scene at the end in which Max shakes Avon's hand and Avon looks at it as though Max has left some nasty substance on it is also very funny and totally unscripted, as is Tarrant and Avon simultaneously requesting teleport.

Boucher's fondness for Westerns comes to the fore in this episode; the script explicitly says that the weapons used in the combat should be either Magnums or Smith and Wesson .38s. The gunfighter sequence, complete with Deeta's not being able to shoot an enemy in the back, and his slow-motion death collapse, is very much indebted to classic Westerns, for instance those directed by Sam Peckinpah, Sergio Leone and George Stevens. The idea of a hired gun fighting on behalf of another organisation references such films as *The Magnificent Seven* and *Once Upon a Time in the West*. The name 'Vinni' also recalls the name 'Vinny,' common in Mafia and East-End-gangster films; the actor playing this character has a London accent and a swarthy complexion. We also get some shrewd politics in the premise of Servalan setting up a war and then invading on the pretext of restoring order.

This story has a rather large number of continuity references, although none of them is gratuitous, being motivated entirely by the plot. Dayna's father's death is used as justification for her to claim a blood-feud with Servalan, and Tarrant talks about Dayna 'fighting hairy primitives with a bow and arrow.' Avon refers to Servalan 'almost' paying a vast sum for Orac, and we again get Cally telepathically sending information to people, as in "Shadow", "Star One" and "Volcano". We learn some additional backstory on Tarrant, although this is limited: the last time Tarrant saw his brother was about seven or eight years ago, and Deeta has been on Teal for more than four years (as this is how long he's been First Champion).

We also get some idea of what has happened to Servalan since the sequence of her chained to the wall of the underground room in

"Rumours of Death". We have seen in earlier episodes (and will see in the season's finale) how it has affected Avon; Servalan, for her part, seems to be dealing with her trauma by redoubling her efforts to rebuild and expand the Federation. At the outset of "Rumours of Death", her empire consisted of Earth and the Inner Planets; now it extends as far as Teal and Vandor, and she is looking to include them as well. Her ore ships are now so numerous as to be regularly getting past the *Liberator*. Much as people who have been burgled invest in expensive security systems as a means of making themselves feel safer, so Servalan is constructing a secure empire around herself.

The episode also contains a kiss between Servalan and Avon, which is unscripted, but nevertheless says a good deal about their characters. As far as Avon is concerned, we have two possible interpretations for his actions. One is that, by employing her own techniques of sexual harassment against her, he is making her aware that he is wise to her tactics; the other is that he is suggesting that he could still be open to offers of future friendship, in order to deceive her as to his intentions. Either way, he is not expressing a wish for them to become lovers; he describes her twice as 'a sick friend,' and he is too shrewd not to be aware of the threat a relationship with her would pose. Servalan, for her part, seems to be using the idea of a relationship between them as a tactical manoeuvre to contain Avon; her triumphant smile at the end of the scene suggests that she interprets the kiss as a sign that she is succeeding (which does not rule out the fact that she may also have enjoyed it).

This scene also flags up the theme of the media and its artifice. In the original script, the line 'After all, it's only a minor violation' was spoken before Avon dematerialised; as it stands, it is spoken afterwards, with Jacqueline Pearce looking directly at the camera, in a breach of the fourth wall. This is also evidenced when Zen's main screen shows, as it so often does, a starscape, but then the voice-over reveals this to be an artificially created and maintained environmental chamber, reminding the viewer that all *Blake's 7* starscapes are equally fake. There is, in addition, the scene in which the Commentator has a snippy off-camera argument with a rather camp director, again exposing the mechanism behind the television programme. On a more humourous note, Boucher deliberately shows the *Liberator* crew watching a broadcast that begins with a starscape and the words 'Space, the final frontier,' and goes on to say '– as it was once called,' symbolically putting *Star Trek, Blake's 7*'s predecessor and in many ways its antithesis, in the past. This sly joke is a bit ironic, however, when one considers that the idea of wars being settled through an agreed competition run by computers and the loser having to give up an agreed penalty in the end is a direct reference to the *Star Trek* episode "A Taste of Armageddon"; the name 'Vandor' references the name of one of the planets in that story, 'Vendikar.'

We also see a slightly more bitter commentary on the media, focusing on the voyeurism it inspires. The experiencing of the combat by the viewers is explicitly linked to the idea of media as catharsis; as Tarrant puts it: 'Murder without guilt, death without loss.' The scene at the beginning, in which a seeming 'fan' approaches Deeta and gushes, 'You're taller than I expected,' is followed by one in which the same 'fan' tries to kill him, perhaps in a pointed reference to cases of media-obsession and stalking. Deeta's dying words to his brother are heard by millions of viewers, again in a condemnation of media voyeurism at times of crisis. Del Tarrant's refusal to shoot Vinni in the back, even though he knows he is an android and has previously stated that he has no scruples about playing fair, is simply a performance of honour for the benefit of any viewers watching, undermining his apparent scruples. As Dayna says: 'The machines are more sophisticated... but the principle isn't, and the people certainly aren't'; sophisticated technology does not change human nature.

"Death-Watch" is a more-than-usually clever episode for the third season, with some darker overtones leading into the pessimistic season finale.

C13: TERMINAL

UK TRANSMISSION: Monday 31 March 1980: 7.15pm – 8.10pm
DURATION: 54:00
VIEWING FIGURE: 10.0m
CHART POSITION: 26
WRITER: Terry Nation
DIRECTOR: Mary Ridge

CREDITED CAST: Gareth Thomas (Blake); Gillian McCutcheon (Kostos); Heather Wright (Reeval); Richard Clifford (Toron); David Healy (Sphere Voice)

UNCREDITED CAST: Stuart Fell, Gareth Milne (Stuntmen / Links); Deep Roy (Link); Nicholas Frankau, Tony Christopher, Peter Farmer (Guards)

SYNOPSIS: Avon has set the *Liberator* on a course that he will not reveal to the other crew-members, following a series of signals. On the way, the ship encounters a cloud of mysterious fluid particles, which Avon insists they fly straight through, despite the others' misgivings. The ship finally arrives at Terminal, an artificial planet built by a consortium of United Planets scientists four hundred and eleven years ago as a sort of laboratory to study the evolution of life; originally it was positioned near Mars, but it is now in Sector Six. Avon teleports down and orders the others not to follow, but Tarrant and Cally disobey him. Avon is guided to a hatch leading to an underground tunnel system; he seems to find Blake, who is badly injured and on a life-support system, but who promises to share a discovery he has made that will make them rich and invincible. Meanwhile, the *Liberator*, affected by the fluid particles, begins to decay. Avon is seemingly captured and brought to Servalan, who offers him Blake in exchange for the *Liberator*; Avon refuses, but when Tarrant and Cally are captured, they, knowing the situation on board the ship, agree. Servalan reveals that Avon's encounter with Blake was an illusion, and that Blake is dead. She teleports up to the *Liberator* with her followers, but the ship finally disintegrates and explodes; the *Liberator* crew, after witnessing this event, turn to finding a way off the planet.

ANALYSIS: "Terminal", originally to have been called "Finale", is one of the most postmodern and allegorical episodes of *Blake's 7*, strongly reminiscent of the 1960s Patrick McGoohan series *The Prisoner*.

The final story of the third season was, at the time, intended to be the last of the series; at the end of this episode, there is no reason for the audience to believe that Blake is *not* dead. Appropriately enough, it contains a number of references to other *Blake's 7* episodes, particularly those that were turning points in the series: "The Way Back" (drugs, hallucinations, social control, the triumph of totalitarianism); "The Web" (experiments with evolution); "Orac" and "Aftermath" (a civilised group living underground with primitives above, and hidden secrets); "Pressure Point" (a dangerous illusion; a *fait accompli* gone terribly wrong, with disastrous results); "Voice from the Past" (a leader acting under external control and opposing his crew); "Hostage" (an enemy desperate to get the *Liberator*); "Weapon" (a duplicate Blake); "Volcano" (nobody wins in a state of war); "Deliverance/Trial" (a planet with an allegorical meaning) and "Rumours of Death" (Avon seeking someone from his past). It is also worth noting that Vila undergoes a character shift back to the first season, and is not silly at any point in the story. This may be simply Nation reverting to his original perception of the character (although the camera script has Vila rigging the electronics of the Cosmos board game to allow him to win, but instead causes it to explode). Cally, for her part, refers to the Links, the primitive apelike creatures roaming the surface of

Terminal, as '*our* ancestors' (emphasis added), further suggesting that the Auronar have human origins.

"Terminal" also develops the Avon narrative to its most logical conclusion since the killing of Anna Grant. In "Rumours of Death", Avon sought out Anna to learn whether or not she really did betray him; now, with Anna dead, Blake has replaced her in Avon's behavioural patterns. If Blake is alive and has access to a wonderful new resource, or if Blake is dead, then he has not betrayed Avon; if Blake is helping the authorities to trap Avon, then he has. Like Anna, however, Blake proves to be an illusion. That Avon says, 'I always thought that his death and mine might be linked in some way,' immediately before, effectively, condemning himself and Blake to death through refusing to give Servalan the *Liberator*, is also significant; he has seen that Blake is compromised, being on life-support and a prisoner of Servalan's, and, by killing Blake along with himself, he would ensure that his idealised vision of Blake is preserved unsullied. Avon is again in denial about his own motives; when we first see him in this episode, he is covering his eyes with his hands. Later, he says: 'Sentiment breeds weakness; let it get a hold of you and you are dead'; however, it is sentiment that sends him after Blake, and sentiment that causes Dayna and Vila to say that they will follow him blindly. (Cally and Tarrant state other reasons.)

Avon's death-wish, first manifested during his quest for Anna, is strongly apparent here. He goes to great lengths to ensure that the crew do not follow him, urging them to leave if he fails to check in on the hour, programming Zen to fly to Califeron (a name quite likely derived from the place where Nation was shortly to settle, California) in twelve hours if he does not return, and finally ordering Vila to run rather than to sell Servalan the *Liberator*. Like Blake in "Trial", he is ensuring that, if he chooses, there is a convenient way for him not to return; although, unlike Blake, he forces the crew's hand, ensuring that the choice rests with him alone. Avon's (unscripted) smile at the end of the story serves three possible functions; the first is as a memorably dramatic end for the story, the second as a means of marking Avon as the focus of the episode, and the third as a means of implying that, for Avon, his image of Blake is untarnished by any hint of betrayal. This, however, means that, for Avon, Blake has now become an ideal rather than a reality, allowing him to deceive himself about the nature of the man.

There is also something odd about Servalan's role in the story. When we last saw her, she was President of a rapidly expanding Federation; here, she has a team of people who are not dressed as guards or mutoids (although this does not necessarily mean that they are not Federation; the script is ambiguous on this point), is in an old ship that has crashed, and has not sought rescue. Kostos addresses her as 'Servalan,' rather than 'Madam President.' Whereas the *Liberator* has been a low priority for her for several episodes, here it is her main goal. Although she has run secret projects in the past (for instance in "Orac" and "Weapon"), here she has been on the planet for some time and has left herself no way out bar the *Liberator*. The only indication that she might still have some form of power is her assertion that she has a team of scientists capable of duplicating the *Liberator* under her control, and we never discover whether this is a lie or not. It seems likely that either the Federation has erupted into civil war, and she is trying to take possession of the *Liberator* in the hope of using it to turn the tide in her favour, or she has actually been deposed, and is trying to obtain it in order to start rebuilding her forces, using a side project that has been kept on the back burner for some time.

In the vein of "Gambit" and "Death-Watch", also, this story is very postmodern, containing no fewer than three breaches of the fourth wall: first, Tarrant's and Avon's exchange: 'Not up to your usual standard.' 'Yes, well, I'm tired' (reminding the viewer that these quips are not just come up with on the spur of the moment, but are manufactured); secondly, Avon's line: 'I have also recorded a full explanation of everything I am doing.... The only thing missing is the end' (as for the viewer, at this point, viewing another recording); and thirdly, Kostos's: 'We must keep the continuity right.' These breaches point up the fact that the whole story is not a straightforward narrative, but is an allegory of something deeper.

The science of "Terminal" is manifestly unworkable by today's standards (to say nothing of those of 1980's). Even if one could create an artificial planet and generate life on its surface, it would take an impossible effort to control the conditions so carefully as to evolve a group of humans, let alone to project human evolution into the future with any degree of accuracy. However, it is worth noting that we have seen a number of things impossible by the standards of modern science that are commonplace in *Blake's 7*, such as faster-than-light travel and teleportation; the people who built the planet were, after all, capable of moving it from the solar orbit of Mars to Sector Six. The second, and more important, point to remember is that, as in "Trial" and "Deliverance", the science of the planet is less important than its role as a metaphor for other things.

The key to what Terminal is (the name means not simply an end, but also a destination) comes in Servalan's explanation of the experiment's conclusions. Humanity, it seems, will evolve not into beautiful Aryan beings (the Aryans we see are not native to the planet), but into hideous beasts. However noble our causes or our activities, evolution is thus, as postmodernists argue, not a forward progression; it will all come to nothing in the end. This is further symbolised in the scene in which the Links trounce the 'civilised' Aryans (who, like the Morlocks of H G Wells's *The Time Machine*, which this story also references, are vulnerable outside of the underground environment). Strong-jawed and blond, the people recall not only the Nazi ideal of human beauty, but also the sci-fi heroes of the 1950s and '60s, who symbolised an ideal of human manifest destiny in space. (Note that the voice of the automatic direction-finder is American, and the camera script describes the Aryans as wearing 'dashing space uniforms'). In the end, however, the Links are more suited to Nietzsche's ideal of the triumph of the strong over the weak; as the Nazis' 'utopia' was built upon bestial acts of extermination, so here the beast triumphs over the beautiful humans.

"Terminal" therefore reflects how, in this story, Avon's bestial, selfish impulses triumph over his better nature. In the final episode of *The Prisoner* (to which "Terminal" is strongly indebted), "Fall-Out", our everyman hero, Number Six, confronts his previously unseen nemesis, Number One, against a background of a recording that repeats the word 'I' in Six's own voice; when he pulls a black-and-white commedia mask off Number One, he sees, first, an ape mask, and then, under that, his own face; but the self that he sees appears to be crazed. All of this represents Six recognising his own egotistical, selfish side. In "Terminal", Avon may be pursuing Blake, but he is doing it selfishly, refusing to tell the crew what he is up to; there is also an appeal to his greed in the fact that the illusory Blake is said to have gained control of a mysterious but valuable resource. Blake himself started to make the same mistake, in "Pressure Point" and "Star One"; in both cases, however, he realised that it was not right to cause death in the pursuit of a selfish dream. Avon, on the other hand, does make this mistake, and pays the consequences, causing the destruction of the *Liberator* and the death of Zen.

Avon's misuse of the *Liberator* is also symbolic. The *Liberator*, by virtue of its name, symbolises the means of obtaining freedom; Avon, however, subverts the democratic process entirely in the pursuit of his selfish ends. He pulls a gun on Tarrant, and Cally, who is in the best position to know, says: 'He would have killed you.' Tarrant is, incidentally, the only one who acts heroically in this story, asking Avon what is going on rather than blindly following, and going against Avon's orders in the best interests of the crew. Avon destroys the *Liberator* by flying it through the particle cloud, against the objections of the others and of Zen; literally, Avon's actions corrupt the cause of freedom. When he goes down to Terminal, an ominous heartbeat-like sound is heard throughout, recalling Poe's *The Tell-Tale Heart*, and therefore symbolising the crime that Avon has committed. Servalan also wants the *Liberator*, not to use in pursuit of freedom, but for her own selfish ends; when she goes on board the ship, she sees, but refuses to acknowledge, the corruption around her. Instead, she goes to the flight deck and, in ordering maximum power, destroys it utterly. The misuse of freedom for selfish ends thus turns the highest ideals into the basest realities.

"Terminal" does, however, finish with a hint of a positive note. After witnessing the destruction of the *Liberator*, Tarrant turns away and suggests that they get on with finding a way off the planet. Even though life may all come to nothing, and causes may become corrupted, the only thing that one can do is carry on living, and make the best of the opportunities one has.

SEASON D (1981)

SEASON D – CREDITS

Series Creator: Terry Nation
Script Editor: Chris Boucher
Producer: Vere Lorrimer
Title Music: Dudley Simpson

Cast:
Paul Darrow – Kerr Avon
Jacqueline Pearce -Servalan (Sleer) (D3, D5, D7 – D12)
Michael Keating – Vila Restal
Steven Pacey – Del Tarrant
Josette Simon – Dayna Mellanby
Glynis Barber – Soolin
Peter Tuddenham (voice) – Orac/Slave

Stunt Co-Ordinator:
Stuart Fell (D1, D2)
Terry Forrestal (D3, D4, D7, D12)
Neil Dickson (D4)
Mike Potter (D10)

Production Manager:
Ralph Wilton (D1, D2, D5, D6)
Rosemary Crowson (D3, D4, D7)
Henry Foster (D8, D9, D13)
Jacinta Peel (D10, D11)
Christian McMillian (D12)

Production Associate:
Frank Pendlebury (D1 – D11, D12 (uncredited), D13)

Production Assistant:
Valerie Turner (D1, D2, D5, D6)
Joan Marine (D3, D4, D7)
Rena Butterwick (D3, D4)
Joan Doig (D4 (uncredited))
Christine Fawcett (D8, D9)
Julia Hanrahan (D8, D9)
Ian Willson (D10, D11)
Patricia O'Leary (D12)
Elizabeth Trubridge (D12)
Winifred Hopkins (D13)

Assistant Floor Manager:
Josephine Ward (D1, D2, D5, D6)
Christopher Moss (D3. D4, D7)
Kevin Mann (D8, D9, D12)
Nigel Taylor (D10, D11)
Laura Gilbert (D13)

Film Cameraman:
Fintan Sheehan (D1 – D10, D12, D13)

Film Recordist:
John Tellick (D1, D2 – D6)
Mike Savage (D3, D4)
Stuart Moser (D7 – D10)
Dick Manton (D12)
Dennis Panchen (D13)

Film Editor:
Sheila S Tomlinson

Video Tape Editor:
Sam Upton (D1 – D4, D6, D8, D11)
Malcolm Banthorpe (D5, D7, D9, D13)
Ian Williams (D10, D12)

Visual Effects Designers:
Jim Francis
Andy Lazell (D1 – D6)
Mike Kelt (D7 – D13)

Video Effects:
Robin Lobb

Graphic Designer:
Douglas Burd
Dick Bailey (D5 – D7, D9 – D13)
Iain Greenway (D8)

Properties Buyer:
Francis Smith

Technical Manager:
David Hare (D1)
Terry Brett (D2, D4, D5, D6, D8, D10 – D13)
Terry Wild (D3)
Jack Walsh (D7)
Bob Warman (D9)

Senior Cameraman:
Dave White

Vision Mixer:
Nigel Finnis (D1 – D5, D7 – D13)
Mary Kellehar (D6)

Studio Lighting:
Warwick Fielding (D1 – D6, D8 – D13)
Brian Clemett (D7)

Studio Sound:
Malcolm Johnson (D1 – D6)
Trevor Webster (D8, D10 – D13)
Richard Partridge (D7, D9)

Special Sound:
Elizabeth Parker

Costume Designer:
Nicholas Rocker

Make Up Artist:
Suzanne Jansen

Incidental Music:
Dudley Simpson

Designer:
Roger Cann (D1 – D7, D13)
Nigel Curzon (D3, D4)
Graham Lough (D5 – D7)
Eric Walmsley (D8, D9)
Ken Ledsham (D8 – D11)
Paul Allen (D12)

SEASON D: INTRODUCTION

The announcement over the final credits of "Terminal" that the series would be returning the following year took everyone in the cast and crew by surprise (apart from Steven Pacey, who had not realised that "Terminal" was meant to be the final episode). Paul Darrow thought that he had been written out without anyone telling him. Although the general feeling among the cast and crew had been that this would be a natural place to end the series – with Maloney and Chappell wanting to move on and Nation now in the USA and working on other projects – Bill Cotton, the Head of BBC Television, had liked "Terminal" so much that he rang up the Presentation Department and asked them to announce that the series would be returning.

This sudden development resulted in that the fourth season having a more hastily-produced feel than the others, due to the fact that it had to be pulled together very quickly. 'We had the go-ahead very late in the day,' confirms Boucher, 'so we were in a godawful rush to get enough scripts together, to select the directors, and then get the first film block rolling. After you've done that, you've got a bit more time to think, so that, I suspect, is why the second half of the season works better than the first; we simply had more time.' Although a revised version of 'General Notes and Baffle Gab Glossary' was produced, there was uncertainty at least up to the time of writing of the first draft of the third transmitted episode, "Traitor", as to what would be the names of the ship and the base that would feature, and as to how the teleport device would work. (The name of the planet on which the base was located was also initially rendered as 'Zenon' rather than, as would later be settled upon, 'Xenon'.) The notion of having another continuing storyline (involving Avon collecting together various scientists and items of equipment to mount a strong attack on the Federation) was considered but then abandoned, as it was felt that this would impose too rigid a running order on the episodes and make the rebels ultimately too powerful. Elements of it were, however, adapted for incorporation into individual episodes (with the advantage generally being lost at the end in order to maintain the status quo).

One idea mooted for the season conclusion was a story called "Attack", featuring Avon's group returning to Earth for a final conflict with the Administration; the notion of including the return of Blake in the final episode was suggested early on, although in the end this would be the only aspect of the original concept to survive. Another submission, "Ragnarok" by Graham Williams, who was producer on *Doctor Who* from 1977 to 1979, was abandoned after being commissioned on 27th March 1981. Paul Darrow, with encouragement from incoming producer Vere Lorrimer, wrote a full script entitled "Man of Iron", which ultimately never got made. As Writer's Guild regulations prevented Chris Boucher from writing more than two scripts per season, he took a leaf out of Nation's book and wrote the first and last stories, on the grounds that these are the ones that usually get chosen for repeats.

The chaotic situation with regard to commissioning the scripts was further complicated by the fact that Jan Chappell, who was initially offered the chance to continue as Cally for the whole season, then, when she turned this down, six episodes, then three, then one, finally agreed only to say two words in voice-over: 'Vila' and 'Blake.' Due to a misapprehension by Vere Lorrimer and Boucher that she would be staying on, the first six scripts were originally written to include Cally, and consequently had to be hastily rewritten (in some cases leading to characterisation and continuity problems). No swansong episode was ever written for Cally, as Chappell's decision to leave came after these scripts had been finished, and Boucher did not have the opportunity to commission a story in which to write her out.

Soolin, a professional gunfighter played by Glynis Barber (who had previously appeared as a mutoid in "Project Avalon"), was developed by Chris Boucher as a Cally replacement. (Lynda is

Chris's wife's name, although he professes not to know where the 'Soo' came from.) His 10th December 1980 outline for the character runs as follows:

SOOLIN
BORN: EARTH
AGE: 25

Parents emigrated to frontier world DARLON IV when Soolin was two years old.

The family farmed a Registered Homestead on DARLON IV until it was re-designated an OPEN PLANET on the discovery of vast mineral wealth.

Since OPEN PLANET designation suspends all normal law, the murder of Soolin's family by the enforcers of a mining consortium was not technically a crime. Soolin was eight years old.

Assuming, wrongly, that the child was too young to understand fully what had happened KEER, the mining consortium's project director on Darlon IV, adopted Soolin. An ex-enforcer himself, Keer made a second and ultimately fatal mistake when he taught the child everything he knew about the gunfighter's trade.

By the time she was fifteen Soolin was an expert with any sort of handgun. Having grown up on an Open Planet, she was also thoroughly familiar with all the less appealing traits of human nature.

When she was seventeen Soolin killed the enforcers who murdered her family and Keer, the project director for whom they worked. She then left Darlon IV and made her way to the base world of the mining consortium where she spent the next four years systematically killing the management board for whom Keer worked.

When the vendetta was completed she returned to Darlon IV and visited her parents' grave. Then she left the planet for good.

Since that time she has been moving constantly, living by her wits, her gun and her beauty – all of which are considerable.

Not unnaturally, she has a deep mistrust of people which expresses itself in a wry and cynical sense of humour. She is an uneasy friend and an implacable enemy.

The fact that Soolin was effectively given Cally's lines (or, where appropriate, Dayna's) for the first half of the season, with any characterising points removed, meant that she was initially afforded little development. Furthermore, as many of the scripts focused very much on Avon, the characterisation of all the other regulars suffered as a result.

Another complication within the cast was that Jacqueline Pearce was at this point ill, and had in fact been hospitalised for a time after the end of recording on the third season. It was thus unclear whether or not she would be able to return. The decision was apparently taken to develop a new female villain, 'Sleer,' which idea was abandoned once it was learned that Pearce could come back. However, the two plans appear to have become amalgamated, with the result that Servalan adopts the alias 'Sleer' and the position of the leader of the Federation's pacification programme; this somewhat surprising decision makes for a lot of script problems, leading one to suspect that it would have been less difficult just to have had her return as Servalan. Boucher was also keen that the suggestions of a burgeoning relationship between Avon and Servalan in the previous year's stories should not be developed, and kept contact between the two characters to a minimum.

David Maloney having moved on, Vere Lorrimer (who visited Terry Nation in Los Angeles in order to discuss the series' future with him) took over as producer on Maloney's recommendation; Lorrimer had now left the BBC and was working freelance. Mary Ridge and David Sullivan Proudfoot were the staff directors for this season. Jacqueline Pearce has said that she felt that Lorrimer didn't really have a hold on the series. Communication between the various departments was less good; perhaps as a consequence, some of the costumes and the make-up are worse than formerly. (Paul Darrow, who had been told by make-up technician Ann Ailes always to request a particular combination of make-up, suffered the least from the changeover.) Lorrimer also penned lyrics for the iconic *Blake's 7* theme tune, with the idea that Steven Pacey should sing them over the closing credits; it is to everyone's benefit that Pacey's agent was not keen on this idea, although the lift-music version that ultimately was placed over the closing titles is not much better. New, *Liberator*-less opening titles were designed by Doug Burd, who also designed a new series logo.

The late commissioning of the new series raised some issues with regard to production. 'As Terry had blown up the *Liberator* at the end of the previous season,' says Boucher, 'we were faced with the problem of having to provide the crew with a new ship, new handguns and all the rest of the paraphernalia.' Visual effects designer Jim Francis (assisted now by Andy Lazell, Steve Drewett having been assigned to *The Day of the Triffids*) created the model for the replacement ship, *Scorpio*. He also designed the *Scorpio* clip-guns – more conventional handguns than the wand-like *Liberator* weapons – which could have different sorts of magazines (the eponymous 'clips') slotted into them. An alternative design was supplied by visual effects assistant Bill Pearson, who developed a sort of modular 'kit-gun,' which would start as a handgun and then have pieces added on to it that would allow it to perform different functions. (One of these guns can be seen in the episodes "Warlord" and "Blake".) Francis eventually chose his own design over Pearson's. The design changes as a whole resulted in the season having a very different feel to it; there is more of an industrial aesthetic in contrast to the opulent, organic style of the *Liberator*. Whereas the *Liberator*'s design suggested richness and alienness, *Scorpio*'s grey metal and chrome (following Lorrimer's suggestion to make the ship resemble the *Nostromo* from the film *Alien*) suggests utility and cheapness, with the stark lighting on the *Scorpio* set adding to the effect. The crew were issued with only two costumes each this season, by contrast to earlier seasons in which they had changed costumes frequently, and these were similarly intended to look functional.

Ratings were down on the previous year, generally averaging about 8.5 million viewers. Ironically, the lowest and highest ratings went to the first and last episodes respectively: "Rescue" with 7.8 million and "Blake" with 9.0 million. The reason for the overall drop is unknown, but it may have had something to do with the season being shown later in the year than its predecessors.

It has sometimes been suggested, and Chris Boucher has claimed in a number of interviews, that this final season can be viewed almost as a new series entirely. It looks and feels quite different from what has gone before; the crew's ship is no longer luxurious and desirable, but ordinary, and they have a planetary base, with neighbours. There is a noticeable shift in crew dynamics, with the

Tarrant-Avon antagonism fading, and Dayna's backstory and anti-Servalan vendetta being downplayed. (Note that Dayna no longer wears her father's graduate medallion.) Certain terms, like 'visplay' and 'spacials,' are no longer used. On the other hand, however, the set-up is very similar to that of previous seasons, involving as it does a ship with unusual capabilities, a teleport and a computer with a personality; and the Federation is still the main antagonist. Although Servalan's adoption of the role of 'Sleer' is problematic, the idea of her being deposed and taking on a new role with the aim of clawing her way back to the top does follow on logically from the situation at the end of the previous season. Tarrant's fading antagonism, and Avon's gradual descent into obsession and madness, are also not out of line with developments we have seen before. On balance, then, it seems safe to say that the fourth season is more or less in line with earlier seasons.

D1: RESCUE

UK TRANSMISSION: Monday 28 September 1981: 7.20pm – 8.10pm
DURATION: 49:51
VIEWING FIGURE: 7.8m
CHART POSITION: 75
WRITER: Chris Boucher
DIRECTOR: Mary Ridge

CREDITED CAST: Geoffrey Burridge (Dorian); Rob Middleton (The Creature)

UNCREDITED CAST: Stuart Fell, James Muir* (Links); Jan Chappell (Voice of Cally); Harry Van Engel, Peter Finn, Albert Welch (Disintegrating Dorians); Bruno Tonioli (Dead Young Man)
*Not in finished episode

> **SYNOPSIS:** Stranded on Terminal, the crew discover that not only is the landscape full of perils, but that Servalan has booby-trapped both the ship and the base with explosives, killing Cally. The survivors encounter a mysterious new arrival on the planet: Dorian, a self-styled salvage operator. They hijack his ship, *Scorpio*, only to find that it is following a pre-programmed flight path back to his base on the planet Xenon. There, they meet Dorian's associate Soolin, a gunfighter. It transpires that Dorian is over two hundred years old, and has sustained his youthful appearance through the use of a mysterious room under his base; his own aging processes, illnesses and so forth are projected onto

a creature trapped in a subterranean room. Dorian disarms Avon, Soolin, Tarrant and Dayna and traps them in the room, intending to make them his next victims, but Vila, who has been overlooked, smuggles in a Federation rifle. Avon kills the Creature, and Dorian dies as his own physical excesses are visited back upon him.

ANALYSIS: "Rescue", like all season openers for *Blake's 7*, sets the scene for what is to come, and establishes the changes to the series format.

As this episode is scripted by Chris Boucher rather than by Terry Nation, we do not see the thematic borrowing from earlier episodes typical of Nation's season-openers and enders. We do get other forms of references back, however. There are quoted lines such as Avon's 'It's not really my field,' and direct references to "Mission to Destiny" and "Children of Auron" in the scene in which Avon repeats the saying of Cally's people: 'He who trusts can never be betrayed, only mistaken.' Slave, *Scorpio*'s flight computer, recalling the previous episode's word-play, calls Terminal: 'our destination.' The crew's forgetting of first Tarrant and then Vila is also similar to events in "Seek-Locate-Destroy" and "Deliverance". Boucher chooses to pass up one possible escape route from the planet for Avon and his comrades – a ship that Nation placed there in "Terminal" – by blowing it up (and by disabling Orac, who could have taken control of another ship for them), and instead introduces something of his own devising.

The most obvious changes in the series are the presence of this new ship with new guns; some *Star Wars* influence is visible here, with *Scorpio* and its owner bearing more than a slight resemblance to the *Millennium Falcon* and Han Solo. However, it is essentially the same sort of thing that we have had before: a technologically advanced ship, with a teleport (albeit non-functional) and a computer with attitude. The Federation is still present, although again said to be reduced from its glory days, and there is direct continuity between this episode and "Terminal". If the fourth season is actually a different sort of series than the *Blake's 7* that has gone before, then it is not particularly apparent in the construction or feel of this episode.

The loss of Cally is, however, a rather significant change. The story had to be rewritten to accommodate Jan Chappell's hasty departure, with the introduction of Soolin. It is, however, a particularly good rewrite, with Boucher making Cally's absence into a plot point; the extra glass on the tray when Dorian welcomes the crew to his base suggests that Dorian was expecting to find Cally as well as the others, allowing them to suspect that their presence on Xenon is not unplanned. Cally's dramatic off-screen death is also a good example of how it is possible to use explosions and effects to gloss over a scriptwriting problem. Soolin is not given much of a presence in this story; we learn that she is a very good gunfighter who killed the person who trained her, but little else. The one glimmer of characterisation comes when Dorian kisses her passionately and she does not respond, making it clear that she is her own woman and not subservient to Dorian's wishes.

As at the beginning of the previous season, the crew dynamic also changes. Tarrant is much more subdued, both in script and in performance; although he goes against Avon's wishes in looking for alternative routes to *Scorpio*'s landing silo, he seems unusually inclined to let Avon take the lead. He does not challenge Avon, and complains to Dayna about feeling tired. Vila and Dayna, although they disobey Avon, ultimately follow his leadership. Vila gets a particularly good part in this story; although Keating's performance is still rather superficial, his scripted lines are very edgy and, where Avon and the others are lulled into a false sense of security when Soolin does not shoot them, he remains suspicious and ultimately saves the day. Finally, although Tarrant and Avon are visibly affected by the events of "Terminal", Dayna and Vila are less so; while Dayna's resilience can be explained through her youth, Vila's reasons are not as evident, and we see, in his behaviour, traces of a blind faith in Avon.

Although the production quality is generally good – the snake-creatures on Terminal deserve particular praise – there are several continuity mistakes between the seasons. Vila's outfit changes from the one he was wearing in "Terminal" to the one he was wearing in "Moloch"; the base entrance has been repainted beige, and the video effect through the viewfinder is slightly different. Terminal is round rather than oval (although of course we could be viewing it head-on in this case), and Dorian refers to it as a 'modified' rather than an 'artificial' planet (although it is possible, given his age, that he could have better information than Tarrant does). The snow on the ground is less of a problem, as it may well have snowed between the events of "Terminal" and those of "Rescue". The original script had Dayna and Vila falling into the web of a spider-like creature; while the change to a snake-creature is understandable when one considers production costs, it would have made more sense to have had Dayna walking into a trap rather than simply falling down a ridge. Some viewers recognised elements of a *Doctor Who* monster called a Sea Devil in the costume for Dorian's Creature; a fact that resulted in enquiries from then *Doctor Who* producer John Nathan-Turner to Vere Lorrimer.

The character Dorian is pivotal to the events of the episode. Geoffrey Burridge gives a variable performance in the role; although he is somewhat over the top in the scenes in the room with the Creature, he otherwise gives the character a wonderfully sinister flair. The scene on Terminal in which it is unclear whether he plans to rescue or kill Dayna and Vila is particularly noteworthy. The character is a deliberate homage to Oscar Wilde's *The Picture of Dorian Gray*, a novel about a bisexual man with a magical portrait that allows him to appear young and beautiful while the portrait takes on the effects of his decadent lifestyle. There is clearly a bisexual or gay aspect to Dorian's character; although he kisses Soolin, the look he gives Avon when saying that he can indulge 'any pleasure... any vice...' is plainly suggestive. (Avon responds with, 'you really are insane, aren't you?') He also gives Avon an odd look when saying: 'You really are most welcome here, my friend.' Dorian states that his first victim was his 'partner,' which has a slightly ambiguous note; he calls his computer 'Slave,' suggesting a sadomasochistic relationship as well as exposing him as a control freak. These suggestions that the character is both homo/bisexual and decadent, derive from the novel, which can be read as a condemnation of the hedonistic lifestyle of the upper-class homo/bisexual circles in which Wilde moved. A deleted scene at the end of the story has Avon detonating charges to destroy Dorian's room, removing all trace of him from the base.

Dorian appears to be something of a *Liberator* fan as well. Not only has he thoroughly researched the crew, he has copied all their paraphernalia – fancy guns, teleport systems, computers with personalities. Now he wants to become them, as, by trapping them in the room, he is effectively taking their lives; he appears to be more of a stalker than an enthusiast. It seems something of a coincidence that Dorian turns up at the right place to rescue them, but then, since the room can warn him of approaching death, it is possible that it was able to direct him; we do not know what powers it has, though there does seem to be some kind of supernatural link between Dorian and the Creature. There appears to be a continuity gaffe at one point when Dorian does not contradict Avon's statement about Ensor having been in hiding for twenty, rather than forty, years; however, as Dorian appears to be only about thirty, had he responded with 'forty, actually,' it would have raised the question of how he had managed to meet Ensor. By being enigmatic and not directly contradicting the false figure, Dorian prevents Avon from asking awkward questions, while suggesting something slightly wrong about the character.

Avon, for his part, is becoming not only the leader of the crew, but very much the focus of the series (not just metaphorically but also literally; in any scene in which the character appears, Paul Darrow is foregrounded). Even though it is Vila who obtains the Federation gun, it is Avon who kills the Creature. The big question that this episode raises is whether or not Avon, as Dorian says, really does care about the crew. When Tarrant asks him where Cally is, he pauses before confirming that he is certain she is dead, and Dayna points out that he did go back for her (although Avon then claims that it was to find Orac). Significantly, he quotes Cally's line from "Mission to Destiny" to Dorian, suggesting that he is still thinking of her. Although Cally's dying word is not 'Avon' but 'Blake,' we must remember that Avon did reject her outright in "Sarcophagus", and that Blake is of course the crew's original leader. Avon rescues Dayna, goes back for Tarrant, and in the end saves the whole crew; although Tarrant comments that staying together as a group means that Avon can get away while the rest are attacked, Avon points out that the converse is also true. While Dayna says, 'Beneath that cold exterior beats a heart of pure stone,' she is saying this for Dorian's benefit, and it may not be true – at this point. Although it might be amateur psychology, Dorian is right in suggesting that it would be impossible for someone to have shared so much with a group of others without developing some kind of bond with them. Avon does seem to care about his fellows, but the real question is, how deep does this run, and, if he is already showing signs of becoming domineering and totalitarian, how long will it last?

Finally, we come to the question of Avon's relationship with Blake. At the beginning of the episode Avon is very aware that, in all probability, Servalan has mined the abandoned ship with explosives. Later, he tells Dayna that the underground living quarters would also have been booby-trapped, set to go off using ultrasonic fuses keyed to pick up the first detonation, adding 'That's how I would have done it.' Yet, if Avon believes he is walking into a 'double booby-trap', why does he allow Tarrant, Vila, Cally and Orac to remain at the base? The most likely answer is that Avon was fully intending to make his long-held belief, that Blake's death and his own would be linked in some way, a reality, and that he was going to take the rest of the crew with him. If so, what stops him must have been the realisation that if Servalan was deceiving them over the ship, then her assurance that Blake was dead, may well also be a lie.

"Rescue" sets the stage for the new season; however, it does not constitute a break with the old series format, merely, as with earlier season-openers, a rethinking of its attributes.

D2: POWER

UK TRANSMISSION: Monday 5 October 1981: 7.20pm – 8.10pm
DURATION: 49:56
VIEWING FIGURE: 8.7m
CHART POSITION: 60
WRITER: Ben Steed
DIRECTOR: Mary Ridge

CREDITED CAST: Dicken Ashworth (Gunn Sar); Juliet Hammond Hill (Pella); Jenny Oulton (Nina); Paul Ridley (Cato); Alison Glennie (Kate); Linda Barr (Luxia)

UNCREDITED CAST: Terence Brooks, Gordon Hann, Richard Reid, Steve Kelly, Pat Gorman, David Robert Long, Derek Suthern (Hommiks in Wasteland); John Holland, Ron Tarr, Steve Ismay, Terry Medlicott, Terry Duran, Ridgewell Hawkes (Hommiks in Base); Annette Paris (Unconscious Luxia)

SYNOPSIS: Stranded on the planet Xenon, Tarrant, Vila and Dayna try to open the door to the landing silo in which *Scorpio* is housed. Avon, meanwhile, has gone in search of Dynamon crystals with which to complete Dorian's teleport system, and is captured by the Hommiks, an all-male primitive tribe. Back at Xenon Base, Vila is contacted by Pella, leader of the Seska, an all-female, technologically advanced tribe who are at war with the Hommiks and who agreed to develop a teleport for Dorian in exchange for him providing them with supplies. She informs Vila that there is a nuclear compression charge on the landing-silo door and that this will detonate if a switch is not reset every forty-eight hours. She then seemingly disappears without trace. The Hommiks capture Pella and one of her followers, and we learn that they routinely kidnap members of the Seska, operate on them to remove their special mental powers (which include telekinesis) and use them to breed sons; daughters are exposed at birth (i.e. left on a hillside to die of exposure). Avon and Pella escape, but Tarrant, Dayna and Vila, who have gone to look for Avon, are captured; Dayna fights the Hommik leader Gunn Sar and, unknowingly aided by the Seska, kills him. Gunn Sar's wife Nina, a former Seska, vows to start a new society elsewhere with the remnant of both tribes. Pella returns to Xenon Base and offers to help Tarrant, Dayna and Vila by deactivating the explosive device, using her telekinetic powers; Avon, however, returns and reveals that Pella has been attempting to gain independent access to *Scorpio* under the pretext of developing a teleport system. Pella reaches *Scorpio* and takes off. Avon and Orac meanwhile complete the teleport system, and Avon materialises on board the ship, kills Pella and takes control. Soolin reappears and offers her gunfighting services to the crew.

ANALYSIS: Ben Steed's third story for the series fits its characters and tone well. It is also a strongly anti-sexist story, the dominating theme of which is that men and women cannot survive without each other.

Despite symbolic references to the rape and subordination of women (particularly in the scenes in which the Seska are captured, blindfolded and operated upon), the story's theme is summed up at its conclusion by Avon, when he says that the war between the sexes is the one war that can never be won. The Seska and the Hommiks have complementary but gender-divided skills: the Hommiks have strength and an organised political system, where the Seska have technical know-how. (Although one Hommik, Cato, is also technically adept, he is an exception, and he dies before we learn the reason for it.) Gunn Sar finds Avon's technical knowledge effeminate, and it is Nina who performs the surgery. Both groups are trying to build single-sex societies. However, neither can succeed in this; the Hommiks need (surgically modified) Seska to bear children and perform technical tasks, but the Seska – as Nina points out – need Dorian (an outsider, and a bisexual man) to bring them nutrients. Their tactics are ultimately self-destructive; the Seska refuse to acknowledge that they have any need for male assistance, and the idea that the Hommiks' exposure of female children can be seen as a form of fosterage – as the Seska will find and raise them – is undermined by the fact that they also kill or capture any Seska that they see. At the end of the story, the Seska are finished, but the Hommik society will not endure long without women. Neither group can survive in its current form, but must be replaced, as Nina says, by a new one – one that will not only include both males and females, but will apparently be led by Nina herself. At the conclusion of the story, when Avon says to Pella, 'If you didn't want the answer, you shouldn't have asked the question,' he clearly means the question as to which sex is more powerful; and, in the end, both sexes will lose.

We also see the subversion and questioning of gendered behaviour. In a sequence similar to one in Steed's earlier story "The Harvest of Kairos", Dayna fights, and in this case beats, a powerful and arrogant man (although she does have Seska assistance). In the scene in which Avon defeats Pella, he points out that if she uses male tactics – brute force – against men, she will lose; she pays him back by using female tactics – stealth and subterfuge – to make him shoot Cato, and then knocks him unconscious. We also have the scene in which we see Gunn Sar sewing on an embroidery sampler. Not only does this suggest a society with a gendered division of labour different from our own – as how, in parts of Scotland, knitting is considered a masculine occupation – it also suggests that this is a subtler, more nuanced story than simply a vindication of male privilege; despite the characters' own binary thinking about gender roles, we see a strong man who sews, and a subordinated woman who is in fact very powerful. Twice within the story, Nina responds 'I am a woman' to assertions that she is a Seska. However, this is neither a boast nor a lament. She is simply stating a fact; she has had the surgery, and cannot now return to being a Seska, and so accepts her new role, for better or worse.

This also raises the issue of Nina's feelings for Gunn Sar. She appears to care for him at least somewhat; when he asks why she did not try to escape when she had the chance, she says nothing but kisses the top of his head; and she later weeps when he dies.

However, it has to be said that she has nowhere else to go; as she cannot return to being a Seska, if she does not show affection to Gunn Sar, she will lose the power that she has attained as his wife. Gunn Sar, for his part, appears contemptuous of her at times, trying to strike her and referring to her as a 'sack of offal'; however, he also says to Avon that he would accept the idea of his going in search of Dynamon crystals on the advice of 'his woman,' but not on the advice of a computer, suggesting that he considers Nina's advice worth listening to. Nina's and Gunn Sar's relationship is thus also more subtle than simply one of domination and submission.

Pella, for her part, is not the most sympathetic of characters. She is more interested in her own power than in rebuilding the Seska civilisation; '*You* will follow,' she tells the others, placing herself in control. She has told the other Seska the same lie about building a teleport that she told Dorian, and she ultimately shoots Kate when the other Seska threatens her access to *Scorpio*. Pella also cannot think outside of Seska and Hommik relationship terms, choosing Dayna as a hostage on the assumption that the men will protect 'their woman.' The Hommiks, on the other side, have a code of honour that prohibits Gunn Sar from killing the unconscious Avon, and causes him to treat Avon as an equal and insider on the field of battle, muttering 'Well, I've got to say all that,' to him following his melodramatic pre-combat speech. The idea of the Hommiks' ancestors making a conscious decision to return to the primitive and start over is also a common theme of 1970s and early 1980s television, from *The Good Life* through *The Day of the Triffids*.

Avon's behaviour in this story is interesting: not only does he condemn Gunn Sar's treatment of Nina, but he also stops him hitting her. This from a man who is not only violent towards women, but will later overpower Pella and kiss her after he subdues her (in a parallel with his treatment of Sara in "Mission to Destiny"). However, Avon's violence towards women has in the past always been situational; he is aggressive towards them only when he feels (or knows) that they have betrayed him or are trying to use him. Whatever Pella may have to say on the subject, Avon does not necessarily have any sympathy with Gunn Sar; he is motivated not by a hatred for women or a need to subdue them, but by a desire to ensure his own survival. He also does not tell the crew the real code to the door. (The fake code he gives, 'Narcissus,' is an appropriate one for the self-obsessed Dorian, who wanted to gain immortality and eternal good looks.)

The performances in the story are good, although Darrow shows an occasional tendency to strike poses. The scene in which Vila tries to convince Dayna and Tarrant that he really has seen Pella is slightly weakened by Keating's decision to play the lines straight, rather than sarcastically – suggesting that Vila really does think he is delusional, rather than that he is rubbishing the others' doubts about what he saw. The script also contains, as well as a number of good lines, some interesting moments: Avon, for the first time ever, runs out of ammunition, and Pella's remark that 'The Black woman must win' is the only time Dayna is referred to as 'Black' in the entire series. The script appears to have been rewritten totally, as, although Cally must have been in the original version, she has vanished without trace; since Soolin appears only at the end y in a tacked-on scene, Steed has not simply given Cally's lines to Soolin, as the writers of subsequent episodes chose to do.

"Power" is therefore not the misogynous vindication of male control that it appears to be at first glance, and is actually a sophisticated take on gender relations and prejudice. As such, it is probably Steed's strongest contribution to the series.

D3: TRAITOR

UK TRANSMISSION: Monday 12 October 1981: 7.20pm – 8.10pm
DURATION: 49:20
VIEWING FIGURE: 8.7m
CHART POSITION: 59
WRITER: Robert Holmes
DIRECTOR: David Sullivan Proudfoot

CREDITED CAST: Malcolm Stoddard (Leitz); Christopher Neame (Colonel Quute); Robert Morris (Major Hunda); John Quentin (Practor); Edgar Wreford (Forbus); Nick Brimble (General); David Quilter (The Tracer); Neil Dickson (Avandir); Cyril Appleton (Sgt. Hask); George Lee (Igen)

UNCREDITED CAST: Peter Tuddenham (House Computer/ Tannoy Voice); Ian Ellis, James Muir, Bobby James, Peter Dayson, David Enyon, Paul Baden, Paul Heasman, Barry Holland, Peter Jessup, Bryan Payne, Eddie Sommer, Terry Stuart, Philip Compton, Richard Reid, Bruce Callander, Pat Gorman, Mike Mungarvan, Sue Bishop, Fiona McAlpine, Kevin O'Brien, Barney Lawrence, Maxine Walker, Wendy Smith, Annette Paris, Derek Holt, John Hartley Horton, Richard Olley (Federation Guards/Attendant/Helot Rebels/Adapted Helots)

SYNOPSIS: Curious as to how the Federation has been retaking its old colonies so easily, the *Scorpio* crew go to the most recently reconquered planet, Helotrix, to investigate. Tarrant and Dayna teleport down and meet a rebel leader, Hunda, who introduces them to his Federation forces contact, Leitz. Leitz tells them that the population are being 'adapted' using a new drug, Pylene-50, under a programme run by the mysterious Commissioner Sleer of the Pacification Police. He sends Tarrant and Dayna to the laboratory where the drug is made, without warning them that the door is booby-trapped. Avoiding the trap, they meet Forbus, the inventor of Pylene-50, who is being forced to work for Sleer. He gives them the formula and the antidote and warns them that Leitz is Sleer's agent. Tarrant and Dayna return to Hunda, who is planning a raid on the Magnetrix Terminal (part of the Federation command network), and give him the antidote. Sleer is revealed to be Servalan; she kills Forbus when he makes an attempt on her life with a home-made bomb, and Leitz when he reveals that he knows her true identity as the ex-President.

ANALYSIS: "Traitor" is not a terribly deep script, and is Holmes's weakest for the series. Although it is not, in and of itself, a bad story, it is mainly of interest for what it can tell us about the changes that occurred between the initial and televised conceptions of the fourth season.

The story was the second commissioned for the season, and 'Episode 4' is written on the front of the first draft in biro; it was still scheduled in that position at the time the camera script was distributed. There are a number of changes between the first draft and what finally appears on screen. The first draft, entitled "A Land Fit for Helots", not only includes Cally, but has different names for *Scorpio* and Xenon Base (*Nighthawk* and Eagle Base respectively); as it was unclear what the communicators/teleport devices would look like at this point, Holmes refers to them as 'things' or 'whatsits' (resulting in a stage direction in which Tarrant and Dayna are said to be standing at the end of an alley, 'holding their things' – the word 'Eh??' appears, in Chris Boucher's handwriting, in the margin). Tarrant and Dayna also do not steal Helot clothing (described at this stage as involving 'distinctively baggy pantaloons') as seen in the televised episode, but teleport down wearing it. Slave does not appear in the first draft and, in the camera script, some of his lines were originally Orac's. In the first draft, Orac refers to being 'forty miles' above the surface. This is highlighted, with 'spacials' (the usual unit of distance measurement in the series) written beside it in Boucher's handwriting. In the camera script, however, the word 'miles' has returned (according to Boucher, this was at Lorrimer's instigation); and the word 'spacials' is never again used in the series. Cally's lines were ultimately given to Soolin, with some being modified to reflect the fact that Soolin is not from Auron and did not know Blake. (In the first draft, Vila responds to Cally's line, 'I didn't know Helots were originally from Earth,' with, 'Then you don't know your history,' and Cally retorts, 'Your history isn't mine, Vila.' By the camera script, Vila's response to the same line has changed to, 'Everyone came from Earth originally, that's a well-known fact,' and Soolin's to, 'it's a well-known opinion, actually'.) A comedic scene in which Vila wishes for crumpets, 'an old Earth delicacy,' was abandoned early on.

Some things that made it into the camera script were changed on recording. A reference is made to Tarrant and Dayna slotting control chips (which, according to the writers' guide, contained landing-coordinate information) into their teleport bracelets, an idea that was later abandoned as too complicated. When Avon warns Tarrant not to get involved, the scripted 'Sure' is delivered by Pacey as the more ambiguous: 'You know me, Avon.' In both the first draft and the camera script, the scenes on Helotrix are set in a city – which would have made more sense than the transmitted versions' mud-flat and jungle – and Forbus's death follows from him attempting to attack Servalan by pressing the contacts together and detonating the nitroglycerine (whereas, as transmitted, it appears that she threatens him and then, seemingly at random, kills him). Servalan also, in both versions, ends up shooting Leitz rather than – in a notable improvement in the transmitted episode – embracing and stabbing him. In another change for the better, the transmitted episode omitted an intended insult by Avon when Tarrant refuses to return to *Scorpio*: the first draft script had Avon calling Tarrant 'You dumbo', and in the camera script this was changed to: 'You dumb–'.

Perhaps the most interesting change between the scripts and the transmitted version is that the former two contain three separate references to the idea that Avon is acting like Blake, which is cut down to one – Vila: 'Blake would have been proud of you, you know'; Avon: 'I know, but then he never was very bright' – in the latter. The first excised line, from the scene in which Avon announces that they must go to Helotrix, had Vila saying, 'You're getting worse than Blake used to be. You're turning into a hero, Avon!' (Avon responds with: 'Whatever the occasion demands...'). The second ran as follows:

AVON: Vila is not at his best hanging around. He's an action man.

VILA: I'll tell you what kind of man I am, Avon – I'm a running man, the way you used to be before you caught terminal Blakitis.

SOOLIN: I suppose it isn't possible that you and Blake do have something in common after all?

AVON: No, it isn't. We're different in every way possible.

SOOLIN: For instance?

AVON: For instance I survived, he didn't.

In the final version, Avon is acting in a more intense way than formerly, putting the viewer in mind of Blake's demeanour at the end of the second season and suggesting that he is beginning to adopt some of the personality traits of his former leader. However, most of the overt scripted references to this are gone.

The major point of the story is the return of Servalan, in the guise of Sleer. This development maintains continuity with the previous season, tying in with the idea that, in "Terminal", Servalan was fleeing a coup, and with the renewed expansionism of the Federation of that time. Servalan's title, 'Supreme Empress,' also reflects the growing grandiosity of her titles over the course of her Presidency. However, the guise in which she returns, that of a high-profile security officer, is not terribly sensible – it is rather as if the Shah of Iran had taken a new job as the Ayatollah's head of security without anyone noticing. Her return is also rather unsubtle; after we see someone appear in a feathered wrap, kill the President-elect of Helotrix and burn the painting of Servalan (which shows her in the dress she wore in "Terminal"), it would be more surprising if it *wasn't* her.

Jacqueline Pearce, who was dissatisfied with Servalan's sudden acquisition of a double identity, has in the past maintained that this was an attempt by the production team to 'diminish' her. Certainly, it is true that in other series, tensions between an actor and the production team have been manifested in the production of scripts in which the actor appears as a double of, or a changed form of, the character that he or she normally plays. Chris Boucher has, however, stated outright that this was not the reason; and also there was some uncertainty as to whether or not Pearce would be returning to the series at all. It is on record that the original idea was to introduce a new villain in the person of Commissioner Sleer (although, as the first draft script features Servalan, this idea cannot have progressed beyond the storyline stage); rather than bringing in the new character, then, the script ultimately reintroduces an old one.

The other characters are superficially developed; while Hunda and Igin do get more backstory than we normally find for rebels – and we learn that they come from a teaching rather than a military background – not much is made of this. Although the colonial-official dialogue of the Federation officers is somewhat clichéd, they do fare better; Quute and the Tracer show signs of having a real working relationship, sharing jokes, playing (unscripted) a chess game, and so forth. This, and the fact that the Helot President-elect is pro-Federation, superficially recalls "Horizon"; the name 'Helots' is also shared with a group of classical Mediterranean people who were enslaved by the Spartans. There is an unusual reference by Vila to computers with solid-state circuitry – the first direct acknowledgement that the technology of the series predates the software revolution. Finally, the fact that there are four columns of Helot rebels lends itself to what can only be described as a subtextual pun – as, of course, the adapted Helots are the fifth column.

The production quality is also variable; there is a very good battle on film between the rebels and the adapted Helots, followed by a very bad battle in the more limited confines of the studio. The much-vaunted 'stock equalisation programme' (another rare reference to Dayna's ethnic origin) is represented by a single Black extra. The makeup is also not particularly effective: the General looks like a *Thunderbirds* puppet, and the less said about Servalan the better. (Jacqueline Pearce has remarked of her makeup in this episode, 'I looked like a man in drag'.) We also see the reuse of several costumes from earlier seasons (with Tarrant wearing Avon's black-leather suit from "Killer" for half the episode) as well as a black feathered wrap for Servalan.

"Traitor" is a run-of-the-mill story, which is significant mainly for the return of Servalan and for the differences between the transmitted version and its earlier drafts.

D4: STARDRIVE

UK TRANSMISSION: Monday 19 October 1981: 7.20pm – 8.10pm
DURATION: 49:02
VIEWING FIGURE: 8.8m
CHART POSITION: 65
WRITER: Jim Follett
DIRECTOR: David Sullivan Proudfoot

CREDITED CAST: Barbara Shelley (Dr Plaxton); Damien Thomas (Atlan); Peter Sands (Bomber); Leonard Kavanagh (Napier)

UNCREDITED CAST: Mike Potter (Double for Atlan); Terry Forrestal (Double for Bomber); Sue Crosland (Double for Dr Plaxton); Jim Dowdall (Stuntman/Space Rat); Stephen Whyment, Reg Woods, Annette Paris, Sally Sinclair, Martin Kennedy, Lisa Clifton (Brig/Space Rats in Base)

SYNOPSIS: *Scorpio* is damaged while attempting to use an asteroid as cover to enter the Altern system and obtain selsium ore for fuel. While making repairs, the crew witness the destruction of three Federation pursuit ships by a small craft moving at an impossible speed, which Orac interprets as meaning that the ship has been fitted with a new space drive system, the Stardrive. This was being developed by the head of the Federation Space Drive Research Centre, Dr Plaxton, who is presumably now with the ship's owner – one of a group of speed-obsessed psychopaths known as 'Space Rats.' The crew travel to the Space Rats' base on Caspar; Avon sends Vila and

Dayna down first, intending for them to be captured as a distraction while he, Tarrant and Soolin break in elsewhere. The crew steal the drive and persuade Dr Plaxton – who is unhappy with the work the Space Rats are forcing her to do – to go with them. They escape the Space Rats and take off in *Scorpio,* but find themselves under attack by pursuit ships. Dr Plaxton fits the ship with the Stardrive, allowing it to evade the attackers, but is killed when Avon activates the Stardrive prematurely.

ANALYSIS: "Stardrive" is one of the weaker episodes of the series. Although it does have some redeeming features, it comes across in general as padded and inconsistent.

From a production point of view, the story is variable. There are, for instance, some lovely model shots of *Scorpio* in space and on Caspar; conversely, we have appalling blue-screen pursuit ships, as well as a very fake-looking dust cloud when *Scorpio* strikes the asteroid. The direction of the chase sequence is inspired, featuring some rather unusual shots in which the camera moves along with the buggy and the motor-trikes; the sequence where Avon detonates explosive devices under the trikes, then casually throws the remote activator away, is particularly good. For most of the story, however, the direction is somewhat lacking; for example, it is rather obvious that Dr Plaxton is being doubled for in the filmed sequences (somewhat mysteriously, as Barbara Shelley was present for the location filming). There is also a strong debt owed to *Star Wars,* particularly with regard to the screen wipes and the combat sequences in the sand dunes. The repair device used on *Scorpio* is unconvincingly realised – a laser that apparently can fill in the hole in the ship's side so that one can see no damage at all. Paul Darrow's performance contains impressions of Burt Lancaster and Steve McQueen; overall during the first half of this season, he appears rather like Rod Steiger playing Napoleon in *Waterloo.*

The script also has some problems. Vila's reference to 'Murphy's Law' is anachronistic, and Time Distort (or 'TD') appears here to be almost exactly equivalent to Standard as a speed measurement, which contradicts the implication in "Hostage" and "Duel" that the ratio between Standard and Time Distort is somewhere around 3:2 or 2:1. There is also a lot of obvious padding in this story, suggesting that there was not enough material for a full script; the longest gap between lines is one minute and forty-five seconds, in the sequence with Avon, Tarrant and Soolin running across the sand dunes; later, on *Scorpio*, the crew stare at the approaching pursuit ships on the rear screen for a full twelve seconds before saying or doing anything. At the end of the story, Dr Plaxton spends a lot of time gazing into space rather than making the final connection on the Stardrive.

The Space Rats are one of the worst aspects of the story. Follett explicitly based them on the Hell's Angels (recalling John Fletcher's 'space-age Hell's Angels' story suggested for the previous season); this idea is bad enough, but the combination of design and scripting gives the overall impression of contemporary youth culture as described by someone who is over forty and rather conservative. Their slang terms (e.g. 'gooks' and 'flagging') and names for each other (e.g. 'Bomber') are contrived, as is their habit of biting the heads off lizards. In production terms, that their costumes feature lots of padding seems odd for a group that prides itself on toughness. (Atlan, their leader, also has quite a bit of pink in his uniform.) More seriously, the fact that they all have Cockney accents – bar Atlan, who appears to be Mexican – and Mohican haircuts draws an unfortunate association between working-class people, punks, foreigners and mindless violence, making the episode more than a little suspect on this level.

As villains go, Atlan is not the most sophisticated. He claims that he isn't a Space Rat, and yet his behaviour corresponds completely with Vila's description of them as psychopaths who live for 'sex and violence, booze and speed.' He kisses Dr Plaxton and puts his hands around her throat, and is obsessed with having the fastest ships possible. We also never learn what he is, if not a Space Rat. His threat to turn Dr Plaxton over to the Space Rats, and 'let them deal with [her] in their own fashion,' is pretty much a case of saying: 'My men will kill you, but first they enjoy themselves.' Dr Plaxton is equally poorly drawn; it is more than a little out of character for a top scientist to work willingly for a group of interstellar yobbos. The fact that she actually wonders how she came to be mixed up with the Space Rats three years ago (a statement that, as she was said to have been working for the Federation at the time of its collapse, gives us an idea of when said collapse took place) further suggests that the writer himself recognises this to be an unbelievable scenario; although a plausible explanation could have been developed – that she was kidnapped, perhaps, or found herself in debt – none is advanced. We never find out what happens to her assistant Napier at the end of the story; he is simply left with the Space Rats.

The regulars are also inconsistently characterised. Although it is unsurprising that Avon would not reveal until the very last minute the full details of his rather dangerous strategy for using the asteroid as cover, and that he would send Dayna and Vila into a trap on Caspar (although it seems a bit of a convoluted plan, which relies on coincidence), it is more surprising for Tarrant not to raise objections to Avon's behaviour, considering that last season he was shown to have more of a conscience than Avon; the cold gunfighter Soolin is the only one to comment on Dayna's and Vila's plight. Neither Vila nor Dayna appears to be aware at any point in the story that they have been sent into a trap, and none of the others is willing to enlighten them. Avon's response, '"Who?', to Dayna's question, 'What about Dr Plaxton?', at the end of the story does flag up Avon's development into a harder, more amoral character; however, his excuse for killing Dr Plaxton makes no sense, as it is not true that she was 'dead anyway,' whatever he did. He programs in the main circuit drive thirty seconds before the impact of the plasma bolt, and the drive is activated five seconds before impact, meaning that he could easily have waited twenty-five seconds before giving up on her. Vila, however, does get an unusually intelligent scene, in which he pretends to be drunk in order to give Avon and Tarrant the solution to their problems without being asked to volunteer for it; he says that he was sent to a penal colony at the age of 14 which, although it does not contradict what we know of Vila's backstory, suggests first that he must have found a way of escaping (or else that penal colony sentences can, in some instances, last for only a couple of years), and secondly that he is a real hard case.

"Stardrive" is inconsistent and trite, containing some dubious stereotypes, shallow plotting and lazy characterisation. It adds nothing to the series, and has very little to say as a story in and of itself. Although admittedly not the worst episode of the series, it come pretty close.

D5: ANIMALS

UK TRANSMISSION: Monday 26 October 1981: 7.20pm – 8.10pm
DURATION: 49:58
VIEWING FIGURE: 8.9m
CHART POSITION: 59
WRITER: Allan Prior
DIRECTOR: Mary Ridge

CREDITED CAST: Peter Byrne (Justin); William Lindsay (Captain); Max Harvey (Borr); Kevin Stoney (Ardus); David Boyce (Og)

UNCREDITED CAST: Jill Goldstone, Janine Orgill, Ellison Kemp (Mutoids on Sleer's Ship); Ralph Morse (Animal on Screen); Nick Joseph, Mike Vinden, Colin Cook, Joe Phillips, Ray Hatfield, Ian Durrant, Mark Howard (Animals in Forest and Cages); Anite Jayne, Olwen Atkinson, Amanda Gee (Mutoids on Bucol 2)

SYNOPSIS: Dayna makes contact with her former tutor Justin, a geneticist, in the hope that he will help the *Scorpio* crew develop an antidote to Pylene-50. She discovers that he was involved in a wartime programme to genetically engineer radiation-proof fighting creatures; although the programme was abandoned, he is continuing to develop the animals. *Scorpio*, meanwhile, comes under attack from Federation pursuit ships, and Tarrant is forced to abandon Dayna and run back to base. Servalan, intrigued by the presence of a planet-hopper that can accelerate to Time Distort Twelve, investigates, and learns from Ardus, a former wartime intelligence officer, of Justin's project. She goes to the planet, kidnaps Dayna and conditions her to hate Justin. Dayna betrays Justin to Servalan, who offers to recondition her to love him again in exchange for his cooperation. The *Scorpio* returns and the crew attack Servalan's forces; Dayna escapes, and Justin's chief creation, Og, is killed. Servalan beats a hasty retreat, killing Justin in the process.

ANALYSIS: "Animals" is one of the worst stories of *Blake's 7*. Although the premise of experimenting on deserters (in the first-draft script, 'enemy prisoners') to create genetically engineered fighting machines is clever, being reminiscent of H G Wells's *The Island of Doctor Moreau* and Philip George Chadwick's *The Death Guard* (and, to a certain extent, Terry Nation's *Genesis of the Daleks*), the story is rendered meaningless through internal inconsistencies, illogical plotting and risible design.

The script's main problems stem from the fact that it was originally written with Cally, rather than Dayna, in the central role, and has undergone little revision; in the revised first draft, Dayna's name (spelled 'Deyna') has been crossed out and Soolin's written over the top, and Cally's struck out and Dayna's name (again misspelled) written in. The change in characters means that we have the unresolved question as to why Dayna's father, supposedly in hiding, brought in tutors for his daughter – particularly when one of them appears to have sympathy for the Federation – and why he would get in a top-level geneticist to teach a girl who appears to have no interest in biology (whereas, as Cally's twin was involved with genetics and they do not appear to have grown up in hiding or in exile, it is less inconceivable for Cally to have known Justin, even been taught by him). In the first-draft script, it is stated that Justin was Cally's teacher at the Academy (despite the fact that he is not an Auronar), and he says that he knew she had feelings for him while there – 'The very relationship of pupil and teacher encourages such things…. They are inevitable,' he says, adding that the reason why her feelings have lasted for so long is that she is from Auron. She counters by saying that she has 'enough of the Auron gift left' (throughout the script, it is implied, somewhat against series continuity, that Cally is losing her psychic powers) to tell that: 'Your own attitude to me isn't exactly fatherly.'

Despite the changes made to this scene, the switch from Cally (who appears to be in her late twenties or early thirties) to Dayna (who appears to be about twenty-four) in the final version strongly suggests that Justin and Dayna had a relationship when she was in her mid-teens. If one makes the – rather unlikely – assumption that Justin started working on the project shortly after he finished tutoring Dayna, and that a couple of years have passed since the Galactic War, the oldest Dayna could have been at the time she last met him is sixteen. As Justin appears to be in his forties here, moreover, he would have been in his thirties at the time, which, given that he appears to have reciprocated her feelings ('My little pupil Dayna,' he calls her affectionately), creates a subtext that was perhaps unintended.

The swap also makes for some characterisation problems. Dayna, who normally expresses few moral qualms about anything, suddenly develops a conscience for one episode only; her disgust also comes on suddenly, without any warning, and her subsequent change of heart is equally rapid. It is a little difficult to square Dayna's feelings of deep love for Justin with the way in which she rapidly gets over her quick snog with Avon in "Aftermath", and with the fact that it has been eight to ten years since she last met Justin. Dayna also seems to think that the animals will trust her rather than Justin, despite the fact that she has brutally gunned down two of them, and has gone into Justin's bunker (meeting him at the entrance) in their presence, thoroughly associating herself with him. Dayna also appears to be romantically involved with Tarrant. His dry, wordless stare when she remarks salaciously that she hopes Justin remembers her suggests jealousy; and her side glance back at him suggests that she is aware of this. This is an idea that is not extensively developed elsewhere in the series.

The description of Justin's project is also inconsistent. Although the references to the Galactic War are compatible with the timeline presented in the third season – the base was set up six years prior to the Galactic War, during which time the animal-development project appears to have been started – one has to ask why, if the project was finished at the end of the War as Justin says, the vessel carrying the other scientists was subsequently attacked by an enemy gunship. We also never learn why the project was abandoned – although one does have to ask what value there is in designing creatures that can fight in high-radiation environments, as there would not be anyone to fight against while they were there – or why Justin, having reduced the intelligence of his experimental subjects through genetic engineering, is now reaugmenting them through brain grafts. Design-wise, the animals are ridiculous, with huge blond wigs, yak horns and wart-like growths (giving them a more than passing resemblance to certain full-body costumes on *The Muppet Show*); they are also far too well-groomed for wild creatures. Justin's morality is more than a little suspect, as he appears to feel that synthesising an antidote to Pylene-50 is more reprehensible than genetically engineering a race of fighting creatures for the Federation. Finally, one has to ask why he destroys all his work when believing Dayna to be dead – it seems an extreme reaction to obliterate many years' work (on a project that he apparently cared enough about to endure remaining isolated on a barren planet rather than terminate it) for someone whom he has known for very little time.

The sequences involving Servalan (garbed yet again in feathers) are little better. Her attempt to gain control of Justin's programme – which would bring her to the attention of her superiors in the Federation – seems odd behaviour for a woman in hiding; and if she intends to use the programme herself, the question remains, what for? The fact that Ardus recognises her means that either she has, by a massive coincidence, again found one of the very few people who could identify her, or else that she is quite widely known in Federation circles, in which case one would think that she would be taking greater care to hide. One has to ask why, if Federation Central Intelligence Control are capable of tracking down Ardus, they have not yet connected Sleer with Servalan; it also makes little sense for the head of the Pacification Police to have the authority to make rules about flight plans. Also, if Servalan was able to get the information that Bucol 2 was the site of a secret project involving Justin, this suggests that Dayna, who is surprised to learn that he worked for the Federation, did not discover his whereabouts from Orac (who, having access to communication channels, could easily have picked up information on the project while it was in operation) – which then begs the question how she knew he was on Bucol 2 at all. Although we know from "The Web" that genetic-experimentation projects of this sort have been banned for centuries, this is not mentioned here, which might lead some viewers to question why the project is such a closely-guarded secret. While Kevin Stoney is very good as Ardus, the character seems fairly superfluous; his blindness and brutal murder by Servalan recall Dayna's father, but there seems to be no narrative reason for this. His realisation of the true identity of 'Sleer' is also too blatant to be realistic. Had Stoney reprised his role as Counsellor Joban from Prior's earlier script "Hostage", the scene might have highlighted the political development of the Federation over the past three seasons; as it is, it serves little purpose.

The brainwashing of Dayna is also rather unbelievable. Even leaving aside the implausibility of the idea that Servalan can somehow, in a relatively short length of time, not only destroy but totally reverse Dayna's love for Justin, instructing her to hate him is not going to cause her to love the Federation and work for her father's murderer, Servalan (and there is no suggestion that any of this features in her conditioning). While we don't see the conditioning process, Servalan refers to it as 'simple aversion therapy,' and the reversal process appears to involve playing soft music and saying 'You love him' over and over again. Dayna, moreover, appears to be unconscious during all this. She also exclaims 'Justin, what happened?' afterwards, implying that she does not remember anything, which is further inconsistent with the idea of undergoing 'aversion therapy.' In the original script, the scene was longer and plainly indebted to the sequence in which O'Brien destroys Winston's love for Julia in Orwell's *Nineteen Eighty-Four;* even then, however, the conditioning was to have taken place in far too short a time to be credible. One wonders why Servalan did not save herself a good deal of trouble by just shooting Dayna and reconditioning Justin. We also never learn why the Federation pursuit ships approach *Scorpio*, given that they don't know that Avon and his crew have acquired the planet-hopper (which seem to be pretty common in any case; until the point at which it outruns the pursuit ships, there is no sign that there is anything unusual about it), or why they are in the vicinity at all, aside from pure coincidence.

Finally, other areas of the story are inconsistent. Avon, Soolin and Tarrant break into the supposedly impregnable bunker awfully quickly, and we do not know why they go in via the side door when the main hatch is open. There is some confusion as to whether Bucol

2 is the name of the sun or the planet: the Captain refers to 'Bucol 2's planet' but Servalan then says 'the planet Bucol 2.' There is a homing device on Dayna's bracelet, but how it works is never explained. Adrenaline and soma (which Justin inaccurately describes as a 'stimulant') seems to have gone from being a medicinal invention of Cally's to the Federation equivalent of coffee. The mutoids (who are never named as such, though notes written on the first-draft script confirm that this is what they are) have undergone a redesign from creepy, vampiric cyborgs to something resembling the backup dancers for a 1980s techno group. Orac's remarks about the fault in the 'anti-grav gyro' being located in the 'inertial guidance glycolene ballast channels' are pure technobabble, and one has to ask why a spaceship needs 'ballast' at all. (Although this is in line with the 18th-century technology feel of the series as a whole, the idea seems totally counterproductive.) The first draft of the script, like that for "Traitor", also contains terminology that differs slightly from that which was finally used: Slave is named 'Grovel,' Servalan is said to be 'Senior Space Commander,' and *Scorpio* is described as a 'Bucket Ship.' Finally, the story ends far too rapidly and conveniently, with one of the mutoids apparently disobeying her orders and gunning down Og for no apparent reason, and with everyone else who is surplus to requirements meeting a sudden and violent end in the last few minutes.

"Animals" is an episode that disappoints on all levels, and is inconsistent both within itself and with the premise and backstory of the rest of the series.

D6: HEADHUNTER

UK TRANSMISSION: Monday 2 November 1981: 7.20pm – 8.10pm
DURATION: 49:32
VIEWING FIGURE: 8.9m
CHART POSITION: 64
WRITER: Roger Parkes
DIRECTOR: Mary Ridge

CREDITED CAST: John Westbrook (Muller); Lynda Bellingham (Vena); Douglas Fielding (Technician); Nick Joseph (Android); Lesley Nunnerley (Voice)

UNCREDITED: Nick Joseph (Muller's Corpse)

SYNOPSIS: Tarrant and Vila travel to Pharos in response to a call from a former pupil of Ensor's named Muller, who wishes to leave the Robot Development Cartel for which he works. Muller teleports up to *Scorpio* with Tarrant; however, he becomes violent when he discovers that Tarrant has also brought up with him a sealed box that was in Muller's room. Vila strikes Muller with a wrench and apparently kills him. Slave becomes rebellious when Vila attempts to investigate the contents of the box; when Orac warns the others on the base not to allow teleport contact with *Scorpio*, the ship's life-support systems are mysteriously cut off, forcing Dayna and Soolin to go up to the ship to rescue their comrades. Muller seemingly returns to life and teleports down to the base; the crew discover that 'Muller' is in fact an android, which decapitated its creator and took his head as a disguise. In the box is the android's real head, which contains an inhibitor system. The android wishes to join with Orac and become the master of the human race. The crew lure the android out on to a metal footbridge, which they have electrified using an abandoned power station, and shock it into immobility long enough for them to put the inhibitor head on it; against Avon's wishes, Tarrant and Dayna destroy the android with explosives.

ANALYSIS: After the transmission of "Headhunter", a viewer wrote in to the *Radio Times* to accuse the story of 'irrational Luddism,' complaining that it was playing on fears that intelligent machines were predisposed to the enslavement of humans. He needn't have worried, as not only is the android in this story not going to frighten anyone over the age of five, but the episode does not stand up to repeated viewing or close analysis.

"Headhunter" was referred to in advance publicity material as a 'horror-comedy,' and this description seems to sum the story up. It does have some clever lines (Tarrant: 'He probably just wanted to get you away from the base, to avoid more bother over Muller's lady.' Vila: 'I was a perfect gentleman towards her.' Tarrant: 'That's what bothered us'; Avon: 'Well?' Soolin: 'Not very, by the look of it'; Vena: 'Our relationship is more...' Avon: 'Recreational'; and many others). There is also some very good direction from Mary Ridge, and we see for the first time crew-members sleeping on bunks contained within the walls of *Scorpio*, as well as, set into one bulkhead, a life-support/medical capsule, which is first mentioned in the notes of the script for "Rescue". Soolin gets some nice character development – she rather resembles a female version of Avon from the previous season, even getting some very Avonish lines – and Glynis Barber's performance is excellent. Tarrant's former personality resurfaces, with him taking the decision to blow up the android without consulting Avon; and Dayna once again shows her old interest in weapons design. Vila's attempt to turn Orac over to the Muller android reflects his previously-seen selfish cowardice, and the scene in which Soolin surprises Vila hiding in the cupboard and he creeps out self-consciously is well-played by Michael Keating. The story also fits with series continuity: Muller's apparent age (50-60ish) tallies with the idea that he was Ensor's pupil as a child; and the concept of the android having the same voice as his creator is taken from "Orac". The hydroelectric power station is undoubtedly from the pre-Hommik/Seska society; we do not see any of the natives in this episode, but presumably Nina's group have moved on by now.

Unfortunately, the story's only gimmick is the fact that the android isn't Muller, but is in fact wearing Muller's head, and once the gaff is blown, the inconsistencies rapidly become apparent. Why does Muller want to leave the Robot Development Cartel? Why has Vena, his mistress, contacted Avon for help, and why is she so surprised at the idea that the Cartel might use force to prevent him leaving? As a character, Vena is not up to much, doing little beyond providing some expository dialogue and then dying, apparently from being squeezed around the middle. Leaving aside the question why anyone would build an android with homicidal tendencies and messianic pretensions in the first place, it also seems incredible that Muller would develop an inhibitor system that is physically separate from the android itself, and not try to install it until after the android is activated. We never learn how the android managed to decapitate its creator without any blood and gore, anchor the severed head to its own body securely, and manage to make the head's mouth and eyes move, or why it collapses when Vila hits it with a wrench across the shoulders. It is likewise unknown why the production team did not get a shorter man to play the decapitated android; and the use of a thunderclap to represent the sound of a power surge is a little odd.

The android's behaviour is rather unbelievable. It seems incredibly thick, trying to kill Tarrant rather than using friendly persuasion to steer him away from the box; it staggers around the base bellowing 'Orac! Orac!' which, not surprisingly, alerts the crew as to what it is after. It falls for the oldest trick in the book when Soolin allows the crew to escape under the pretence of fetching Orac; it lurches up to Dayna's grenade and stands still while it blows up. We never learn how it is able to take over other mechanical devices; Orac's abilities in this regard have been explained as his being due to his ability to communicate with any device containing Tarial cells, but these are not mentioned in the story, nor is it explained how the android is able to take over Orac. One might also ask why the android wants to unite with Orac anyway, as it can do anything Orac can do, plus move; it is tempting to speculate that it is because it wants Orac's intelligence, but since Orac under the influence of the android simply babbles messianically, it seems a bit pointless. It is also an improbable superweapon, as it can be beaten by bombs and electricity; although it talks about taking over from humans, this seems rather unlikely under the circumstances. Why Avon wants the android is therefore a mystery, as there is little that it can do that Orac – a much more reliable device – cannot.

Avon does not fare terribly well in the story. He has a good moment when he takes the time to change his clothes despite being pursued by a mad android, showing his increasing vanity. He also takes off the helmet of his 'rescue suit' (improbably named, as, if Vila and Tarrant wear them on the ship, they cannot be for rescues alone) as soon as possible, and shakes out his hair. However, his putting the base at risk in order to rescue Tarrant and Vila – and his violently emotional reaction at the thought of their deaths – seems at odds with the increasingly amoral Avon of this season, who was unconcerned at Dr Plaxton's death and callously allowed Dayna and Vila to be captured by Space Rats. We also never learn how a 'rescue suit' with an exposed neck and *Rocketeer*-style fin is supposed to be any use at all.

Orac is, additionally, somewhat inconsistent. His line, 'There is nothing original about domination, as you will discover,' implies that he has worked out what is going on, as he is not yet under the android's control at this point; had he simply told everyone the truth instead of uttering oblique, doom-laden phrases, he would have saved a lot of trouble. As we have seen in "Power", Orac will give a straight answer when his own survival is at stake, so why he does not do so here is inexplicable. His performing medical functions (as opposed to psychological, as in "Voice from the Past") is something seen in this episode only.

In summary, "Headhunter" is a story with flaws that might be forgiven on first viewing. When returned to a second time, however, its many inconsistencies and failings become painfully apparent. Like many horror B-movies, the episode relies on a surprise twist to cover an utterly unbelievable scenario.

D7: ASSASSIN

UK TRANSMISSION: Monday 9 November 1981: 7.20pm –
8.10pm
DURATION: 49:30
VIEWING FIGURE: 8.8m
CHART POSITION: 71
WRITER: Rod Beacham
DIRECTORS: David Sullivan Proudfoot and Vere Lorrimer
(uncredited)

CREDITED CAST: Betty Marsden (Verlis); Richard Hurndall
(Nebrox); Caroline Holdaway (Piri); John Wyman (Cancer); Peter
Attard (Benos); Adam Blackwood (Tok); Mark Barratt (Servalan's
Captain)

UNCREDITED CAST: James Muir (Pirate Guard on Cell); Harold
Messias (Pirate Guard in Fight); Les Clarke, Carl Graeme, Nelson
Ward, Bryan Godfrey, Raymond Sargent, John Gooch, Jonathan
Truss, Bruce Guest, Harold Gasnier, John Brattle, Wayne Reed, Ken
Halliwell, Glen Francis, David Browne, Lee St. John, Alan Hardy,
Nigel Skeete, Keith Daly (Pirate / Slaves / Bidding Agents /
Attendants); Karen Willis, Diane Graeme, Sue Dorning (Slaves)

SYNOPSIS: Vila intercepts a message from Servalan to an
assassin, Cancer, naming a planet (Domo) and a date (the ninth),
and mentioning 'five subjects.' Suspecting that they are the
targets, Avon goes to Domo, a planet known for its trade in
slaves, and allows himself to be captured by slavers in order to

take the battle to Cancer. In the process, he loses his teleport bracelet, and an old slave named Nebrox helps him to recover it in exchange for a promise to free him; Nebrox also tells him that Servalan's ship and a mysterious black ship had both landed, and Servalan had purchased a slave that she had brought to the black ship, which had then taken off. After escaping with Nebrox, Avon tracks down the black ship; teleporting over, he and Tarrant capture a man who appears to be Cancer, and discover a dancing-girl named Piri who claims to be the slave that Servalan bought. Nebrox and Soolin teleport over to the ship. Cancer apparently escapes and Nebrox is killed. In searching for the culprit, Avon is knocked out by Cancer, who proves not to be the man but, in fact, Piri. She has killed both Nebrox and the decoy Cancer, and plans to kill him and Soolin and persuade Tarrant to take her back to Xenon Base, where she will kill the others. Soolin, however, works out who the assassin really is and, with Tarrant, rescues Avon and calls *Scorpio*.

ANALYSIS: "Assassin", one of the first television commissions for actor-turned-writer Rod Beacham, is not a deep story, and lacks subtext, but is much better than any episode of this season since "Power". Although it may be superficial, there are enough entertaining aspects to it to keep the viewer coming back after the gaff has been blown.

The dialogue, for one thing, is more than usually clever (Vila: 'You're going to kill an unarmed prisoner?'; Soolin: 'When did you get religion?') and there is a clear Boucher influence, particularly on lines like Avon's: 'The tape said five subjects. You can use your fingers if you like, Vila.' The exteriors are also very good (Vere Lorrimer, who took over to direct the location sequences when David Sullivan Proudfoot was taken ill, deserves extra kudos); the scene of Avon walking across the mudflats is well-filmed, as are the fight sequences. (Darrow reportedly insisted on doing his own stunts, and injured his hip in a fall doing so.) Although the plot is not deep, it has only one major flaw (see below) and makes for a welcome break from the 'collecting scientists' stories of earlier in the season. We also get some nice continuity, with Dayna's feud with Servalan being referred to for the first time since "Death-Watch". The space-pirates theme is highlighted in the location sequences and the slavers' costumes; the script also reveals Verlis's full name as Ohnj Verlis, an anagram of 'John Silver' (although the association between the two characters is tenuous at best).

The main flaw in the story is Nebrox. The reason why Avon keeps his promise to take him back to *Scorpio*, at some personal risk, is unknown; Avon is not particularly honourable, and has been seen to break his word on occasion when it suits him (for instance, in "Rumours of Death"). We also do not know why he takes Nebrox onto Cancer's ship with him. (As Avon says, he is 'not holding a convention for liberated slaves'.) At one point Avon does say to Nebrox, 'You could be in the way; on the other hand, you could be useful,' but he neither states nor implies how he thinks Nebrox could be a help or a hindrance. The general effect is rather as if the writer hasn't been able to think of a reason for Nebrox to come along either, and so has put in the line in the hope that the audience will believe Avon knows something that they don't. Nebrox's presence on *Scorpio* and, later, on the black ship is thus a case of plot taking precedence over character.

There are other, more minor, quibbles with the story. The sequence where Avon and Tarrant run around to the front of the captain's chair in order to shoot the figure they see in it (rather than simply shooting it in the back) is contrived, as its only purpose is to allow the false Cancer to ambush them; before they had shot the figure, it should have become apparent to them that it was a dummy, which would have aroused their suspicions. The spider used to assassinate Cancer's victims is very slow-moving, and the sequence where Soolin raises her hands just as it is about to bite is predictable. The writer cleverly got around the fact that the budget would not run to large crowds of extras for the slave-auction scene by making the apparent buyers brokers for dozens of real buyers. However, the brokers' outfits are ridiculously over-the-top, and it is painfully obvious that only one of them is allowed to speak. Proudfoot's fondness for *Star Wars*-style screen wipes is once again in evidence, to the point where it becomes intrusive. The make-up is also somewhat crude; Josette Simon and Jacqueline Pearce visibly suffer under the early-eighties fashion for blue and purple eyeshadow, and in certain of the studio shots one can see the shading under Darrow's cheekbones. Although Servalan gets a respite from the feathers for most of the episode, they do return briefly in the location sequences. The attentive viewer will be able to spot a number of clues pointing towards Piri's real identity; even leaving aside the fact that her name recalls that of the beautiful but malevolent Arabian spirits, we have Verlis's prurient chuckling over Servalan's purchase; the fact that she has never eaten mangon, the food of the slaves; and the crab badge that she wears.

Steven Pacey has gone on record as saying that he does not like this episode, chiefly because it shows Tarrant in a very bad light. He falls in love with Piri, who appears to be a brainless bit of fluff; she effectively calls him thick to his face ('I don't really like clever people,' she says, snuggling up to him); and later she says that once Avon and Soolin are dead, she expects Tarrant to take her innocently back to the base. This behaviour is very out of character for the Tarrant we have seen thus far, who is impetuous but never downright stupid, and he loses a certain amount of credibility as a result. As Pacey has remarked: 'Once your character has done something foolish or ridiculous, the audience remembers it, and you lose a little bit of respect, and it's very difficult to get that back.'

Avon, for his part, has a good day. Darrow, who is once again playing Avon rather than a version of Napoleon, is on top form; his new costume (all of the regulars having been issued with new outfits from this story onwards) also suits him well. (Darrow would revert to his earlier costume four stories later, finding the new one restrictive.) We get a few self-referential jokes at the character's expense; Benos's line, 'Bit on the skinny side, aren't you?' for instance. The same character's remark about Avon 'talking soft' seems like a dig at the received pronunciation accents of the series. However, the scene in which Avon sits back and watches 'Cancer' beat up Tarrant is excellent, as is his plan to sell himself as a slave. (The bit where he approaches Benos for help, sounding slightly unconvincing, is an outstanding acting job by Darrow.) There is a slight edge of bondage-and-domination to Servalan's line: 'I would prefer my slave to call me Mistress.' Soolin also has a good day, again resembling the Avon of last season, and her lack of sympathy for Piri is particularly well played. She, too, gets some of the best lines of the story: (after Nebrox expresses a wish to visit Piri) 'Why, do you fancy a little chat about the good old days on the chain gang?'; 'I expect a little suffering will have helped to make her a better artist'; (after slapping Piri) 'There are two classic ways of dealing with an hysterical woman. You didn't really expect me to kiss her, did you?'; and finally (in an epitaph for Piri): 'All sweet things have one thing in common: a tendency to make you sick.' Although Dayna and Vila get little to do, it quite clearly is not their episode.

"Assassin" may not be the deepest of stories, but it is well worth watching, and a welcome respite after some of the stories earlier this season.

D8: GAMES

UK TRANSMISSION: Monday 16 November 1981: 7.20pm – 8.10pm
DURATION: 49:28
VIEWING FIGURE: 8.0m
CHART POSITION: 95
WRITER: Bill Lyons
DIRECTOR: Vivienne Cozens

CREDITED CAST: Stratford Johns (Belkov); David Neal (Gerren); James Harvey (Guard); Rosalind Bailey (Gambit)

UNCREDITED CAST: Michael Potter (Stuntman/Burning Mecron/ Guards); Michael Gaunt (Computer Voice); Tim Oldroyd, Graham Cole (Gerren's Associates); Ken Halliwell, Harry Fielder, Pat Gorman, Sean Islip (Federation Guards); Trisha Clarke (Mutoid)*; John Brattle, David Browne, Les Clarke, Harold Gasnier, Nelson Ward, Bruce Guest, Wayne Reed, Raymond Sargent, Nigel Skeete, Vaughn Collins, Bobby Hart, Alan Hardy (Mecronians / Federation Guards)

SYNOPSIS: Avon, together with a corrupt Academician named Gerren, plots to acquire a cache of Feldon crystals – gems that concentrate energy and are thus a source of unlimited power – from the Federation. These have been stolen by Belkov, the man running a Feldon mining operation on the planet Mecron II, and, apparently, hidden on a ship, the Orbiter, stationed above the planet. Belkov is obsessed with games, and has modified his computer, Gambit, into a powerful game-playing device; the Orbiter is defended with booby-traps and games controlled by Gambit. Servalan, meanwhile, suspects Belkov of stealing the crystals and arrives on Mecron II to investigate; Belkov contacts *Scorpio* and offers to make a deal with the crew in exchange for his escape. Tarrant, Vila and Dayna teleport down with Gerren, but Belkov plays them and Servalan off against each other while organising his own escape, trapping Tarrant, Dayna and Gerren below the launch bay. Vila rescues them and, under orders from Avon, retrieves a circuit from Gambit, which appears to be upset that Belkov has ordered it to self-destruct on his departure. The crew escape, but Gerren is captured; Servalan extracts the apparent location of the crystals from him. Avon, Soolin, Tarrant and Orac go to the Orbiter and, with Gambit's help, overcome a series of trials; the final game, however, is really a trap, as its completion will focus the Orbiter's Feldon panels onto a black hole. Gambit refuses to allow Belkov automatic control of his ship, self-destructing instead, and Belkov is killed; Avon counters the effect of the black hole on the Feldon panels through a burst of power at short range from *Scorpio*'s weapons. The crew then reflect that their trouble has been for nothing; even a necklace of Feldon crystals that Vila stole from Belkov's quarters proves to be fake.

ANALYSIS: "Games", by Bill Lyons, an actor who had become an award-winning scriptwriter, is an entertaining episode that shows an improvement on some of those earlier in the season, although it does contain a few problems and logical inconsistencies, and lacks depth.

The episode was originally to have been directed by Gerald Blake; Vivienne Cozens, a former production assistant whose only previous credit as a director had been on a single programme (*Some of My Best Friends*), took over at short notice when Blake dropped out.

The premise of the story is one very much in keeping with the era: the early 1980s were the time when computer games first became popular with the general public. Although the realisation of the games in this episode – in particular the screens, the lettering and the presence of computer chess – is slightly dated, the concepts are quite advanced, including a shoot-em-up that reads and anticipates the user's skill levels, and a flight simulator as envisioned by the BBC Visual Effects Department. The depiction of the Gambit computer is more sophisticated than normal, drawing on the idea (of which *Blake's 7* first made use in "Orac") of an owner's personality (or one compatible with it) being transferred to, or exhibited by, a computer. Although Gambit is still hardware-based, we are seeing moves towards a more software-based concept of computing, with Belkov adding and removing games from the system as it pleases him, and Gambit's knowledge and abilities seemingly being contained in the circuit board that Vila removes without any loss of these faculties to the computer itself (suggesting multiple copies of a program rather than the physical alteration of a computer).

The story in general is refreshingly Machiavellian. Everybody is on the take, from Belkov to Gerren to Servalan herself; there are some excellent moments when Avon explains about Gerren's forays into manipulating the stock market, and when Belkov tricks Tarrant, Dayna and Gerren into trapping themselves under the launch bay. As for the *Scorpio* crew, Tarrant makes it clear that they must use the crystals rather than sell them and risk them getting back to the Federation, and Dayna agrees with him; Vila comes down on the side of profit; and Avon does not say what he intends to do. We also see Avon presenting the crew with a Blake-like *fait accompli*, and the crew objecting to it. Unusually, too, the embattled Mecronian resistance remain in the background; rather than becoming characters in their own right, they are restricted to being shady figures, creeping about assassinating guards and being duped by unscrupulous entrepreneurs. There is also a minor subtext as to where the crystals are hidden; although their location is never stated, they are neither on the planet nor on the Orbiter, implying that they are on the craft that Belkov uses to escape. Stratford Johns does a good job in the role; however, there are two problems with his character. The first comes at the end where, although the camera script has a sequence in which Belkov's ship is destroyed after Gambit refuses to give him automatic control, the explosion is not shown in the televised version, implying that Belkov has somehow made a clever escape. Secondly, Stratford

Johns' tendency to ad-lib some of his lines means that the phrase 'Lock the Orbiter panels into Cygnus XL' is rendered as 'Lock my controls into Cygnus XL and the Orbiter,' which turns the scene into nonsense, suggesting as it does that Belkov is locking his controls into a black hole.

There are also a number of differences between the transmitted version and the rehearsal script, most of which make sense, as they involve the removal of redundant information or the shortening of overlong scenes. Originally, for instance, when Belkov ordered a security scan, Gambit was simply to have shown a series of images, without Belkov specifying particular areas; and the final version makes it clearer what he is looking at. An early line referring to 'bloody traps' is changed to 'booby traps,' presumably with a view to avoiding shocking sensitive viewers. When the Gambit computer asks Vila, 'Would you like to play something? I'm programmed for all games,' Keating ad-libs the word 'madam' when he replies, 'That's very kind of you, madam, but not at the moment, thanks,' giving his response a more salacious character.

One change made at the recording stage was the removal of a camera-scripted scene in which pursuit ships fire on *Scorpio* after the Orbiter, which it has been using as a shield, has 'ceased to exist'. The removal of this scene – which makes for a cleaner ending to the story – also, however, necessitated the cutting of another line from the camera script, which stated that the planet was being pulled out of its orbit by the black hole. Had this not been done, it could have appeared, with the pursuit ships' presence unaccounted for, that Servalan had perished either with the destruction of the Orbiter and, as noted by Orac, everything in its immediate vicinity – or on the planet as it moved off-course; as it is, we can assume that Servalan remained on the planet and was able to leave with impunity later on.

There is, however, one deletion of scripted lines that seems to make little sense. This occurs after Orac reveals that the Orbiter's position depends on the distance and intensity of each star the Feldon panels are locked into. In the rehearsal script, the scene continued after Orac says, 'The successful completion of a game continues the sequence':

TARRANT: Different stars, different power levels. If we win this one, will we get back into orbit?

ORAC: Insufficient data.

Another scripted line that would have helped to make sense of the sequence was also cut. This was Avon's statement that 'the crystals concentrate negative as well as positive' energy, explaining, in story terms at least, why the crew are so concerned about the crystals being focused on a black hole. This, however, would have gone no way toward remedying the biggest flaw in the story: the idea that crystals that concentrate energy would amplify the power of a black hole, which is in fact a collapsed star with intense gravity that sucks in all matter, light and energy within its vicinity. This betrays a lack of knowledge, on the writer's and/or production team's part, as to what it is that a black hole actually is and does.

Although "Games" is another good story for lines – Vila in particular makes up for his relative lack of presence in "Assassin", both in dialogue terms and in his rescue of his fellow-crew-members on Mecron II – it also contains an abnormal number of production mistakes. Gerren is shot in the left shoulder on the Orbiter, but later he is seen holding his right shoulder.. After Orac has been transported over to the Orbiter, he is still visible on the *Scorpio*. (Admittedly, a fake Orac will turn up three episodes later in "Orbit", but under the circumstances, it's more likely to be a production error than deliberate foreshadowing.) There is an accidental camera wobble in the scene when Vila is talking to Gambit. Servalan is once again in extreme make-up and feathers, and the plain-chant heard during the Mecronian religious ritual is an inexcusable cliché. The model shots, however, are very good, as is the unscripted sequence of a burning Mecronian fleeing the explosions; the excellently-choreographed fight scene that culminates in a Federation guard being tipped into the mining machinery is reminiscent of a similar scene in the film *On Her Majesty's Secret Service* in which a skier falls into a snowblower, turning the snow red. This is also the only time that we see *Scorpio* fire what the script calls its 'main beam weapons.'

Finally, this story clearly demonstrates the problem with having Servalan go by the name 'Sleer.' Different people over the course of the narrative call her by different names, which must be incredibly confusing for viewers who happen to have missed earlier episodes. Although it does demonstrate that the Federation is much the same no matter who is in charge, Servalan's new role does not work terribly well in most episodes: either it causes confusion (as here) or else it is a liability to the plot (as in "Animals").

Although "Games" is an enjoyable story, and one that actually shows a little more depth than many of its contemporaries, it also contains a number of production gaffes and confusing script omissions that mar its overall impact

D9: SAND

UK TRANSMISSION: Monday 23 November 1981: 7.20pm – 8.10pm
DURATION: 48:51
VIEWING FIGURE: 8.3m
CHART POSITION: 87
WRITER: Tanith Lee
DIRECTOR: Vivienne Cozens

CREDITED CAST: Stephen Yardley (Reeve); Daniel Hill (Chasgo); Peter Craze (Servalan's Assistant); Jonathan David (Keller); Michael Gaunt (Computer)

UNCREDITED CAST: Andy Bradford (Stuntman/Double for Reeve)

SYNOPSIS: A Federation expedition consisting of three men and Servalan goes to the planet Virn. Their mission is to locate a unique trace element first identified by a team that was mysteriously lost five years ago. On landing, the pilot stays with the ship and the rest go in search of the base, with one of the men dying mysteriously on the way. *Scorpio* also heads for the planet with similar intentions; Tarrant and Dayna teleport down, but Dayna is wounded in an engagement with the Federation team and returns to the ship, unknowingly bringing traces of sand with her on her boots. Tarrant kills the other male Federation team-member; he and Servalan then declare a truce, while remaining suspicious of each other, and investigate the abandoned base of the original expedition. On board *Scorpio*, meanwhile, Vila seems afflicted with lethargy, and the computers apparently go haywire. Both Tarrant and Avon realise that the sand on the planet is a living being, which feeds off the cellular energy of humans; it kills off most males in any given group and keeps the females and the dominant male for breeding stock. The trace element turns out to be a preservative that keeps corpses fresh so that the sand can feed off them. Tarrant and Servalan, drawn together by their plight, make love. Later, both Tarrant and Avon discover that water destroys the sand; Avon uses *Scorpio* to alter atmospheric conditions on the planet and cause a rainstorm. Tarrant and Servalan allow each other to escape to their respective ships.

ANALYSIS: "Sand" (another story originally to have been directed by Gerald Blake and taken over by Vivienne Cozens at short notice) is one of the better episodes of this season, as well as one that, rather unusually for this period, refers back to earlier stories in the series.

Tanith Lee apparently based the script on conversations she'd had with Jacqueline Pearce about Pearce's own life (including an incident in which she moved into a houseboat adjacent to one in which Steven Pacey was living). The premise of the story is also in keeping with much of Lee's fiction, which frequently involves vampires, sexual entanglements and powerful magical forces. Soolin, unusually for *Blake's 7*, introduces a fantasy element by suggesting that Cally's death and the *Liberator*'s destruction point to a curse on the crew, although she then says that she does not really believe it. The sand also appears to multiply on its own (a few grains of it on Dayna's boots having in a couple of hours noticeably increased in volume), like some creature from a horror film.

There are also elements of the earlier *Blake's 7* episodes "Trial" (a living planet) and "City at the Edge of the World" (a couple seemingly trapped for eternity who settle down, make love and then hit upon the solution to their problems). Servalan going back for Keller recalls Dayna going back for Justin earlier in this season. There are also references in the dialogue to earlier episodes, including "Death-Watch" and "Terminal". Servalan reveals that she was able to use the *Liberator*'s teleport systems to escape destruction in the latter episode – which, as Tarrant notes, seems impossible, but then again we never do learn the full extent of the *Liberator*'s capabilities, particularly while it is in its death throes. We also get the first reference to Cally's death since "Rescue"; the hostility of everyone bar Soolin to discussing the issue suggests that it has been a taboo subject and a sore point for some time. (Vila's remark, 'If I died, it would be a real joke,' implies that Cally's death has raised fears for him that no-one would care if he were also to perish.) This is one of the few stories this season to suggest outright – as was common in earlier seasons – that the characters have lives and adventures beyond those that we see on-screen. Soolin refers to the events of "Sarcophagus", saying that the others have told her about them at some length, and elsewhere Servalan refers to the Presidency as having been 'stolen during [her] absence' – as the coup appears to have taken place before "Terminal", but after "Death-Watch", this is also an incident that occurred off-screen.

The pairing of Servalan with Tarrant, although unusual (as, up until now, Avon's name has normally been linked with hers), does develop all characters involved in new directions. There is also a clear attraction between them – the fact that both characters are emotionally affected by their parting at the end of the story indicates that their affair was not simply the result of mental manipulation from the sand (and in any case, Avon, Dayna and Soolin show no signs of mutual sexual interest in the scenes on *Scorpio*, even though the sand is clearly exerting enough of an influence to render Vila lethargic from the draining of his cellular energy). The fact that both Orac and Keller's computer, when going haywire, declare passionate love (and quote variations on the same phrase, 'We will be lovers for a little while, maybe for a long while, who knows?') seems to have more to do with the author flagging up the romantic themes of the story than with the sand's influence upon their dialogue. Tarrant and Servalan have an incredibly chaste love scene, with a torrid love-making session represented by a single kiss and a reference in the next scene on Virn to Servalan having been asleep. Dayna is the first to react when Tarrant reveals that he slept with Servalan, leaping out of her chair and stalking off, in what may be an understated reference to the implication in "Animals" that they had feelings for each other (both, perhaps, intended to build on their comic clinch in "Ultraworld"), but is more likely a now-rare allusion to Dayna's blood-feud with

Servalan. Tarrant is also very bright in this story, coming independently to the same conclusions as Avon about the nature of the sand and the trace element, and without using the 'probability square' that Avon employs to make sense of the facts in his possession.

The idea that Servalan's love affair with Keller at the age of eighteen, followed by his leaving her, fuelled her lust for power is also in keeping with what we have previously learned of the character's past. We know from "Pressure Point" that she was a spoiled brat, and it is possible that she channelled her frustration upon being rejected into her ambitions. There are, in addition, evidently power issues involved; Jacqueline Pearce has interpreted Servalan's actions after Keller left as being in her words, 'motivated by the mistaken belief that power brings invulnerability.' Servalan has apparently taken a while to get around to looking for Keller (we learn that the expedition disappeared five years ago, but Servalan is plainly older than 23, so he did not go off to Virn immediately upon leaving her); however, the break-up of the relationship has affected her greatly. Servalan's remark about how the tapes may not have reached the highest Federation authority at the time they were made very likely refers to herself, as she would have been at least Supreme Commander five years earlier. The absurdity of her new identity is again flagged up, as, although she notes that anyone close to Servalan was purged, the fact that Reeve recognises her suggests that there are many people left who would be able to identify her.

Apart from a slightly lame piece of poetry at the beginning from Keller, and a rather dated reference to 'running the tapes,' the dialogue is generally good. There is a return to some of the grimmer, more amoral lines of earlier seasons, with Dayna remarking that, as there are only four Federation personnel on the planet, they need only four of the bullets to work. Tarrant and Servalan also get some impressive pieces of dialogue, notably: 'Oh Tarrant, I'm just the girl next door'; 'If you were the girl next door, I'd move'; 'Where would you move to, Tarrant?'; 'Next door.'

The production quality is not always, however, up to standard. The Federation soldiers are risibly costumed in uniforms recycled from "The Harvest of Kairos", Stephen Yardley sports a silver bomber jacket, and Servalan wears an evening gown (with the ubiquitous feathers) to explore a remote desert (in contrast to the relatively sensible clothing she wore under similar circumstances in "Orac"). The fact that the triggers on the *Scorpio* clip-guns were set within their handles, and were very sensitive, has left an out-take sequence in which Steven Pacey tries repeatedly to pick up his gun without it immediately going off, and using colourful language as he does so. Pacey also accidentally broke the cube of spring water just prior to Tarrant's and Servalan's kiss, soaking them both.

"Sand" is a welcome – though long overdue – return to the mood and style of earlier seasons, which develops the characters of all the regulars in new directions.

D10: GOLD

UK TRANSMISSION: Monday 30 November 1981: 7.20pm – 8.10pm
DURATION: 48:29
VIEWING FIGURE: 8.0m
CHART POSITION: 86
WRITER: Colin Davis
DIRECTOR: Brian Lighthill

CREDITED CAST: Roy Kinnear (Keiller); Antony Brown (Doctor); Dinah May (Woman Passenger); Norman Hartley (Pilot)

UNCREDITED CAST: Mike Potter, Mark McBride (Stuntmen/ZVP Guards); Maurice Connor, James Muir, Derek Suthern, Reg Woods, Les Conrad, Malcolm Harvey (Guards on Space Princess); Bookie Daniels, Pauline Lewis-John, Elaine Williams, Doris Littlewood, Pat Butler, Chris Bradshaw, Leslie Adams, Giles Melville, Charlie Stewart, Les Conrad, Malcolm Harvey, Anne Higgins, Kathleen Heath (Passengers on Space Princess); Lee St John, David Browne, Carl Grahame, Nelson Ward, Harold Gasnier, Keith Daly, Nigel Skeete, Bryan Godfrey, Wayne Reed, John Gooch (ZVP Guards/Federation Guards)

> **SYNOPSIS:** Keiller, the purser of the pleasure cruiser *Space Princess*, contacts Avon with a proposal for a scam. The liner, unknown to its passengers, also ferries consignments of gold from Zerok to Earth, but the gold's atomic composition is affected by a process that turns it black and renders it worthless;

he suggests that they secretly prevent one consignment from being processed, and then steal it *en route*. However, when the *Scorpio* crew attempt to tamper with the processing, they are attacked by guards carrying different weapons from rest of the personnel around the plant, allowing the consignment to go through, and the processor is destroyed. Avon and Soolin investigate and learn that Keiller used to work for a Federation president; they accuse him of intending to double-cross them. He protests that he was forced to contact them by a mysterious third party who claims to have access to a way of reversing the process. Avon decides to continue with the plan; the crew smuggle the black gold off the cruiser and meet with Keiller's original contact, who turns out to be Servalan. Servalan seemingly admits defeat and pays them for the black gold; when they return to *Scorpio*, however, Orac informs them that Zerok has ceded to the Federation, meaning that Servalan is now able to recover the value of the black gold… and that the money she has paid them, being from the Bank of Zerok, is now worthless.

ANALYSIS: "Gold" is easily the best story of the season so far, and continues the high standard set by "Sand", returning to the tightly-plotted, subtext-heavy narratives of previous years.

The episode (one of four storylines that Davis, a former drama teacher, had submitted for consideration) stands out not simply for its good dialogue and efficient structure, but for being unusually hard-edged, even for *Blake's 7*. The body count is massive, with the crew gunning down non-Federation security guards on Zerok without compunction. This is in stark contrast to "Seek-Locate-Destroy", in which the crew were careful to either knock out or round up the Federation guards on Centero. It is also at odds with Tarrant's and Soolin's disgust when Keiller kills an unarmed man on the *Space Princess*, implying a situational morality. The crew are plainly after the gold for themselves, rather than reflecting on any ethical considerations as in "Games"; they have either become a sort of Baader-Meinhof group, or else have followed the course begun in the third season into a career as pirates. (Chris Boucher has stated that a descent into criminality was an inevitable development for the characters once Blake had left.) Rather than the leader-follower scenario seen elsewhere in the season, Avon describes his relationship with the others by saying: 'They're not my gang.... We are together for mutual convenience. I imagine that if I double-crossed them, they would try and kill me.' The reasons for this (as Avon is very much the group's leader during this season) are twofold: first, to frighten Keiller by implying that they are out of Avon's control, and secondly, to diplomatically suggest to Tarrant, Dayna and Soolin that they have more power within the group than in fact they do. The concept of the *Space Princess* is decidedly cynical: the passengers think that they're getting a luxury cruise (and are no doubt paying for it), when in fact, they are being shown a series of films of natural wonders while the ship flies directly to Earth, and being kept drugged so that they don't notice. Keiller makes some wonderfully offhand comments about the ship's doctor being a drunk and the plainclothes guards being rotten actors; the ship's new (and presumably sober) doctor seems unsurprised when Dayna pretends to be a drug addict in withdrawal, again suggesting a corrupt and decadent system. Finally, we get a hint as to the reason behind some of the confusion in earlier seasons as to whether Cally is 'human' or 'alien,' as the doctor uses the term 'alien' in such a way as to refer to humans not born on Earth.

Although the ability to change the atomic constitution of gold is plainly what Boucher calls 'baffle gab' (as is the idea of the gold having undergone a 'subneutronic overlap shift,' which conveniently rules out the use of the teleport, since Orac says that gold that has been treated in this way cannot be safely teleported), the concept does bear a resemblance to a famous real-life fraud: the Nigerian 'wash-wash' scams. In these, victims are approached and told that they are due to come into money, but that the money has been rendered worthless by being stained with dye. They are then persuaded to pay vast amounts for a – non-existent – solution to wash the dye off. The idea of Servalan giving the crew banknotes that she knows will shortly be worthless also recalls the Fritz Lang film *Doctor Mabuse the Gambler*, in which the eponymous antihero, who has manipulated the stock market to drive down the currency rates, gives a large amount of now-worthless banknotes to a pathetically grateful beggar.

This story also sees the return of the extensive subtext. Servalan (who, for once, is not referred to as 'Sleer') knows that Keiller has a previous acquaintance with Avon, and so orders Keiller to put the scam to him. However, she realises not only that Keiller will try to double-cross her, but also that Avon will still not trust him, even after he has realised that Keiller has nothing to gain from obeying her. Consequently, she brings in guards to attack them at the plant to stop them from preventing the gold being processed; as the processor is destroyed in the attack, the crew cannot simply wait and try the scam again on a new batch, but must go through with the plan as intended, meaning that they will have to come to her in order to obtain any profit from the venture. She knows that Keiller will go along with Avon until they arrive on Beta V, but also that Keiller's greed will ultimately override his instincts and he will therefore believe that she will uphold her end of the bargain. She has falsely told Keiller that after the heist has taken place, she will be acting as an intermediary for the Zerok Government to buy the processed gold back (as she is not acting for the Federation, and, without the equipment to restore the gold herself, it is otherwise worthless to her). She has also told him, presumably in order to convince him that he will not become surplus to requirements after the gold has been handed over, that once the transaction has been completed, he will stay on with the *Scorpio* crew and later, through some further ruse, reacquire the money for Servalan. This is evidenced by the fact that he says, 'I don't suppose I'll get paid now, will I, Servalan?' after Avon leaves him behind on the grounds that the crew do not trust him. She also deliberately leaves a clue to her presence in Keiller's record, knowing that, first, it will encourage Avon to follow through on the scheme in the hope of defeating her and, secondly, Avon will abandon Keiller to her tender mercies. (Servalan needs to dispose of Keiller because he knows too much.) Finally, she is aware, while they are not, that Zerok is on the verge of ceding to the Federation. Significantly, Vila – who, as Avon notes, is a professional thief and a good one – is suspicious of Keiller's plan; he is no doubt familiar with the underlying logic of scams of this kind. There is also a continuity link between this story and "Sand", in the exchange of looks between Avon and Tarrant when the latter says that Servalan is not a 'greedy gangster' and the former asserts that she is. The fact that – as in "Games" – the crew lose at the end (with Servalan making a clear profit of seven billion) adds considerably to the episode's entertainment value, as does Avon's almost insane laugh when he realises what has happened.

One slight drawback is that Soolin, Dayna and Vila are not as well-characterised as formerly, despite some good scenes such as the one in which Keiller tries to put his arm around Soolin and she threatens him calmly with her clip-gun. Paul Darrow and Jacqueline Pearce – allowed to meet, for the only time in this season – play their scene together to the hilt. Roy Kinnear is also excellent. Despite the fact that surviving behind-the-scenes footage from this story (Brian Lighthill's first ever directing job) reveals some problems with the recording of the fight sequence on the cruiser – at one point, for instance, the doors fail to close on time, and Darrow is consequently able to join the others on *Scorpio* rather than being left behind, much to the amusement of the cast and crew – the production is also good. The hotel-style décor and cheesy lounge music on the *Space Princess* set the tone nicely; and Servalan, although she does sport an opera-cloak, has at least shed the feathers for a change.

"Gold" is a good, solid story that acts as a marker to demonstrate how much, in the absence of Blake, the crew have lost their initial idealistic bearings, seeking personal profit rather than fighting oppression. By taking this path, furthermore, they wind up, appropriately enough, working for Servalan.

D11: ORBIT

UK TRANSMISSION: Monday 7 December 1981: 7.20pm – 8.10pm
DURATION: 48:37 – Viewing Figure 8.0m
CHART POSITION: 91
WRITER: Robert Holmes
DIRECTOR: Brian Lighthill

CREDITED CAST: John Savident (Egrorian); Larry Noble (Pinder)

SYNOPSIS: *Scorpio* approaches the planet Malodar in response to a message from a scientist, Egrorian, who has been missing for ten years. Egrorian requests that Avon come down alone and unarmed (stating that he will be subject to a weapons scan), in an automatically-guided shuttle, and that *Scorpio* stand off in deep space. Avon insists on bringing Vila, and also smuggles a small gun on board the shuttle. Upon their arrival, Egrorian offers to trade his invention, the tachyon funnel – which can destroy distant planets in seconds – for Orac; Avon agrees, and he and Vila return to *Scorpio* to fetch Orac. Egrorian is in fact working with Servalan, who helped him to flee the Federation; they plot to leave Malodar together, abandoning Egrorian's assistant Pinder. Avon exchanges a fake Orac for the funnel, and leaves with Vila on the shuttle; however, the shuttle proves too heavy to achieve escape velocity. Avon and Vila jettison all nonessential objects – including the tachyon funnel – but they are still seventy kilos short. When Avon asks what else could be jettisoned, Orac suggests Vila. Avon goes looking for Vila, who hides; Avon then discovers a speck of ultra-heavy neutron material, contained in a plastic block, which Egrorian has placed on the shuttle to weigh it down. He jettisons it and pilots the shuttle back to *Scorpio*. Servalan, angry at the failure of Egrorian's plan, abandons the scientists; Pinder ages both Egrorian and himself to death by exposing them to Hofel's radiation.

ANALYSIS: "Orbit" is a disturbing, cynical and subtext-heavy piece. Inspired by Tom Godwin's 1954 short story "The Cold Equations", it continues the upward trend in overall script quality in the last third of the season.

The crew continue to develop along the amoral lines seen in the previous episode. Egrorian states that he is offering the tachyon funnel to Avon because he knows that he will use it to crush the Federation 'ruthlessly' and set up his own command structure in its place. Vila's vision of this new order, furthermore, is hardly democratic or liberal, being aimed solely at his own personal comfort. ('All we have to do is knock out a few planets for target practice, then name our own terms... I'll have an imperial palace with solid diamond floors, and a bodyguard of a thousand handpicked virgins in red fur uniforms'.) Avon remarks, deadpan, that the crew's killings were committed in pursuit of liberty, and Egrorian says, 'Oh liberty, oh liberty, what crimes are committed in your name?' (in a quotation attributed to Marie Jeanne Roland, a victim of the French Revolution), after calling them 'ruthless desperadoes' and before referring to their leader as greedy, egotistical and cunning. Avon in particular shows increasing selfishness and ruthlessness: not only does he express a deliberate intention to put Tarrant (and Dayna) in the line of fire, but he cares more about keeping Orac than saving Vila's life, as, while he gets rid of the tachyon funnel early on, it never appears to cross his mind once to jettison the computer. Similarly, although Vila smiles when Avon talks of sending Tarrant down to deal with Egrorian, it seems not to have occurred to him that Avon might consider him equally expendable.

Tarrant, for his part, reciprocates Avon's attempt to use him as cannon-fodder later on, in a scene in which he prevents Dayna from teleporting over to the shuttle with bracelets. He states that *Scorpio* cannot dock without being stationary, but in "Gold" it is seen making two in-flight dockings; also in that episode, Avon is teleported from one moving object to another, rendering void Tarrant's second objection. It is worth noting that, while Boucher corrected other inconsistencies in Holmes's script, and did alter this line slightly, he allowed it to stand, assisting the implication that Tarrant doesn't particularly want Avon to survive the crash and is willing to lose Vila and Orac in the process.

Tarrant is the only crewmember who knows about Avon's plan to substitute a fake Orac for the original. (The decision to use the replica, which Avon had built some months ago, must have been taken fairly late in the day, after Avon became suspicious that the tachyon funnel could have been booby-trapped.) It is possible that Tarrant worked this out for himself, although it is more likely that he raised objections to Avon's stated intention to trade Orac for the funnel, so that Avon had to confide in him. (Note that Avon and Tarrant walk onto the flight deck together before Avon and Vila return to Malodar with Orac, suggesting an off-screen conversation.) This, incidentally, is yet another *fait accompli* on Avon's part; he will not tell the crew about the scam until after he has pulled it off.

The balance of power within the story is carefully worked out. Egrorian takes precautions against the crew using the teleport, and warns them that they will be subjected to a weapons scan. Avon and Vila do not then simply hide bracelets on the shuttle, because they are not anticipating trouble anywhere but on the base. Avon does not kill Egrorian and Pinder and steal the tachyon funnel upon first meeting them because he is, as he later says to Vila, concerned that it is booby-trapped; he does not kill them after the funnel is safely disconnected and loaded on the shuttle because he is aware that such a possibility will have occurred to Egrorian and that he will have devised some counter-measure – Egrorian, for his part, knows that Avon's caution will hold him back. Although Avon believes that he is going to be double-crossed, he is hoping that his double-cross is cleverer than Egrorian's.

Egrorian, like Krantor in Holmes's earlier episode "Gambit", is a sleazy, decadent and unscrupulous bisexual man. It is all but stated that his relationship with Pinder was originally sexual; he refers to the man, who was eighteen when they ran away together, as 'my golden-haired stripling,' and there is visible jealousy from Pinder whenever Servalan is present. Egrorian remarks that he would like to get to know Vila better (having Vila sit next to him and stroking his arm at one point); there is a model of Michelangelo's famous male nude, *David*, in the lab. Egrorian is also, however, cloyingly affectionate towards Servalan and speaks of them getting married and sharing power (in a reflection of the similar proposal that the bisexual crime-lord Rafiq makes to Triad leader Lily-Lee Tang in *Gangsters*; like Lily-Lee, Servalan plays along with this in order to get what she wants). It is worth noting that virtually all of Egrorian's physical behaviour, apart from his torturing of Pinder and his falling on his knees before Servalan at the end of the story, is unscripted, suggesting that it was perhaps worked out between John Savident and the director. Now that Pinder has aged due to his exposure to Hofel's radiation, Egrorian's sexual interest in him has been sublimated into physical torment; the scene in which Egrorian injures Pinder's arm is described in the first-draft script as 'sado-sexual,' and this implication remains in the televised version (particularly in Avon's and Vila's exchange of uncomfortable looks upon witnessing the performance, and Egrorian's later excusing of it with the line: 'Naughty boys must be punished'). However, Pinder would rather be tormented in this way than be left alone on the base by Egrorian and Servalan; any form of human contact, even cruelty, is preferable to isolation for him.

The script as it stands is one of the more salacious in *Blake's 7*, with Vila suggesting that Avon take one of the girls to Malodar with him to 'interest' Egrorian, and describing his imagined bodyguard of virgins as 'Vila's royal mounties' (suggesting that they won't remain virgins for long). The original script gave the planet's name as 'Turdes' (with Vila remarking that this was appropriate), allowing Holmes to work in bits of scatological humour about Egrorian 'sitting on Turdes' and being at 'Turdes command.' At one point, however, Tarrant's line 'I'll be darned' becomes, in the televised version, 'I'll be damned,' a rare example of language being toned-up rather than toned-down in *Blake's 7*.

The original script also contains a number of scenes subsequently cut. One of these shows Servalan loading a gun on her ship and concealing it on her person, strongly implying that she intends to kill Egrorian and Pinder whatever the outcome of their plan. Another has Vila asking how, if the tachyon funnel has just destroyed a satellite seventeen light years away, they can see the results instantaneously; Egrorian explains that this is related to the properties of tachyons, and demonstrates by training the beam on *Scorpio* and having Avon ask Tarrant to revolve the ship on its axis, so that they can see that the image on the tachyon funnel is operating in real time whereas that on the regular scanner isn't. (This is quite sinister, as the implication is that Egrorian could destroy *Scorpio* at any point.) Orac, on board the vessel, detects the beam. This leads on to another cut scene in which Tarrant, Dayna and Soolin reflect, after Avon and Vila have left with Orac, that Egrorian could conceivably now destroy the ship, as Orac's presence no longer protects them. The phrase 'Tarial cells' has been added to the description of the computer, presumably by Chris Boucher. The scene of Avon looking for Vila was originally to have featured Avon treading on Vila's hand and Vila struggling not to cry out. A shot of Vila sobbing as Avon searches for him (which was not scripted, but was recorded) was later cut as it was felt to be too disturbing.

There is a slight discrepancy in the script, in that the unit of measurement for distance is (Imperial) 'miles' but that for weight is (metric) 'kilos'. (The story title was originally to have been "A Few Kilos More".) There is also one in the production, when Egrorian takes thirty seconds to age to death, although we have heard that being exposed to Hofel's radiation for a fraction of a second aged Pinder fifty years. If Egrorian and Pinder left the Federation ten years ago, as the script states, and Servalan was the 'head of Federation' at the time, then the timeline for the past two seasons would now have to stretch over about ten years. There is also a continuity point, in that the stage directions state that *Scorpio* is at 'Roche's Limit' (first mentioned in "Traitor") above Malodar, after which Slave remarks that they are ten miles above its surface.

Darrow is very good in this episode; as this script is an intelligent one in which Avon is seen to be clever and calculating, his performance suggests that his mind is working away under a mannered exterior. When confronted with Savident's wonderfully over-the-top performance as Egrorian, Darrow wisely becomes very still, which means that he is in maximum contrast to the other actor. (Pearce's attempt to out-camp Savident fares less well.) The sequence with Egrorian failing to activate Orac, and Avon coolly producing the key, is entirely unscripted. Servalan has again shed the feathers, although the cubist metal shoulder brooch is not much of an improvement, nor are the earrings.

"Orbit" is sharp and disturbing, with the relationships between the regulars continuing their descent into amorality and mutual suspicion.

D12: WARLORD

UK TRANSMISSION: Monday 14 December 1981: 7.20pm –
8.10pm
DURATION: 49:07
VIEWING FIGURE: 8.5m
CHART POSITION: 74
WRITER: Simon Masters
DIRECTOR: Viktors Ritelis

CREDITED CAST: Roy Boyd (Zukan); Bobbie Brown (Zeeona);
Dean Harris (Finn); Simon Merrick (Boorva) Rick James (Chalsa);
Charles Augins (Lod); Brian Spink (Mida)

UNCREDITED CAST: Walter Henry, Mike Vinder, Arthur Parry,
Barney Lawrence, Douglas Auchterlionie, John Giles (Zukan's
Technicians); Ina Claire, Jean Channon, Sally Carpenter (Inhabitants
of Zondawl); Maykel Mills, Joe Phillips, Salo Gardner, Denis
Hayward, Ray Knight, Fred Reford, Ray Martin, Phillip Shelley,
Toby Byrne, Harry Fielder, Bryan Jacobs, Tony Pryor, Stephen
Whyment, Michael Gordon-Browne (Inhabitants of Zondawl/
Federation Guards on Zondawl and Betafarl)

SYNOPSIS: With the Federation increasingly gaining control of
other worlds through the use of Pylene-50, Avon arranges a
summit with the leaders of five powerful non-Federation planets;
he suggests that they band together to produce and distribute the
antitoxin. The leader of the most powerful group, Zukan of
Betafarl, arrives late, but with the necessary equipment; he also

says that he has the raw materials, but *Scorpio* will have to go to Betafarl to collect them. Unknown to Zukan, his daughter, Zeeona, has also arrived, having fallen in love with Tarrant during his visit to Betafarl. When he discovers this, Zukan orders her to return home on *Scorpio* with Avon and Soolin. Soolin, however, teleports Zeeona back to Xenon without Avon's knowledge. When they arrive on Betafarl, they discover that they have been deceived and a troop of Federation guards is waiting for them; on Xenon, meanwhile, the base is damaged by a series of explosions and an airborne radioactive virus is unleashed. It transpires that Zukan has arranged the betrayal with Servalan, in exchange for being let alone by the Federation to pursue his territorial ambitions; she, however, plants a bomb on Zukan's ship, and it is disabled in the explosion. Avon and Soolin escape but are unable to reach Xenon before the base's usable air supply runs out. Zukan, overhearing this, contacts them and offers to tell them how to obtain fresh air in exchange for rescue. Learning that Zeeona is on the base, however, he sinks into madness, and Avon has to work out the solution to the air-supply problem. Zukan is killed when his ship explodes. Once the crew have been safely transported to *Scorpio*, Zeeona volunteers to decontaminate the base; however, she dies when her skin is exposed to the virus.

ANALYSIS: "Warlord", by Simon Masters, a writer and script editor who was first published while still in his teens, is a story that is much better then its poor production values might suggest.

Somewhat surprisingly, considering Viktors Ritelis's excellent track record on series such as *Secret Army* and *Colditz*, the direction of "Warlord" is quite strikingly bad. Although there are a few effective model shots (particularly the sweep of *Scorpio*'s nose towards the camera as it takes off from the surface of Betafarl), and Zukan's ship is well-designed, these assets are for the most part outweighed by poor costuming decisions, trippy hallucination sequences and inexplicable close-ups on people's eyes. There is a dreadful (if mercifully brief) blue-screen effect when Avon and Soolin first reach Betafarl; and the electric-charge effect, on the cups when the delegates toast their alliance, and later on the virus victims, is also regrettable. Zeeona's costume and wig appear to have been modelled on those of contemporary singer/actress Toyah Willcox; as the other Betafarlians have normal-coloured hair, there is no reason for hers to be pink (and the fact that the person responsible also does her father's hair in a similar colour means that both characters suffer from a lack of credibility). The various delegates are dressed in an assortment of costumes from *Doctor Who*; Rick James (giving a truly dreadful performance) looks rather like American drag queen RuPaul in his bouffant, pearls and cloth-of-gold. On the other hand, we get the chance to see Bill Pearson's alternative *Scorpio* weapon, wielded by a Federation guard, and the 'rescue suit' returns, now with the neck covered and the word 'rescue' dropped. Although she is still cursed with overdone makeup, Jacqueline Pearce's dress is actually rather nice for a change; however, the actress recalls that costume designer Nicky Rocker originally wanted to cover it with a yellow feather waistcoat, which Pearce refused to wear on the grounds that it made her look like a canary.

The script can be clumsy at times, and there is a slight error when Avon and Soolin are said to have been on Betafarl for three hours, suggesting that they have been standing around in a desert muttering 'Something's wrong' for all that time. The 'airborne radioactive virus' central to the latter part of the story is also ludicrous, particularly as it appears to strike victims down instantly with electric discharges and then eat the flesh from their bones in minutes.

The characterisation of the regulars is, however, for the most part in line with what we have seen elsewhere. Vila especially is developed well; as in "Sand", he is a maudlin, selfish coward with a tendency to get drunk and snipe maliciously at his colleagues rather than simply a figure of fun. Dayna is also good, if underused. Servalan gets a brief final appearance in the series; Jacqueline Pearce was very disappointed by her lack of a proper send-off. Soolin, however, enjoys a particularly strong episode; as in "Assassin", she appears to work out that something is wrong before the others do, and acts strategically upon her suspicions. When Zeeona says that she believes her father does not want her involved in the venture because he wishes her to retain an image of respectability, Soolin responds: 'Yes, it may be politically expedient to be allied with us, but we're hardly respectable. It could explain it – *I suppose*.' [our emphasis]. This suggests that she is actually having some doubts about Zukan's behaviour and attitude. She then helps Zeeona to return to Tarrant not out of some form of romanticism, but because having her on the base will provide them with a bargaining chip should Zukan prove untrustworthy (although she does also seem to feel that Zeeona should stand up to her father). Later, Soolin claims to be Zeeona in order to keep the guards from killing her, signifying that she knows Zeeona's value to her father and that she is willing to use this knowledge.

Zeeona herself has interesting aspects to her character. It is, for instance, implied that she may be lying about being a biogenetic engineer, in order to justify her presence to Tarrant; she shows no evidence of actually being one, and the fact that she takes her glove off in a contaminated area strongly suggests that she doesn't know much about biology. Her death, unfortunately, has a tacked-on feel rather than flowing naturally from the events of the story, which is a pity.

The beginning of the episode also shows a return to the earlier, quasi-serial, format of *Blake's 7*; direct connections are made with "Traitor" and with other early stories of the season. Several months, at least, appear to have passed after the events of "Orbit"; since we last encountered it, Pylene-50 has been developed further and is now a standard pacifying agent in the Federation colonising programme. It is fairly safe to assume that, once resistance has been crushed, the levels of Pylene-50 will be reduced and the natives turned again into a productive workforce. The sequence in which two soldiers gun down several drugged natives on Zondawl, however, indicates the problems with this strategy; although the Federation now needs fewer soldiers to control their subjects, the guards are bored and consequently inclined to cause trouble. Initially, we see one soldier idly pretending to shoot the drugged people, which develops into a massacre when his comrade indicates that they don't need to pretend. The drug programme therefore does not necessarily mean a reduction in violence or loss of life.

Avon's alliance is well-thought-out. As the plan stands, Avon will gain regardless whether or not the alliance itself succeeds; if it fails, he can, by distributing the formula for the antidote, ensure that at least some people can resist the Federation. Together, however, the allies have a chance of actually presenting a united front against the invaders, rather than simply engaging in piecemeal acts of resistance.

The presence of Zukan is, nevertheless, critical to the formation of the alliance, as he is a powerful warlord behind whom the others might, ultimately, rally against their common enemy. He is apparently given to the grand gesture, as when he turns up providing not only the raw material as he was requested to do, but also the equipment. He is, however, a problematic figurehead; he has been engaging in pre-emptive strikes against his neighbours in the name of pursuing a 'defensive strategy', keeping them in a weakened state and worrying away at their territories. Servalan's offer, to give him free rein in the area in exchange for the alliance's destruction, suggests to him a strategy that serves his own interests better than the one offered by Avon; by obtaining the antitoxin from Avon beforehand, and then breaking the alliance, he can effectively indulge his own territorial ambitions unimpeded, implying that he would never have been content with simply pursuing 'defensive' aims. Like many, Zukan thus underestimates Servalan's duplicity (to say nothing of her ability to conceal bulky explosives in form-fitting dresses) and believes that he can get the better of her.

The key to Zukan's character is established in the speech he makes about life on Betafarl (which contains a slight suggestion that he is not native to the planet, as he is not accustomed to its natural conditions): 'It never sleeps. Perpetual light. All that energy. There are times when I miss the darkness. It is hard to live always in the light.' Earlier, in the freight bay, he shines his torch full onto his accomplice Finn, hiding himself in the shadows. Zukan therefore seems to experience a sense of discomfort with his own duplicity; the fact that he has something to hide means that he finds the constant light uncomfortable and yearns for the concealing darkness. His guilty conscience appears also in his slightly histrionic speech to Finn about dreaming of the faces of those whom he has killed, and later in his denial that Zeeona is on Xenon. Although he has no qualms about sacrificing Finn (despite Finn's apparent surprise at this action), to kill his daughter would be one murder too far. Rather than a ruthless and selfish leader, and in stark contrast to Avon, he is one who is uncomfortable with the necessity for sacrifice demanded by the role he has adopted.

At the end of the story, events have conspired to utterly destroy

Avon's seemingly foolproof scheme. Not only does he not have an alliance, but he also does not have the antitoxin, and he does not appear to have shared the formula with any of the delegates other than Zukan, who is now dead. With Zukan out of the way, the area is destabilised and easy prey for the Federation; the *Scorpio* crew, meanwhile, have lost everything in their attempt to produce an effective force for resistance, including their own base.

D13: BLAKE

UK TRANSMISSION: Monday 21 December 1981: 7.20pm – 8.10pm
DURATION: 49:38
VIEWING FIGURE: 9.0m
CHART POSITION: 77
WRITER: Chris Boucher
DIRECTOR: Mary Ridge

CREDITED CAST: Gareth Thomas (Blake); David Collings (Deva); Sasha Mitchell (Arlen); Janet Lees Price (Klyn)

UNCREDITED CAST: Terry Forrestal (Stuntman/Technician); Michael Bauer, Max Mundy (Bounty Hunters in Cabin); Steve Durante, Mike Mungarvan, Tony Starr, Cy Town (Technicians); Michael Bauer, Max Mundy, Pat Gorman, Jeff Wayne, Douglas Roe, Steve Durante, Mike Mungarvan, Tony Starr, Cy Town, James Muir, Harry Fielder, Peter Benfield, Graham Cole, Peter Gates Fleming (Federation Guards); Barry Summerford (Tando); Stephen Whyment, Steve Kelly (Bounty Hunters in Plantation)

SYNOPSIS: Fearing that their location may have been revealed to the Federation by Zukan, the *Scorpio* crew are forced to abandon and destroy Xenon Base. Avon announces that he has found a new figurehead around which to build an anti-Federation alliance: Blake, who is now a bounty hunter on the frontier planet Gauda Prime. Upon reaching this location, *Scorpio* is attacked by gunships and crashes on the surface; all the crew teleport to safety except Tarrant, who is injured while trying to land the ship. Tarrant is found by Blake, who takes him to a base and then appears to arrest him and turn him in; Tarrant escapes before he can learn that Blake is in fact recruiting a new band of rebels under cover of his bounty-hunting activities. The rest of the crew arrive in time to hear Tarrant's story, and Avon, believing Blake to have betrayed them, kills him. Dayna, Vila, Soolin and Tarrant are shot by a squad of Federation guards summoned by Arlen, one of Blake's followers who is secretly a Federation officer. Avon, surrounded by Federation soldiers, stands over Blake's corpse, raises his gun and smiles…

ANALYSIS: "Blake" is the final story of the series and, arguably, the best of all. Certainly it ends *Blake's 7* on a strong and dramatic note.

The content of the episode was kept a closely guarded secret by the production team, with scripts being released only a few days before the rehearsals began. The regular cast professed themselves to be shocked upon reading it, particularly by the final shoot-out.

Taking a leaf from Nation's book, Boucher's script reaches back into the series' past to echo key episodes. The scenario strongly recalls "Terminal": the action again centers around an allegorical planet with an element of destiny and of society degenerating into anarchy; and the ship is ultimately destroyed (the shot of Tarrant sliding down a floor-panel as *Scorpio* breaks up recalling an almost identical shot on the *Liberator* in "Terminal") due to the crew ignoring the ship's computer, which reaches out to them at the point of its demise. There are also, however, echoes of "The Way Back" in the story of an underground resistance movement infiltrated by a Federation spy, and in the sequence with the guards gunning down the protagonists; the enforced pacification of Gauda Prime recalls Vargas's story of his ancestors' activities in "Cygnus Alpha". There is a direct reference to "Terminal" at one point, and Vila's line about being 'harmless and armless' recalls a similar quip in "Time Squad"; there are references to the events of "Warlord" at the beginning of the story; and Avon uses another form of the Pearson kit-gun to kill Blake.

Boucher also uses the classic Nation bait-and-switch device by hinting early on (when Deva refers to the imminent arrival of a representative from the Federation High Council) that Servalan may appear, but never having her arrive or even confirming that the mysterious representative is in fact her. (Lorrimer says that it was felt that Servalan was overused, and also that it would be more surprising for the audience if she were *not* to turn up.) Soolin's history has also been referred to before (although here, for the first time on-screen, her planet of origin is given a name, 'Gauda Prime' – strangely, different from that, 'Darlon IV', given in the original character description), making this the culmination of a series of allusions that have been building up over the course of the season.

References to scenes from classic Westerns are again in evidence at the climax of the story: notably, the slow-motion shoot-out sequence in *The Wild Bunch*, and the freeze-frame ending of *Butch Cassidy and the Sundance Kid*.

This script is also thankfully free of coincidence. Even the arrival of the Federation guards is not simply down to ill-fortune; Arlen, having infiltrated Blake's base, has obviously contacted them and ordered them to close in on short order. Klyn refers to 'one or two transports' crossing without clearance, suggesting that the Federation troops were arriving in the area around the same time as Avon and the others. The story is also rather metaphysical, exploring the idea of tracing a single line through the pattern of infinity, and of the effect that the actions of individuals have on the rest of the universe. The setup on 'GP,' as the locals call it, derives from Boucher's love of Westerns, which often focus on territories where the law is officially suspended and then reintroduced by force following the exploitation of its resources. The idea of criminals being used to eliminate the lawless is particularly appropriate: set a psychopathic killer to catch a psychopathic killer. The production quality more than does the script justice, with the location scenes being particularly dramatic; there is also a clever sequence in which, during Avon's speech about 'thieves, killers, mercenaries... psychopaths,' the camera lingers on Vila, the women, Tarrant and Avon in turn, suggesting that there is an element of appropriateness in the crew finishing up on Gauda Prime.

Avon's behaviour in this episode marks the culmination of the hints throughout the series that he is not just an ordinary white-collar criminal but a man with a severe personality disorder. His relationships are either shallow or obsessive; he shows no emotion at the deaths of his crew, but has become obsessed with Blake to an all-encompassing degree. As well as emulating aspects of Blake's behaviour (although, since Avon lacks Blake's conscience, the morality of his actions is more dubious) he is determined to track Blake down no matter where he might be, or in what situation, in order to, effectively, force him into the mould of the heroic figure that Avon wants him to be. Darrow turns in an excellent performance, being particularly cold and psychopathic; note especially his casual killing of Klyn (originally to have been a male character; the change of gender lends an extra edge of nastiness to the murder), played by Darrow's real-life wife Janet Lees Price. Although Avon's speech about the necessary qualities of a figurehead leader is mannered, Darrow implies that this is a deliberate performance by smiling cynically as he adds, in a more naturalistic tone: 'Idealism is a wonderful thing.' Keating also acquits himself well, with his line 'You think it's Blake, don't you?' being particularly well-played; the only point at which Vila approaches being a figure of fun is when Soolin quips that he wanted to leave the base because the wine had run out, but in the context, this is neither inappropriate nor silly.

Soolin continues to develop as a character, speaking with a much harder tone than usual. Although she is normally very cool, in this story she reacts strongly no fewer than three times: once upon hearing the name 'Gauda Prime,' once during her exchange with Vila in the abandoned hut after the bounty hunters' flyer passes over, and once when she finds out that Avon was using a distress beacon to call the bounty hunters in. This indicates that Soolin is, for a change, totally on edge.

It should be noted, first, that the crew's lighting a fire is not as stupid as Avon suggests, as they weren't expecting bounty hunters to have been looking for survivors so far from the crash site, and secondly, that Avon is in fact using the crew as bait, whatever he may say; he was watching the hut, and so would have known who was in it.

Blake himself has changed since we last saw him, in more ways than the physical: Tarrant says, 'What on earth happened to you?' and he replies, 'Oh, most of it wasn't on Earth.' He has lost his faith in people, relying instead on tests designed to assuage his paranoia. The original description of Blake in the camera script says that 'One eye is covered by a black patch exactly like that once worn by Travis' (a scar was ultimately adopted instead at Gareth Thomas's suggestion), drawing a parallel between the Federation man who became an outlaw, and the outlaw who became a Federation man (as he must have been turning in or killing the outlaws who failed his test, thus doing the Federation's bidding). The trick he pulls on both Tarrant and Arlen is a test to find people suitable for the organisation, to see how they react when betrayed by an apparently friendly figure. He tells Arlen his real name (it is unlikely that his identity is widely known on Gauda Prime) to see what her reaction will be, and the 'information' that she has for Deva, by which she passes the test, is that Blake is a known revolutionary.

Blake's statement, in the wreckage of *Scorpio*, that he was shooting at gun-runners is clearly a lie; in fact, he was preventing other bounty hunters from killing or capturing Tarrant. He is playing a complicated game with Tarrant here; if Tarrant suspects that he is Blake, then the idea that he is trading with gun-runners (and Blake's implication that Jenna was killed running guns for him) implies that he is preparing a revolutionary force. It also puts them both on the same side, rather than suggesting that Blake is a bounty hunter. Having gained his trust, Blake can test Tarrant to find out if he is who he seems to be; as Blake cannot be unaware of Avon's activities (given that they are well-known to such individuals as Keiller and Egrorian), one obvious way to infiltrate Blake's organization would be to crash a Wanderer Class Planet Hopper on Gauda Prime and have the sole survivor claim to be a crewmember whom Blake has never met.

Although it is true that the resistance movement will need a figurehead, it is also plain that there is more to Avon's quest for Blake than mere expediency. As the cases of Anna and Avon's brother have revealed, Avon subconsciously divides the people he respects into two categories: those who betray him and are alive, and those who are true to him but dead. If Blake is alive, this puts him in the same category as Anna: someone who, by living, has betrayed Avon. In addition, the finding of Blake is a blow to Avon's psyche; the discovery that Blake is alive, and as such no longer an ideal figure for him to live up to, affects him greatly, feeding into his self-destructive urge. When Tarrant commits his act of self-sacrifice by remaining on *Scorpio*, Avon pauses before running to the teleport, suggesting a new-found respect for Tarrant; idealism is not dead in Avon. It is therefore not the case that, had Blake explained to Avon what he was doing, Avon would not have killed him; Blake's mere physical presence was the sign of his betrayal, and so Avon would not have believed anything that he said. But when Blake dies, Avon realises that he did not betray him after all; he stands over Blake (which is a scripted move), as if protecting his body.

The biggest question that has been asked about this episode is, however, whether or not there could have been a fifth season, had the BBC decided to renew the series. Chris Boucher was under instructions to 'wrap the series up,' but he still maintains that, had circumstances changed after this episode had been broadcast, he could have written a story that brought back those of the regulars who were willing to return. While his abilities in this regard are indisputable, in this case, unlike the Nation season-enders, there is little way out of the scenario as seen for any of the protagonists. Leaving aside the fact that the effects of the shots on the crew appear conclusively fatal, at no other point in the series has any Federation soldier possessed a stun weapon (making it unlikely that this is the case here), and the usual pattern has so far been that, when a group of guards arrive, they kill everyone. Furthermore, there is no indication that this is some convoluted plan of Servalan's; and, in any event, she has never shown interest in the crew's long-term survival. As for the possibility that the Blake we see die is in fact the clone that appeared in "Weapon", it's worth noting that the clone was programmed with the Clonemasters' reverence for life, which is scarcely in keeping with a future career as a bounty hunter. Although it is possible that one or more of the crew were merely wounded rather than killed, this would be an extremely lucky occurrence that would rather go against the grain of the episode, and Blake himself would certainly be dead.

Although the final scene goes to a freeze-frame before we see Avon die, his chances of survival are even more remote than those for his crew. At the end of the story, he raises his gun, not to surrender but to aim it at the guards; we then hear, as the credits roll, the sound of his gun ringing out followed by other shots. (Although we hear what sounds like Avon's gun again, it might not have been his, as the troopers carry different types of weaponry.)

Orac is not present during this scenario (probably hidden or left in the flyer by the crew, as they would not bring him into a potentially dangerous situation), but it is difficult to imagine what he could usefully contribute. The possibility that what we hear over the credits is in fact a firefight between the guards and the Security force called in by Klyn earlier in the episode is not one that raises the odds on Avon's survival any more than a scenario in which he faces the guards alone. There seems no way out for Avon.

This story is an appropriate end to an excellent series. Blake is now conclusively and visibly dead (whereas at the end of "Terminal" there was always the possibility that Servalan was lying), and the rest of the crew have also apparently been killed in a firefight that brings to a conclusion many of the themes and running plots of the season. From the very beginning, we have been left under no illusion that being a rebel is a safe occupation, with the deaths of characters who were introduced as if they were to be regulars, followed by the deaths of the actual regulars Gan and Cally, and the destruction of Zen and the *Liberator*. We have also seen an idealistic movement degenerate, over the course of four seasons, into a marginal band of pirates and criminals who, in the end, are more supporters than attackers of the system that exists. The whole series has thus been predicated on the idea that revolution is a grim process, which is easily co-opted by greed and venality, and whose practitioners tend to meet violent ends. It is fitting, then, that as the credits roll, there is no Seven anymore, and certainly no Blake.

AFTERWORD

Blake's 7 has an enduring legacy, which still remains influential over a quarter of a century later. It was a series of a type only really found in the 1960s and 1970s: a pulp show that was intelligently written and tackled controversial themes that are still relevant today – perhaps, considering the recent spread of international terrorism and some of the new developments in biogenetics and computing technology, even more so.

The four years of the series' initial broadcast also saw considerable social change. Leaving aside the fact that, as noted, it was a very White and middle-class series at the outset but gradually came to incorporate more multiethnic and working-class actors as disadvantaged groups came to new prominence in British society, it also straddled the changeover from a declining Liberal-Labour government and rising social unrest to the more confident, although no less controversial, reign of Margaret Thatcher's Conservative government. In America, the same period saw the shift from Jimmy Carter's ultra-liberal administration to Ronald Reagan's hard-nosed, corporate-materialist government. There were also a number of celebrated terrorist situations, from ongoing conflicts in South Africa and Northern Ireland, to the Iranian Embassy crisis and CIA covert operations in South America and Afghanistan. In some ways, the series became prophetic within its own lifespan, as the world shifted to the right and charismatic leaders of both genders became popular figures.

Blake's 7 also had a strong influence on many telefantasy series that came afterwards. *Red Dwarf*, for instance, was a story about space exploration not from the point of view of heroes, but from that of a small band of acerbic characters of a range of ethnic and social backgrounds (one, like Orac, a dead man's personality revived as a computer program) and an attitudinous ship's computer. *Red Dwarf* episodes abounded with downbeat endings, knowing postmodern winks at the audience and explicit sexual and scatological humour (resulting in the banning of one episode in the USA), and the series also developed story arcs and end-of-season cliffhangers.

Another series even more directly influenced by *Blake's 7* was

Babylon 5, the creator of which, J. Michael Straczynski, was an avowed fan of the former series (and even attempted to get some of the original cast of *Blake's 7* to make guest appearances); he also took on a Nationesque role, writing large portions of the series himself. Ron Thornton, a designer on both series, has said that the form of the *Whitestar* (which also, incidentally, boasts an auto-repair system) was a deliberate homage to that of the *Liberator*. As well as borrowing the story-arc concept and the idea of getting around a low budget by concentrating on deeper social and political themes, *Babylon 5* featured a number of characters (Londo and G'Kar, Garibaldi, Kosh, Talia and Lyta, for instance) whose personalities incorporate both heroic and villainous aspects. The steady descent of Earth into Fascism over the course of the first three series, as well as the running themes of psychic manipulation through technology and genetic engineering, also echo many of *Blake's 7*'s preoccupations. The main difference between the two series, however, is that in *Babylon 5*, the protagonists actually win.

The late 1990s have seen the development of not one but two series involving living ships with motley crews of unpleasant and acerbic people on the run (at least initially) from totalitarian organisations. *Lexx* features as its protagonists a humourless, possibly undead assassin (who is forced, mutoid-like, to ingest a bloodlike substance in order to stay alive), a beautiful woman, a decidedly unheroic pilot, and a randy computer (with a portion of a human brain as one of its components) that is carried about by the other cast members. The series' stories explore ideas of reality versus hallucination, mind transference, morality and the abuse of human rights. *Farscape* has a more conventional hero, but his crew includes a female warrior, mystical psychic women, a comedic cowardly alien, and a strong man who may or may not have killed his own wife in a blind rage. The chief villains of the series are a leather-clad near-psychopath with whom the hero has a close emotional relationship, and a short-haired female military commander who is over-fond of black and white evening gowns.

Some of the more big-budget American series have also picked up on aspects of *Blake's 7*. *Star Trek: The Next Generation* featured an empathic character (played by Marina Sirtis, who auditioned for the parts of Cally and Dayna) and end-of-season cliffhangers; its sequels featured story arcs (albeit probably poached from *Babylon-*

5), hostile, invading shape-shifters from an unexplored region of space, social allegories, and the presence of a potentially destructive element (*Voyager's* Seven of Nine) in the ship's crew. Joss Whedon, another self-confessed fan of *Blake's 7*, has filled his series *Buffy the Vampire Slayer* and *Angel* with story arcs, ongoing character development, postmodern jokes and fourth-wall breaches: one episode of *Angel*, "She", is a deliberate retread of "Power"; Spike is a villain forced onto the side of the good guys by virtue of having a limiter (albeit a different sort of device from Gan's); and Willow descends gradually into evil – with the best of intentions – in a way recalling the corruption of Avon and Blake.

Also worthy of note is Dennis Potter's posthumously-produced teleplay *Cold Lazarus*, which was an explicit homage to *Blake's 7*. Featuring another strong female villain and anti-establishment terrorists, it focused around a future dominated by corporations and unscrupulous scientists seeking to exploit the preserved memories of a long-dead writer. The story had the hallucinatory feel and reality-questioning message of such episodes as "Terminal" and "The Way Back".

Finally, it is worth considering whether or not *Blake's 7* could have been viable in the 21st century, with our increasing acceptance of regional and non-White actors, cheaper yet better effects and fewer curbs on violence. On the one hand, the answer would seem to be yes; attitudes and technology have changed such that, if it were to be made today, one would get a much more polished product that did not pull its punches about sex and violence. On the other hand, however, it is doubtful whether a series about terrorism from the point of view of the terrorists would even be considered in the present political climate; modern telefantasy is much less experimental and controversial, and more hesitant to tackle serious issues of the sort that might touch a nerve with the public. Furthermore, stories of this relevance and complexity are now limited to arts programmes and European cinematography (perhaps explaining why *Blake's 7* has a small but thriving Continental fan-base), not in family shows going out at quarter past seven at night; since the series ended, only Dennis Potter has really been able to claim the same achievement.

Blake's 7 may have been ahead of its time in many ways, but it is also a series that could not have been made at any other point in television history. The coincidence of excellent writing and innovative attitudes to storytelling with a particularly experimental period within mainstream television production has made it unique in the history of telefantasy, if not of television itself.

INTRODUCTION: APPENDICES

Despite the fact that a number of ideas for *Blake's 7* merchandise (including action figures) were considered at one point or another, and despite Nation's reputation as an aggressive salesman (David Maloney recalls that the BBC Enterprises representatives with whom they spoke were visibly terrified of him), relatively little spin-off material was actually produced. A few items of fairly standard merchandise – novelisations (*Blake's 7*, *Blake's 7: Project Avalon* and *Blake's 7: Scorpio Attack*, all by Trevor Hoyle), annuals, spaceship models etc – were produced during the lifetime of the series. Further items, both official and unofficial, have been issued since, including factual reference works, more items of merchandise – replica props, badges and so forth – and a good deal of fan-fiction. The series has been released on video in its entirety a number of times. Also, between 1985 and 1990, the BBC released four 'compilation' tapes, each of which featured three or four episodes compressed into a two-hour story. These were: "The Beginning" (comprising "The Way Back" to "Time Squad"), "Duel" (comprising "Seek–Locate–Destroy", "Duel" and "Project Avalon"), "Orac" (comprising "Deliverance", "Orac" and "Redemption"), and "The Aftermath" (comprising "Aftermath", "Powerplay" and "Sarcophagus").

Following the mandate of our book to explore the series, its themes and its development, we are going to concentrate in this section on those spin-offs that are best known to fans of *Blake's 7* and that have, in one way or another, sought to advance or add to the series. (The annual and comic strip stories, however, fall outside the scope of this book.) Appendix A covers and analyses the two BBC audios – *Blake's 7: The Sevenfold Crown* and *Blake's 7: The Syndeton Experiment* – and two original novels – *Blake's 7: Afterlife* and *Avon: A Terrible Aspect*. Appendix B covers the two not-for-profit audios – *The Mark of Kane* and *The Logic of Empire* – sold through various *Blake's 7* fan organisations,; and the *Kaldor City* series of original audio adventures, which feature Carnell, a character created by Chris Boucher for the episode "Weapon". In this instance, due to the nature of the material, we have opted not to provide any analytical coverage.

APPENDIX A

BLAKE'S 7: AFTERLIFE

PUBLISHER: Target Books (1984)
AUTHOR: Tony Attwood

SYNOPSIS: Five months after the events of "Blake", Avon is being held captive on Gauda Prime by a mysterious woman named Korell. He escapes and encounters Vila, who has been hiding in a freighter. Together with Korell and Orac, they plan to flee the planet and upgrade the freighter, but are partly thwarted when Servalan arrives and confiscates both Orac and Caro, a second Orac-like device built by Ensor. They go to the planet Skat to obtain sygnum ore for shielding, and stumble across a means of travelling into parallel universes through 'white holes'; they also visit the planet Ghammar, where the natives offer them the materials with which to build a teleport in exchange for the technology, but Avon double-crosses them and flees with the materials. They then go to Terminal and set up a base there, from which Avon plans to steal ten thousand million credits from the Federation banking cartel. A civil war breaks out between Servalan, the Federation's military wing and the Earth Administration, with the Ghammarians also involved. Captured as he attempts his bank fraud, Avon bargains for his freedom by offering to help the Federation defeat the Ghammarians. Servalan arrives on Terminal, and is killed by Korell, who turns out to be an agent of the Administration. Avon and Vila are rescued by a group led by Tor, Avon's sister; she has been controlling Avon through a technique known as Machine Induced Neural Deviance (MIND), and plans to take over in the wake of the chaos of the civil war. The story ends with Tor poised to make her plan a reality…

ANALYSIS: It would be an understatement to say that *Blake's 7: Afterlife* is not a worthy sequel to the series. It is far worse than any of the series' lowest moments, riddled with internal and continuity errors, and with a plot that is difficult to follow at best.

The premise of the story itself is based on a misunderstanding.

Attwood's stated intention was to tie up the loose ends from "Terminal" and "Blake"; the problem is that there don't appear to be any. Failing to see a simple answer for Avon's behaviour in these episodes – that his obsession with Blake was causing him to become unhinged – he opts for a complicated one, that Avon was being mentally manipulated by an outside force (which, incidentally, contradicts Attwood's own assertion, in his preface, that Avon acted as he did on Gauda Prime because he suspected a trap). The story that follows feels very much as if Attwood is trying to rewrite *Blake's 7* along the lines that he wanted it to run, getting rid of characters he doesn't like (e.g. Tarrant, Servalan and Orac) and introducing ones of his own devising (Korell, KAT, and the Blake computer).

Furthermore, there is a serious flaw in the plotline involving Servalan's plan to sell weaponry obtained through a white hole to the Federation, and thus, as anything brought into another universe deteriorates rapidly, leave it in a weakened state. If, as the novel says, the plan has been operating for only a few months, this implies that the Federation, somewhat improbably, would have replaced half its troops' weaponry in less than a year. It also implies that the guns deteriorate at a very rapid rate indeed (as, if they break up at a slower rate, too few will be affected to make any difference), which begs the question why the Federation haven't noticed by now, unless Servalan is operating on a very small scale, which would be totally ineffectual. If the imports in question were mechanical parts to be fitted into extant armaments, this would make more sense; however, as the text clearly states that it is whole weapons that are to be replaced, the scenario becomes unworkable.

The way in which the regulars are characterised is also at odds with their portrayal in the series. Servalan is said to be a 'crude fighter' who kills anything she comes across (which appears to stem from Attwood's taking her line 'Where there's life, there's threat' to be a literal statement of her beliefs); Blake is said to have been a homicidal maniac and a lunatic. Avon, who is mostly described in terms of gestures and movements, is very much portrayed as an action hero, where Vila is even more moronic than he was in "Ultraworld". (By the time it is asserted that he was an 'alpha plus' [sic], it's hard not to groan.) KAT, Vila's handheld computer, is nothing more than annoying, and the ship's computer, named

'Blake,' although said to be programmed with a personality, gives no evidence of having one. There is also an unfortunate undercurrent of misogyny running throughout the story. Servalan and Tor are characterised as mad, ruthless bitches, where Korell (whose physical description, being very much of the 1980s, gives the book a rather dated feel) gets virtually nothing to do at all, and there are hints at the end of the story that she too is a ruthless bitch.

Structurally, the novel is a mess; the plot wanders through unconnected set-pieces for three-quarters of the text, then ties them all together at the end, which consequently has the feel less of clever Dickensian prose and more of someone desperately trying to fit all the incidents that have occurred into a single conclusion. Orac and Caro (a somewhat unimaginative backward spelling) are introduced with great fanfare, then, after they are appropriated by Servalan, we hear nothing more of them bar a couple of passing references. Tor, by contrast, appears only one chapter before the end of the story (on a spacecraft named the *Blake's 7*), with no foreshadowing, and the very premise of having Avon's sister being a fanatical revolutionary strains credibility to the breaking point. Tarrant appears, wanders around for twelve pages and then, apparently, dies. MIND is mentioned at least once per chapter, to no apparent purpose.

The book is also riddled with elements that contradict information given in the series; to cite only two of the most glaring, it is stated that Ensor intended to sell Orac to the Federation, and that Terminal is in Sector Five, and was established by a business consortium in order to develop fast-growing food. The idea of the fauna instantly evolving to fit the changing environmental conditions is also at odds with the description of the project given in "Terminal". Furthermore, the book contains several typos; most notably, it is unclear whether the name of the second Ensor computer is Caro or Cora. A former member of the *Scorpio* crew named 'Sollin' is also mentioned.

In its defence, *Blake's 7: Afterlife* does have two good points. One is a scene in which the Federation Chief Commander Rodin and his men cannot verify the identities of Avon, Vila and Korell because, on the project with which they are involved, there is 'so much secrecy and security… that we don't even know who is doing what and where.' The other is the revelation at the end of the novel that the Administration has been secretly fomenting and supporting rebellions – including Blake's setup on Gauda Prime – in order to keep the Federation military occupied. Unfortunately, neither of these is enough to raise this book to the standard of even the weakest stories of the series itself.

A sequel, entitled *Blake's 7: State of Mind*, was planned but never written. Considering the problems with *Blake's 7: Afterlife* (with which Terry Nation was reportedly unimpressed), it is probably just as well.

AVON: A TERRIBLE ASPECT

PUBLISHER: Citadel (1989) [US]/Carol Paperbacks (1991) [UK]
AUTHOR: Paul Darrow

SYNOPSIS: Rogue Avon, a dissident against the Federation, is being pursued by his half-brother, Axel Reiss, who wishes to kill him in revenge for an old injury. Rogue is killed by Reiss in single combat, but before that fathers a child, Kerguelen ('Kerr'), by a woman named Rowena. Rowena flees with her son to Saturn, where she becomes the consort of a surgeon named Pi Grant, who has two adopted children, Del and Anna. Kerr is raised with them and, in time, undergoes military training to become one of the Federation's elite Iron Guard. He also becomes Anna's lover. Determined to avenge Rogue's death, Rowena kills one of Reiss's associates. In the process, however, she comes to his notice, and Reiss has both her and Grant killed. Some time later, Kerr learns of the true circumstances of his mother's death and is offered a position with the Seventh Family, a group that controls the Federation banking system. He fights and kills Reiss, and plans to steal five hundred million credits and flee to a neutral group of satellites with Anna, but is betrayed by his collaborator, Maco, arrested and sentenced to transportation.

ANALYSIS: *Avon: A Terrible Aspect* is an entertaining, often witty, pacily-written story with the only real disappointment being that it bears little relation to the series to which it is supposedly a prequel.

The novel is written in a 1950s pulp-sf style, with action sequences and a macho ethic in keeping with that genre, and the language used seems to be a deliberate homage to such novels (making for some genuinely hilarious sex scenes). It has three main male protagonists, Rogue Avon, Axel Reiss and Kerr Avon, all of whom, coincidentally, resemble each other (meaning that, as Paul Darrow has facetiously remarked, there would be at least one role for him if the book were to be filmed). The novel's main strength lies in its clever treatment of Federation politics, which is complex and multilayered; frequently, what seems to be a cliché or shortcut turns out to be the opposite (as when a prostitute appears to join forces with Rogue, betraying her employers, simply because she fancies him, but is later revealed to be acting as a double agent). It is also very easy to follow despite this complexity, being plainly put and with the political machinations well explained. The book is split into four sections, each focusing on a different character and giving their version of the story's events, allowing multiple perspectives on the action.

There are a few problematic details within the novel. The science is generally quite sloppy, with the Clouds of Magellan (which are, incidentally, two galaxies) apparently having relocated themselves from sixteen thousand light years away to within our Solar System, and one character dropping dead due to having been raised on a planet with a turbulent atmosphere and then travelling to one with a calmer atmosphere. There are a number of unintentionally comic references to 'the wars for Uranus' (including one in the very first sentence of the novel). Some of the names are also problematic, with 'Axel Reiss' being a bit too close to 'axle grease' for comfort, 'Rogue' being something of a dubious name for anyone who isn't one of the X-Men, and Rowena deliberately giving her son a name meaning 'desolation' (which is a bit like giving your child a name that means 'manic-depressive' or 'dreadful' in another language).

The main problem with the book for fans of the series is that, however enjoyable it may be, it seems to have little if anything to do with *Blake's 7*. The Federation is here portrayed as a society along the lines of ancient Rome, with slavery, decadence and Nine Families controlling everything through dynastic principles, and not as the Soviet-inspired totalitarian state we see on the screen. There is also a hint of a patriarchal principle of inheritance, which is at odds with the largely gender-egalitarian Federation of the series. Dissidence seems to take the form of regular, violent revolts rather than political action and terrorism, and the Federation appears to be confined entirely to the Solar System. There is also conflict with the series in that Cygnus Alpha is said to have been acquired only recently, whereas the series paints it as a long-established penal colony. Del and Anna Grant, and Tynus, are also rather different from how they appear in the series: Grant is described as a superficial man who is easily led and susceptible to flattery, where his sister is a weak-willed drug addict whose betrayal of Avon is rather different from that described in "Countdown" and "Rumours of Death". Avon's fraud scheme, which involves siphoning money into a bogus corporation set up on Jupiter, is also different from that described in the series, and is very much secondary to the central plot of him seeking revenge on Axel Reiss.

The portrayal of Avon, furthermore, is at odds with that seen on television. Here he is said to be a man raised in aristocratic surroundings, who was trained to the military at an early age. He is an honourable man who always keeps his word, and who places revenge against his parents' killer above all other goals including personal safety. While this may not be a total departure from the televised version of Avon, it is hard to square it with the self-interested, cold and unstable man we see in the series.

As a prequel for a *Nineteen Eighty-Four*-inspired series, *Avon: A Terrible Aspect* is less than successful. As a pulp-fiction-inspired novel, however, it is eminently readable.

BLAKE'S 7: THE SEVENFOLD CROWN

UK TRANSMISSION: BBC Radio 4. Saturday 17 January 1998: 2.30pm – 4.00pm
WRITER: Barry Letts
DIRECTOR: Brian Lighthill
INCIDENTAL MUSIC: Jeff Mearns

CAST: Paul Darrow (Avon); Jacqueline Pearce (Servalan); Michael Keating (Vila); Steven Pacey (Tarrant); Paula Wilcox (Soolin); Angela Bruce (Dayna); Peter Tuddenham (Orac/Slave); Pip Donaghy (King Gheblakon); Janet Dale (Jelka); Christian Rodska (Dr Kapple); Simon Carter, Kim Durham, Cornelius Garrett, Susan Jeffrey, Katherine Mount, Graham Padden, Rob Swinton (Other Roles)

SYNOPSIS: *Scorpio* travels to Servalan's base on Ferno to acquire new power cells; while there, Avon and Vila learn of Servalan's plan to obtain a mysterious diadem, of which she already has one stone, with the ability to amplify the wearer's psychic power. They trace it to the planet Torella, closely followed by Servalan. They obtain the diadem but are forced to return it in exchange for Vila, whom Servalan has captured. Before they do, however, they learn that the crown is part of a more powerful device. They locate it shortly before Servalan does, but Avon is duplicated in a teleport accident, and a struggle between Avon and Servalan for the crown awakens the Divani – ancient, semi-divine beings who once ruled the galaxy. Avon's duplicate puts on the crown and holds the Divani back long enough for the crew to escape.

ANALYSIS: *Blake's 7: The Sevenfold Crown*, put simply, is not very good, being let down by poor scripting and pedestrian production.

The story incorporates many elements from the first six episodes of the fourth season, plus "Games", "Project Avalon", and Tony Attwood's novel *Blake's 7: Afterlife*, with ideas from Letts's *Doctor*

Who stories (particularly "The Time Monster" and "The Paradise of Death") included in the mix. Although liberal borrowing from earlier stories in the series is not unknown in *Blake's 7*, the combination of antecedents in this case means that the end result is rather more 'Famous Five' than '*Dirty Dozen* in space.' The script also shows a fairly schizophrenic attitude to series continuity: care is taken to explain Servalan's use of the name Sleer, but *Scorpio* and the Federation vessels have all developed the ability to jump into hyperspace. Parts of the story as written also go completely against the themes of the series. In *Blake's 7*, for instance, we usually see monarchies only on the most primitive of planets; here, one is running a holiday world. Avon says he has torn out the throat of a tiger with his bare hands, and has trained himself to withstand pain. The crew use stun-weapons, and show altogether too much altruism. (And why should the crew insist on trading the diadem for Vila's life?) Vila's occasional over fondness for alcohol has suddenly become gluttony for food.

While one could perhaps forgive the continuity breaches, the story is also hampered by more general problems. The dialogue is poor and the characterisation, especially of the women, is lamentable; there is a lot of schoolboy prurience (particularly in the opening scene, in which Avon has a dream of being whipped by Servalan) and fairly gratuitous descriptions of violence (particularly in the hanging sequence). There are massive info-dumps, including some long technical descriptions (which, as well as being dull, are also out of keeping with the series' casual attitude towards science), and a few too many Dickensian coincidences. (Vila and Soolin just happen to come across the man with the information they need, for instance.) The story is also overly padded, and the abrupt introduction of Avon's duplicate (as well as his uncharacteristic self-sacrifice) seems to serve no purpose other than to have someone save the crew at the end of the narrative.

There are also elements of the plot that make no sense whatsoever. Why does Servalan outline most of her plan when she knows that Avon and Vila are hiding behind a couch, listening? Why do the *Scorpio* crew develop such a needlessly complicated plot to steal the diadem, when they could just use the teleport to enter the chamber in the dead of night? Why does Gheblakon suddenly decide to help people who have come to steal his own property? Why does Servalan have Tarrant tortured when the crew's plan is fairly obvious, and why does she not take his bracelet? Why does she teleport up to *Scorpio* to make a deal, and why don't the crew kill her when she does – or at the very least use her as a hostage and get Vila back without trading away the diadem? Even people who are not fans of the series, and therefore not likely to object to the continuity problems, would have trouble overlooking these issues.

The production is also rather flat, and the decision to use upbeat techno-inspired music throughout does not help. Paula Wilcox as Soolin actually sounds quite a bit like Glynis Barber, but plays the role very differently, more flustered schoolgirl than cold killer. Angela Bruce as Dayna has a regional accent, and is audibly much older than Josette Simon in 1981.

Overall, *Blake's 7: The Sevenfold Crown* is muddled, overlong, and not particularly entertaining.

BLAKE'S 7: THE SYNDETON EXPERIMENT

UK TRANSMISSION: BBC Radio 4. Saturday 10 April 1999: 3.02pm – 4.00pm
WRITER: Barry Letts
DIRECTOR: Brian Lighthill
INCIDENTAL MUSIC: Jeff Mearns

CAST: Paul Darrow (Avon); Jacqueline Pearce (Servalan); Michael Keating (Vila); Steven Pacey (Tarrant); Paula Wilcox (Soolin); Angela Bruce (Dayna); Peter Tuddenham (Orac/Slave); Judy Cornwell (Gaskia); Peter Jeffrey (Doctor Rossum); Graham Padden (Vledka)

SYNOPSIS: The *Scorpio* crew and Servalan are simultaneously *en route* to the planet Syndexia in pursuit of Syndeton, a substance that helps ships travel into hyperspace and allows telepathic control of anyone with a chip made from it embedded in their brains. Servalan learns of the crew's plans, foils them, and implants a Syndeton chip in Tarrant's hypothalamus. Tarrant takes control of *Scorpio* and forces the crew to fly to Kapeka in search of Dr Rossum. When they encounter him, he claims to have transferred the minds of everyone on the planet into 'neurobots,' controlled through the Great Neurobot. Servalan, learning of this through Tarrant, goes to Kapeka, connects her brain into that of the Great Neurobot and collapses; Dr Rossum removes Tarrant's chip. Avon reveals that Dr Rossum did not, as he believed, transfer the minds into the robots, but simply copied their personalities. He is therefore a mass murderer, as he destroyed the bodies after the presumed conversion.

ANALYSIS: Following the broadcast of *Blake's 7: The Sevenfold Crown*, the production team came under severe criticism from mainstream press and fans alike. This was a great concern both to writer Barry Letts and to director Brian Lighthill, as they believed it would affect the chances of any future productions. As a consequence, there are three main differences between this audio and its predecessor: the scenario is more cop-show and less children's-adventure; Vila reverts to being a drunkard (although the gluttony does reappear briefly); and the sexual sadism is less overt (although still present, particularly in the scene in which the strapped-down Tarrant double-entendres about what he can do with only one hand). Servalan has also become a bit more sensible, and does her bargaining over a communications channel rather than teleporting straight into her enemies' ship. Unfortunately, these changes do not address the deeper problems of scripting, consistency and characterisation.

Blake's 7: The Syndeton Experiment, in fact, appears to have much the same plot as *Blake's 7: The Sevenfold Crown*: like its predecessor, it features Servalan and Avon both out to get some device that gives the user psychic control over others; corrupt planets with gross rulers; and Tarrant and Avon inveigling their way into a palace. There are even near-identical guided-tour sequences in both stories. The production of the second story is, however, even worse than the first; the fact that many of the regulars audibly double for bit-parts gives it a cheap and confused feel, and the robot voices are sometimes hard to understand. The regulars are still poorly characterised, especially the women; Servalan has suddenly turned into a menopausal housewife, cooking dinner for Captain Vledka and then seducing him. The idea of Avon being at the [Federation Space] Academy (before being kicked out) and visiting a bordello is uncharacteristic – even at his most extroverted and unhinged, he does not seem like the type – and the notion that he was on the Federation wanted list at an early age, while never actually directly contradicted by the original series, simply does not ring true.

As well as the episodes mentioned in the analysis of *Blake's 7: The Sevenfold Crown*, Letts has also drawn on "Breakdown" for the scenes in which the restrained Tarrant persuades Soolin to release him; "Orac" for the idea of a fugitive scientist with a heart complaint; "Shadow" for the scenarios of drugs, mind control and gangster culture; and "Weapon" for Servalan's seduction of a Federation officer. *Avon: A Terrible Aspect* may be responsible for some of the more dubious backstory for this character, and *Afterlife* for the scenario of a mad tyrannical woman determined to gain psychic control over the universe. The scene in which Servalan takes control of the Great Neurobot is heavily indebted to the climax of Letts's *Doctor Who* story "Planet of the Spiders", in which the (female) ruler of the Eight Legs, the Great One, dies after ranting of ultimate power. The names 'Rossum' and 'Kapeka' are drawn from Karel Čapek and his play *R.U.R.* [Rossum's Universal Robots], and there are also references to John Wyndham's short story *Una*, in which a scientist creates a multi-legged, multi-armed, pyramid-shaped 'perfect human.'

Once again, the script is full of anachronistic expressions (e.g. 'Fine words butter no parsnips') and variable continuity (*Scorpio* and the Federation ships still jump into hyperspace). Some of the phrases are dire (e.g. 'boo juice') and the expression 'The Feds' was never used in the series (although it is common in American cop-shows as slang for the FBI). Leaving aside the difficulty of implanting a chip in someone's hypothalamus without extensive neurosurgical training, there is also a logic problem in that, if Syndeton exists simultaneously in our space and in hyperspace, how is it that Servalan's connection with the chip is broken when Tarrant enters hyperspace? One redeeming aspect is the idea of Rossum inadvertently killing two million people in the name of scientific advancement, although this is very much in line with the 'mad scientist' film genre.

Blake's 7: The Syndeton Experiment only really improves upon its predecessor in that it is half an hour shorter. Although there have been some changes, the story appears to be mainly a retread of *Blake's 7: The Sevenfold Crown*, and consequently inherits many of its more problematic aspects.

APPENDIX B

THE MARK OF KANE

FORMAT: Independent Audio (June 1996)
WRITER: Alan Stevens (Part One); Alan Stevens and David Tulley (Part Two)
PRODUCER: Alan Stevens
DIRECTION/Sound Design: Alistair Lock
SLEEVE ARTWORK: Pete Wallbank

CAST: Brian Croucher (Travis); Christina Balit (Mutoid Pilot); Tracy Russell (Valisha/Blossom); Bruce McGilligan (Alien); Steven Allen (Stenner); Alistair Lock (Customer); Terry Molloy (Kane); Pete Wallbank (Royce); Alan Stevens (Morik); Peter Halliday (Barkeeper); Gareth Thomas (Blake); Daniel Bowers (Tando); Peter Miles (Lafayette)

SYNOPSIS: This audio consists of two stories, linked by two characters: Kane and Travis's mutoid. They take place in the interstices, as it were, of "Gambit" and "Blake" respectively, and draw parallels between Travis and Blake. Part One, "War Crimes", is a kind of 'day in the life of Travis,' focusing on the former Space Commander as he makes contact with the Andromedans, goes to a bar in search of Docholli and learns that he is on Disentastra, and has an encounter outside the bar with two bounty hunters named Kane and Royce, in which he kills the latter and maims the former. Returning to his ship, he interrogates his mutoid, who has access to her memories but no emotional connection with them, in a clumsy attempt to reach some vestige of humanity. She confirms that she was once Maryatt's wife, Valisha, placed on the ship by Servalan in order to remind him of his betrayal of Maryatt and thus of his own hypocrisy in defying the system.

Part Two, "Friendly Fire", picks up with Kane on Gauda Prime some years later, as Kane seeks to find Travis and avenge his injuries upon him; he has become something of a stalker, emulating Travis's style and weaponry, having acquired the now-damaged mutoid (semi-affectionately nicknamed

'Blossom'), and yet hating Travis to the point of obsession. Kane joins forces with two bounty hunters, 'Dev Varon' and Tando, to hunt down a fellow bounty-hunter named Lafayette, who killed a friend of Varon's named Jenna. Varon, unknown to Kane, is in fact Blake; Tando is a friend of Gan's from Gan's days as a murderer. During the attack, Lafayette recognises Blake, whom he believed he had killed on Jevron, and states his name before Blake shoots him. Kane, having learned the true identity of 'Varon', asks if he killed Travis, and Blake admits to this. Consumed with anger at being thwarted in his quest, Kane tries to kill Blake, scarring his eye in the process, but Tando shoots Kane, Blossom shoots and injures Tando and Blake shoots Blossom. As they leave, the dying mutoid, in what may be a sudden regaining of humanity or simply a reflex action, whispers the name of her husband.

THE LOGIC OF EMPIRE

FORMAT: Independent Audio (March 1998)
WRITER: Alan Stevens and David Tulley
PRODUCER: Alan Stevens
DIRECTION/Sound Design: Alistair Lock
SLEEVE ARTWORK: Pete Wallbank

CAST: Paul Darrow (Avon); Peter Tuddenham (Orac/Slave/Zen); Trevor Cooper (Kelso); Tracy Russell (Elise); Ian Reddington (Lydon); Alistair Lock (Major Brecht); Jacqueline Pearce (Servalan); David Tulley (Section Leader); Gareth Thomas (Blake); Alan Stevens (Squad Leader 1); Bruce McGilligan (Squad Leader 2); Pete Wallbank (Trooper); Sharon Eckman (P.A. System); Patricia Merrick (Kerrine); Jim Smith (Ric)

SYNOPSIS: Seven years after the events on Gauda Prime, Avon (having survived through unspecified but evidently supernatural means, possibly involving Dorian's room under Xenon Base) is now working as a mercenary and arms dealer; weary and uncaring, he is still possessed with a death-wish, but seems incapable of breaking out of the pattern of his existence. He answers a call from his ex-lover Elise, who has joined up with a resistance group.

Once ten in number, a recent overambitious raid has reduced the group members to three: Elise, the comedic Kelso, and Lydon, their intense, hard-edged leader. They request Avon's help with a scheme to steal gold from a Federation mining station. Avon, unimpressed by this new group that is forced to look to the older generation for help, clashes with Lydon. Unknown to Avon, however, this is all part of a scheme to capture him. The scheme has been developed for Servalan (now restored as President) by a psychostrategist, and there are layers of reality operating of which Avon is unaware. Elise, suffused with a sense of ennui, muses upon the feeling that something important happened in the galaxy, on which humanity missed out. She and Avon sleep together, and Avon has a dream in which he encounters a ghostly Blake who speaks to him in phrases taken from the episode "Terminal", and attempts to warn him of the coming danger. Their stronghold is attacked by Federation Commandos. Avon, deceived by Lydon into thinking that Elise has betrayed them, kills her; discovering that Lydon (who has killed Kelso) is the traitor, he also kills him, but is then captured and brainwashed by Servalan; in this instance, the psychostrategists have won.

Some time later, Avon is found in a domed city on Gauda Prime, where he is joining the resistance under the name Roj Blake, suggesting not only that the cycle of oppression and resistance is never-ending, but that the resistance itself has in fact been under Federation control from the very beginning.

DOCTOR WHO: CORPSE MARKER

PUBLISHER: BBC Books (1 November 1999)
AUTHOR: Chris Boucher

SYNOPSIS: Kaldor City (the capital of a world that does not possess space travel) is a heavily stratified, corrupt and decadent society; but for the presence of a Mafia like aristocratic class, the Founding Families, and for a strong class tension between them and the 'new blood' politicians who have achieved power through meritocratic means, it might as well be the Federation. In the desert beyond the City, an incident occurred in which a robotics genius, Taren Capel, programmed the robots on a Storm Mine, a giant mobile mining complex, to kill the human crewmembers; afterwards, it was hushed up. The psychostrategist Carnell, who arrived in the City some years ago during his flight from the Federation and who has set himself up as advisor to the City's elite, dismisses the reported presence of an unknown man and woman, known as the Doctor and Leela, as a mass hallucination.

Years later, the new Cyborg class of robots seem to be repeating the past, targeting the Storm Mine massacre survivors – Kiy Uvanov, now a Company official, Lish Toos, now a Storm Mine captain, and Ander Poul, whose experiences have rendered him insane. At the same time, the City faces attacks by a group of rebels claiming to be the followers of Taren Capel. The Doctor and his companion Leela, arriving in Kaldor City, investigate. The Doctor assists Uvanov, while Leela falls in with a group of rebels. They learn that behind both sets of attacks is an experimental robot styling itself 'Taren Capel'. They also learn that there is a further layer of manipulation, as Carnell is in fact the author of the whole situation.

Carnell remains an elusive figure; although we learn that psychostrategists are identified early by the Federation's government and trained from childhood to their profession, little is revealed about his background or motivations. His scheme is foiled, in this instance, not because of cultural factors, but because of his lack of flexibility when confronted with an unknown factor; by attempting to explain away the Doctor's and Leela's presence on the Storm Mine, he fails to consider the possibility that they might one day return as mysteriously as they vanished.

At the end of the story, Uvanov seizes the opportunity to become the City's ruler, suggesting that there may be changes in the political structure of the society to come in the near future.

KALDOR CITY: OCCAM'S RAZOR

Magic Bullet Productions (1 September 2001)

WRITER: Alan Stevens and Jim Smith
PRODUCER: Alan Stevens
DIRECTOR: Alistair Lock and Alan Stevens
SOUND DESIGN: Alistair Lock
DIALOGUE EDIT: William Johnston and Alistair Lock
PRODUCTION MANAGERS: Jim Smith and Fiona Moore
DESIGN: Andy Hopkinson
CREATIVE CONSULTANT: Chris Boucher

CAST: Paul Darrow (Iago); Alistair Lock (Voc Receptionist); Russell Hunter (Uvanov); Trevor Cooper (Rull); Brian Croucher (Cotton); Scott Fredericks (Carnell); Robert Lock (Voc 31); Alan Stevens (Voice 1); Mark Christian (Pull Buggy Voc); Patricia Merrick (Justina); Peter Miles (Landerchild); David Bickerstaff (Kyle); Bruce McGilligan (Voice 2); Fiona Moore (Lift); Computer Voice (Tracy Russell); Annabel Leventon (Devlin); Andy Hopkinson (Security Man); Matt Symonds (Voc Server); Peter Tuddenham (Strecker); Robert Edwards (Guard)

SYNOPSIS: Kaldor City is a corrupt and decadent society, in which all power is in the hands of the Company and the aristocratic Founding Families; with most jobs being taken by robots, the citizens live in idleness, and work is a luxury. Some months after achieving the highest office on the planet, Company Chairholder Uvanov finds himself confronted with a series of mysterious and violent deaths among the City's elite, which even top psychostrategist Carnell appears unable to explain. The trail seems to lead to a newcomer to the City, an enigmatic and ruthless robot programmer calling himself Kaston Iago – but how is he involved and why?

KALDOR CITY: DEATH'S HEAD

Magic Bullet Productions (20 April 2002)

WRITER: Chris Boucher
PRODUCER: Alan Stevens
DIRECTOR: Alan Stevens and Alistair Lock
SOUND DESIGN: Alistair Lock
DIALOGUE EDIT: William Johnston and Alistair Lock
PRODUCTION MANAGERS: Fiona Moore and Jim Smith
DESIGN: Andy Hopkinson
CREATIVE CONSULTANT: Chris Boucher

CAST: Scott Fredericks (Carnell); Nicholas Briggs (Sheen); Robert Lock (Rov); Trevor Cooper (Rull); Brian Croucher (Cotton); Peter Miles (Landerchild); Peter Tuddenham (Strecker); David Bickerstaff (Attendant); Russell Hunter (Uvanov); Alistair Lock (Hume); Paul Darrow (Iago); Patricia Merrick (Justina); Tracy Russell (Blayes); Fiona Moore (Voice 1); Bruce McGilligan (Voice 2)

SYNOPSIS: Operations Supervisor Rull, investigating shady dealings at a desert research station, finds a maze of political involvement that points in unexpected directions, and that seems to involve Uvanov's rival Firstmaster Landerchild. Meanwhile, a female security agent named Blayes, assigned to find out who is behind a bizarre and seemingly groundless assassination attempt on Uvanov, makes a discovery that casts a totally new complexion on the incident, and that could put her own life in jeopardy. At the hub of this web of intrigue would seem to be the enigmatic Carnell – but who is he working for, and what does the deceased robotics genius Taren Capel have to do with the situation?

KALDOR CITY: HIDDEN PERSUADERS

Magic Bullet Productions (30 November 2002)

WRITER: Jim Smith and Fiona Moore
PRODUCER: Alan Stevens
DIRECTOR: Alistair Lock and Alan Stevens
SOUND DESIGN: Alistair Lock
DIALOGUE EDIT: William Johnston
PRODUCTION MANAGERS: Fiona Moore and Jim Smith
DESIGN: Andy Hopkinson
CREATIVE CONSULTANT: Chris Boucher

CAST: Peter Miles (Landerchild); Russell Hunter (Uvanov); Nicholas Courtney (Packard); Scott Fredericks (Carnell); Paul Darrow (Iago); Patricia Merrick (Justina); Tracy Russell (Blayes); Trevor Cooper (Rull); Brian Croucher (Cotton); Jim Smith (Crane); David Bickerstaff (Manzerak); David Collings (Paullus); Robert Lock (Guido); Alistair Lock (Bextor); Tony Lang (Voice); Mark Thompson (Leighton); Alison Taffs (Caitlion); Scott Andrews (Corda); Alan Stevens (Berganza); Nickey Barnard (Damon); Jasmine Breaks (Zala); Bruce McGilligan (Voc Voices)

SYNOPSIS: Dismissed from her job at Company Security, Blayes falls in with a cell of religious zealots, the Tarenists, who believe that Taren Capel, the mad robot programmer killed at the end of the *Doctor Who* story "The Robots of Death", is a messiah who will return to judge them all. With the support of their Machiavellian leader Paullus, she stages a raid on one of the plants that supplies the city's oxygen requirements; it rapidly turns into a hostage crisis when things go wrong. With Kaston Iago engaged in clandestine investigations in the outer zones, and the media, spearheaded by ruthless Kaldor City News reporters Danl Packard and Zala Vance, whipping the public up into a frenzy of terror, Uvanov turns to Carnell to solve the crisis. But what is Blayes' real agenda, and who stands to gain the most from her activities?

KALDOR CITY: TAREN CAPEL

Magic Bullet Productions (15 March 2003)

WRITER: Alan Stevens
PRODUCER: Alan Stevens
DIRECTOR: Alan Steven
SOUND DESIGN: Alistair Lock
DIALOGUE EDIT: William Johnston
PRODUCTION MANAGERS: Jim Smith and Fiona Moore
DESIGN: Andy Hopkinson
CREATIVE CONSULTANT: Chris Boucher

CAST: Scott Fredericks (Carnell); Robert Lock (Voc 31); Russell Hunter (Uvanov); Trevor Cooper (Rull); David Bailie (Taren Capel); Paul Darrow (Iago); David Collings (Paullus); Tracy Russell (Blayes); Patricia Merrick (Justina); Brian Croucher (Cotton); Peter Miles (Landerchild); Bruce McGilligan (Security Man); William Johnston (Tarenist 1); Alan Stevens (Tarenist 2); Jim Smith (Tarenist 3); Alistair Lock (Yardley); Nicholas Courtney (Packard); Jasmine Breaks (Zala)

SYNOPSIS: As Kaldor City gradually descends into a siege mentality, Uvanov must defend against political attacks by his rival Firstmaster Landerchild and physical attacks by the Tarenist cult led by the enigmatic Paullus and the rogue security agent Blayes. As his personal assistant Justina and self-styled professional assassin Kaston Iago deal with issues of their own, Uvanov calls on Carnell for assistance. However, unknown to anyone in Kaldor City, the psychostrategist is close to uncovering a dangerous secret about the cult's long-dead messiah, Taren Capel; and when he does, no one in Kaldor City will be safe.

KALDOR CITY: CHECKMATE

Magic Bullet Productions (20 September 2003)

WRITER: Alan Stevens
PRODUCER: Alan Stevens
DIRECTOR: Alistair Lock
SOUND DESIGN: Alistair Lock
DIALOGUE EDIT: William Johnston
PRODUCTION MANAGERS: Fiona Moore and Jim Smith
DESIGN: Andy Hopkinson
CREATIVE CONSULTANT: Chris Boucher

CAST: Paul Darrow (Iago); Russell Hunter (Uvanov); Nicholas Courtney (Packard); David Bickerstaff (Voc 101); Brian Croucher (Cotton); Trevor Cooper (Rull); Scott Fredericks (Carnell); David Collings (Paullus); Tracy Russell (Blayes); David Bailie (Taren Capel); Patricia Merrick (Justina); Alan Stevens (Voice); Robert Lock (Cresswell); Alistair Lock (Yardley); Peter Miles (Landerchild); Courtney King (Kellen); Bruce McGilligan (Voc 13); Mark Thompson (Producer); William Johnston (Announcer); Danny Golem (Ghoul 1); Nickey Barnard (Ghoul 2); Peter Halliday (Derhaven); Miles Gould (Attendant); Rachel Fishwick (Schraeder)

SYNOPSIS: With the contents of Company Central's Archive Room in the hands of Paullus and Blayes, and with Taren Capel's legacy of destruction unleashed upon Kaldor City, no-one is safe. As Paullus prepares to contact a force that could be either the salvation or the destruction of the people of Kaldor, Uvanov faces the fight of his life – not merely to retain his position, but for sheer physical survival. Carnell having apparently abandoned the City to its fate, Iago must make a terrible choice – to save the City, he must sacrifice everything he has gained.

KALDOR CITY: STORM MINE

Magic Bullet Productions (18 December 2004)

WRITER: Daniel O'Mahony
PRODUCER: Alan Stevens
DIRECTOR: Alistair Lock and Alan Stevens
SOUND DESIGN: Alistair Lock
DIALOGUE EDIT: William Johnston
PRODUCTION MANAGERS: Fiona Moore and Barry Ward
DESIGN: Andy Hopkinson
CREATIVE CONSULTANT: Chris Boucher

CAST: Paul Darrow (Iago); Tracy Russell (Blayes); John Leeson (Chief Mover); Philip Madoc (Commander); Alistair Lock (MedVoc); Mark Thompson (Supervoc 6); Gregory De Polnay (Voc 23); Robert Lock (Voc); William Johnston (Voc 65); Wanda Opalinska (Dockmaster); Patricia Merrick (Chief Fixer)

SYNOPSIS: Eighteen months after her final confrontation with Iago, Blayes awakes to find Kaldor City in quarantine and herself on a Storm Mine in the Blind Heart Desert. Her companions are three strangely familiar figures, a vengeful spirit-- and a robot with a dangerous secret. Trapped in a claustrophobic, dreamlike environment, the former terrorist must now undertake a journey which may end in the destruction of her world-- or its beginning.

KALDOR CITY: THE PRISONER

MJTV Productions (24 April 2004)

WRITERS: Alan Stevens and Fiona Moore
PRODUCER: Mark J. Thompson
DIRECTOR: Mark J. Thompson
SOUND DESIGN: Alistair Lock
DIALOGUE EDIT: William Johnston
DESIGN: Mark Spencer and Andy Hopkinson
CREATIVE CONSULTANT: Chris Boucher

CAST: Paul Darrow (Iago); Peter Miles (Landerchild)

SYNOPSIS: Landerchild interrogates Iago, who has been discovered trespassing on the grounds of his estate, but events soon take a metaphysical turn.

KALDOR CITY: METAFICTION

Magic Bullet Productions (7 July 2012)

WRITERS: Alan Stevens and Fiona Moore
PRODUCER: Alan Stevens
ASSOCIATE PRODUCER: Alex Fitch
DIRECTOR: Alan Stevens and Alistair Lock
SOUND DESIGN: Alistair Lock
DIALOGUE EDIT: William Johnston
PRODUCTION MANAGER: Fiona Moore
CREATIVE CONSULTANT: Chris Boucher

CAST: Paul Darrow (Iago); Patricia Merrick (Justina)

SYNOPSIS: Iago reveals he has read this book.

INDEX: NAMES

INDEX: TITLES

Titles in italics are working titles or unmade episodes

ABOUT THE AUTHORS

ALAN STEVENS has been interested in *Blake's 7* since it was first televised. He has written articles for, and edited, many publications on *Blake's 7*, *Doctor Who* and other telefantasy programmes. Since the early 1990s, he has produced a number of documentaries, serials and dramas for radio, as well as two independent *Blake's 7* audio dramas, one *Blake's 7* audio documentary, a *Blake's 7* stage play, and a series of *Blake's 7*/*Doctor Who* spinoff audio dramas, *Kaldor City*. He is currently based in the South East of England, from where he runs his own audio drama production company, Magic Bullet Productions (www.kaldorcity.com), and writes for the theatre, the Web, and print publications.

FIONA MOORE was born and raised in Toronto, Canada. In 1997 she moved to the UK, and has lived there, alternating between Oxford and London, ever since. She has a doctorate in Social Anthropology from the University of Oxford, and is currently Reader in International Human Resource Management at Royal Holloway, University of London. She has written extensively on a variety of subjects, ranging from international business expatriation to the culture of drag queens. Her fiction and poetry have been published in, among others, *Asimov, Interzone* and *Dark Horizons*.

Printed in Great Britain
by Amazon